Hope

Andrew Razeghi

Hope

How Triumphant Leaders Create the Future

JOSSEY-BASS
A Wiley Imprint
www.josseybass.com

Published by Jossey-Bass
A Wiley Imprint
989 Market Street, San Francisco, CA 94103-1741   www.josseybass.com

Jossey-Bass books and products are available through most bookstores. To contact Jossey-Bass
directly call our Customer Care Department within the U.S. at 800-956-7739, outside the
U.S. at 317-572-3986, or fax 317-572-4002.

Jossey-Bass also publishes its books in a variety of electronic formats. Some content that
appears in print may not be available in electronic books.

Library of Congress Cataloging-in-Publication Data

Razeghi, Andrew, 1970-
    Hope : how triumphant leaders create the future / Andrew Razeghi.
        p. cm.
    Includes bibliographical references and index.
    ISBN-13: 978-0-7879-8126-6 (cloth)
    ISBN-10: 0-7879-8126-5 (cloth)
    1. Success. 2. Fortune. 3. Hope. 4. Leadership. I. Title.
    BJ1611.2.R395 2006
    658.4'092-dc22   2006005275

Printed in the United States of America
FIRST EDITION
HB Printing   10 9 8 7 6 5 4 3 2 1

Contents

Hope

For Cindy:
Where would we be without your two-minute rule on life?

And for Charlie:
Keep dancing without music.

Part One

THINKING ABOUT BELIEVING

If you want to make God laugh,
tell him your future plans.
*—Woody Allen, quoting an
old Yiddish proverb*

1

VOICES FROM THE ICE

On the first day of life there is nothing to remember
and everything to hope.

—*Aristotle*

Flashes of color raced by my car window. During the skid, I grew to appreciate why most tourists end their journey at the visitors' center. In the wintry wilderness outside Anchorage, cars are magnetically attracted to everything but the road. And so, like long-lost friends, my fearless front bumper and a petrified snowbank had no other choice than to meet again. And when they did, the car shook to an abrupt stop. "It's a good thing I didn't buy that snow globe," I thought. "What a mess that would have been."

Driving conditions were worse than I had anticipated. The road was nothing more than a permafrost-reinforced ice rink navigated only by those with vehicles or egos larger than the last frontier itself. As for me, my transportation of choice was of the subcompact sort. A quick glance over my shoulder confirmed that no one had witnessed my roadside gymnastics. Fortunately, although my coffee had spilled, my ego was intact. While staring at the reason for my premature exit, I thought, "Is this what the park rangers meant by hearing voices from the ice?" followed quickly by "I shouldn't be here." However, given the fortuitous nature of what I was about to encounter, I couldn't leave. After all, this unexpected "voice from the ice" was touting the virtues of this book. Unlike others at the visitors' center, it seems I was meant to be there—on that road, in that place, at that time. Here's why.

A Chance Encounter

Alaska. It is arguably the most beautiful place on earth. Its native people and sourdoughs still wave at passing trains, live off the land, and—at the Wal-Mart in Wasilla—buy more duct tape than anyone on the planet. Although densely populated with wildlife, Alaska is sparsely populated with the human variety. With over 650,000 square miles, every Alaskan man, woman, and child can stretch out over his or her very own square mile. With over three million lakes and three thousand rivers, William Seward was certainly no fool. Seward's Folly, negotiating this land from the Russians for 2 cents an acre, would make even Donald Trump blush with envy. So spectacular is Alaska's majesty that Henry Gannett, the director of the U.S. Geological Survey and traveling companion of John Muir, wrote in a 1901 essay for *National Geographic*, "If you are old, go by all means. If you are young, stay away until you are older. The scenery of Alaska is so much grander than anything else of the kind in the world that, once beheld, all other scenery becomes flat and insipid." Unfortunately, although I would like to think of myself as relatively young, I couldn't stay away. I had a job to do.

In March 2005, on the twenty-fifth anniversary of the Alaska Governor's Conference on Safety, Health, and the Environment, the governor's office invited me to deliver a keynote speech on leadership. Although I had come to speak, I also learned a few things, including how to wear a gas mask properly, why caribou and the oil pipeline love each other, and how not to dress a moose (take it out of your neighbor's driveway before you gut it). The conference itself was enlightening, but it was the beauty of a chance encounter that left the most memorable impression on me. Then again, aren't most of life's lessons unplanned?

Alaska is thirty minutes from Anchorage—or so I was told. You need to leave it to see it. Therefore, as soon as I arrived, I left. If you have never felt alone—I mean really alone, as if you are the last living being on earth—take a trip into the bush of Alaska during the spring thaw. In today's world of wireless connectivity and therefore perpetual responsibility, I secretly wanted to get lost in the vast emptiness of the last frontier. However, after witnessing the true meaning of wildlife, I opted for the scenic drive along the Turnagain Arm, an open road with dramatic views of Cook Inlet, beluga whales, Dall sheep, and bald eagles. The obligatory tourist stop along the Arm— and therefore my planned destination—was Portage Glacier, fifty miles south of Anchorage. Although breathtaking in its beauty, the glacier was all but lost on this urban dweller as the wind, rain, and overcast skies suggested that I seek refuge among the park rangers in the Begich-Boggs Visitors' Center. They pour a great cup of coffee.

Once inside, I was accosted by that bastion of all visitors' centers, tchotchkes. I must admit that the idea of an Alaskan malamute snow globe did pique my interest. However, I was neither browsing nor buying. Nor did I have the patience to watch the award-winning film about receding glaciers titled *Voices from the Ice*. A map of the area therefore became my de facto excuse for seeking shelter from the storm. While studying the map, and in some sort of cosmic coincidence, my eyes were immediately drawn to a very small dot: a town called Hope. Although it appeared to be about thirty miles farther into the wilderness and despite the inclement weather, as one writing a book on hope, I had to go there. Like *Seinfeld*'s Kramer testing his wits by driving as far as possible on an empty tank, I couldn't resist the urge to keep going. And so I did. Diversion became adventure.

Nestled warmly inside the world's smallest rental car, I eagerly navigated the increasingly less drivable road through the Kenai Mountains. And then it happened. On the road to Hope, I encountered a sign that begat a skid that begat a stop in the middle of the wilderness. It was a sign—not a figurative sign, a road sign—a voice from the ice. It read: AVALANCHE AREA. NEXT 1.5 MILES. DO NOT STOP. As a flatlander and urban dweller, the last thought that enters my mind when I see the word *avalanche* is "do not stop." And so I stopped, got out of my car, and took a photo. "Stupid tourist," I later thought. "But what a great photo!"

With my digital image in tow, I proudly reinserted myself into my four-wheeled rental shelter like a hunter packing out a fallen deer. I then laughed out loud as I envisioned the inevitable expression on my wife's face. I would surely share this act of bravery with her—certain to be embellished. Fortunately, the snow held; I was spared, and forty-five minutes later, I arrived in Hope, Alaska's first Gold Rush town.

An Accidental Lesson

What was once home to more than three thousand people is now inhabited by a couple of hundred hangers-on and one unassuming diner with the best barbequed chicken sandwich on the planet. Over lunch and while reflecting on the gravity of the situation I had just put myself in, it hit me—an epiphany, a metaphor that only nature and man's attempt to coexist with it could yield. Here, in the heart of God's country, stands a poetically coincidental lesson in leadership. Along a weather-beaten road to a forgotten yet once celebrated town called Hope is an encouraging message for all those who make the journey: Drive beyond fear. Do not stop. Hope is just around the corner.

This chance encounter—this accidental lesson—raised a question in my mind: In moments of uncertainty, when hope is on the line, why do some leaders succeed and others fail? How do they think, feel, and act in those moments when the future is up for grabs? What do they believe? Could it be that they have a different relationship with hope? Could it be that triumphant leaders follow an unarticulated methodology of sorts for translating hope, the virtue, into hope, the plan? If so, can it be learned? It appears the answer is yes. As it turns out, there is more to this ancient virtue than we have historically known, scientifically and practically. Hope works; however, like sunscreen, it works only if applied correctly.

Shedding New Light on an Ancient Virtue

Nobel laureate Bertrand Russell said it best in *New Hopes for a Changing World*, "a way of life cannot be successful so long as it is mere intellectual conviction. It must be deeply felt, deeply believed, dominant even in dreams." Intellect is overrated. Don't get me wrong, intelligence is important; however, in moments of ambiguity, intuition, creativity, and beliefs are as important as reason, analysis, and proof. However, since history has not been kind to theoretical mixed marriages—keep your spirituality away from my biology and your emotions out of my intellect—we've stood in isolated admiration of the dogma that we find most convincing. Enter cognitive and behavioral psychology, philosophy, physics, and theology. Therefore, although exploring the power of hope in the context of leadership was not necessarily frowned on, it has simply fallen through the cracks.

However, with the introduction of magnetic resonance imaging and other advanced technologies for studying the "softer side of humans," physics has lost its monopoly on tangible evidence. The soft sciences have become harder, thereby making the study of all things intangible more meaningful, if not more convincing. With similar tools at their disposal, neuroscientists, like chemists in ages past, are just now able to witness the mysterious workings of the mind versus simply taking a person's word for it. This has profound implications for the study of human behavior, not the least of which is leadership.

Hope's New Agent

Human resources—like marketing's ongoing transformation from art to science—is about to undergo the greatest cultural and academic revolution in its history. And you thought Myers-Briggs was invading your space! Try taking your next performance review with your head locked squarely inside a thirty-ton magnet. The 7-Tesla MRI machine holds 250 miles of superconducting wire, making it 140,000 times stronger than the earth's magnetic field. Hope's got a new agent. Next stop: your brain.

2

BRAINFOREST

We think too much and feel too little.
—*Charlie Chaplin*

It happened five years before my Alaskan escapade. It was a day that nothing mattered. Rising laughter, hoots, and hollers drew my attention. In the center of the exhibit hall stood a crowd of twenty to thirty conventioneers formed into a large circle around what appeared, from a distance, to be an air hockey table. If I were at a casino in Vegas, I would have expected dice, tokens, and high fives exchanged between strangers. However, I was at the Earl's Court Convention Center in London attending a futurist conference sponsored by the BBC. There was not a high five in sight.

As my client, Kurt, and I approached the booth, what we thought would become increasingly apparent became progressively more confusing. Two individuals "manned the booth": a thirty-something male wearing the obligatory headset and a tall, attractive, twenty-something female wearing, well, not much. Again, my mind left for Vegas. The poor girl—her clothes fit like a dive suit. She was clearly the obligatory exhibit booth girl. I can only imagine the conversations that take place between corporate event planners and exhibit booth vendors when preparing for trade shows. "So," says the exhibit booth salesman, "on page twelve, you will find carpet options; on page fifteen, a fine selection of chairs; and last but not least, on pages sixteen through eighteen, you will find photos of Mandy, Sandy, and Candy, our booth girls for hire."

As we worked our way through the crowd, the table came into view. Although it was not an air hockey table, it could have stood in for one in a pinch. A chair sat at either end of the table, one for each opponent, along with two small circles marking goals of some sort. A ball about the size of a golf ball sat in the center of the table. And then the more disturbing elements came into view. Hanging on the back of each chair were headbandlike helmets connected to wires reminiscent of something one would expect to find in a Mary Shelley novel. "Electrodes?" I thought. "What on earth are these people doing?" My curiosity sent my eyes on a journey. I followed the wires to two large monitors, one at either end of the booth. The equipment was like that used for administering electroencephalo-grams (EEGs, or "brain wave" tests). The EEG is typically used to detect abnormalities in the brain's electrical activity. However, in this application, it was deployed in a game of sorts.

With the showmanship of a Barnum & Bailey ringmaster and looking directly at Kurt and me, Headset Man cried out, "Gentlemen, step right up!" Kurt and I looked at each other, then at the super-model, then at the electrodes, and finally at each other once again. Nervous laughter followed. With a shrug of the shoulders and given that we were three espressos into the morning and feeling a little ad-venturous, we accepted his offer. The crowd cheered. As we took our places, the electrode helmets were carefully put in place by Booth Girl—the highlight of the morning—who then escaped behind the monitor like a dental hygienist seeking refuge during the X-ray portion of the program. "What am I doing?" I wondered. At this point, feeling that same sinking feeling one has once the harness locks into place and you realize that you can't get off the roller coaster, I played along.

"Gentlemen!" barked Headset Man, "Your task is to *not* think." This statement, of course, sent my mind in all sorts of directions. It was as if a dam broke in my brain. Every thought I had ever pondered yet couldn't remember came flooding forth. With a nervous smile, the subtitles began to run in my mind—"Is this safe? What am I doing? Why is Booth Girl laughing at me? Damn wires! Calm down. Quit thinking. How do you stop thinking? She's still laughing. Do I have food stuck in my teeth?" After *that* rush of thoughts, I calmed myself with some "Little Engine That Could" confidence: "Come on," I thought, "you have been *not* thinking your entire life. Surely, this is *one* game you can win?"

Headset Man continued, "By using your mind, your objective is to roll the ball across the other person's goal line. I repeat. You can only use your mind to move the ball. By *not* thinking, the ball will roll toward your opponent's goal line and you will win. If you *think*, the ball will roll toward your goal line and you will lose. The first person to force the ball across the opponent's goal line wins. A silent mind wins the game." "This is genius," I thought. "It's a game that you can win by doing nothing. It's like watching a football game and actually having a *real* effect on the outcome of the game by simply not thinking. This should come naturally." On this day, nothing mattered—literally.

With an enthusiastic John Madden–like tenor in his voice, yet with a James Lipton air of thoughtfulness, Headset Man continued, "Ready? Begin." It was on. At first, the ball swung wildly back and forth. My end. His end. It rolled uncontrollably. "Oh no! It's coming at me!" I thought, causing the ball to roll with even greater speed in my direction. "Stop thinking, stop thinking," I thought. Then there was sudden silence. My mind went blank. I was *not* thinking, and the ball began rolling away from me. In fits and starts, I was winning. The ball rolled toward Kurt's end of the table only to stop *suddenly*, as if Kurt had leaned into it with all that he could muster (or *couldn't*, as the case may be). As the ball slowly approached Kurt's goal line, the end was in sight. I would surely be crowned the victor, yet I didn't allow myself to gloat. Then, unexpectedly and in some kind of sympathetic act in support of the underdog, Headset Man asked me to begin singing "Happy Birthday." Begrudgingly, I complied. "Happy birthday to you . . ." As I sang, the ball began creeping slowly in my direction. "Happy birthday to you." The ball continued its death march toward me. "Happy Birthday" was killing me. I was losing. "Sing quickly, get this over with," I thought. "Happy birthday dear Kurt. Happy birthday to you." I looked down. The ball sat within inches of my goal line. The crowd cheered. I held it with every *un-thought* thought I could dismiss. Kurt, in anticipation of his win, burst out in sudden laughter. "This isn't fair!" I thought. "Stop thinking! Stop thinking!" Again my mind went dark. Suddenly, the ball shot back toward Kurt, stopping just shy of his side of the fifty-yard line. "Take that!" I tried *not* to think. The crowd cheered. I was back in the game. However, once again, in a cruel and repeated act of unfair advantage, Headset Man went to his ace in the hole. "Andrew!" he ordered. "Look to your right." Again, I complied. There, before me, like the pearl of an oyster opened to the light of day for the very first time—and within inches of my face—was Booth Girl. Smiling seductively in a pose reminiscent of Marilyn Monroe with lips puckered, she blew me a kiss. As I watched—in slow motion—the ball came hurtling toward me with a force of nature like the Hale-Bopp comet streaking across the heavens. The crowd cheered in glory. High fives were exchanged. Kurt had won. I had lost. To add insult to injury, however, I hadn't lost to Kurt. I had lost to myself. My *thoughts* beat me!

I had all but forgotten that experience until I began writing this book. As a student of leadership, the "day that nothing mattered" came rushing back to me like that ball had on that fateful day at Earl's Court. What happened in my mind? What role did my outlook and my beliefs play in affecting my performance? Mostly, why did I lose?

Mind Games

According to Magnus Jonsson, studio director of Sweden's Interactive Institute and team lead on the development of this game, aptly named Brainball, unlike most games of sport, Brainball goes against the conventional notions that success is determined by physical aptitude and strategic thinking. In Brainball, the ability to run, jump, and throw is inconsequential, as is the ability to analyze and reason. How the mind processes information and manages stress determines the victor. For example, strategic thinkers and rational decision makers have no advantage. Nor does concentration help achieve the goal. What matters most in this mind game is the body's own intuition.

In July 2005, I had the opportunity to speak with Magnus about the game, this time on my home turf in Chicago. Since we last met in London, Brainball has been played by more than three hundred thousand people, including yoga gurus, artist-musician Brian Eno, children with attention deficit disorders, and the prime minister and king of Sweden. Dutch journalist Robert van Weperen describes Brainball as "the best invention since the Internet." Apparently, *nothing* matters to a whole lot of people. In my second attempt, certainly, I thought, I would have an advantage on U.S. soil. However, though my opponent had changed, once again I lost—this time to Kevin, my brother-in-law, in a three-game tournament.

In the top photo on page 14, you'll see my brain at work. Notice that I'm winning—the ball is moving away from me. In the bottom photo, you will notice my brother-in-law's response. The ball has moved back to the center of the table. As this photo illustrates, given the ball's center position, we are in a stalemate. (I've chosen not to publish his winning photo.)

Here's why I lost. My brain, like your brain and your television, is electrified. The brain's signals are measured in microvolts. The four distinct brain waves are known as beta, alpha, theta, and delta. Beta waves are associated with an alert state of mind and cycle between 14 and 30 hertz. Alpha waves, in the frequency of 8 to 13 Hz, tend to be strong in a relaxed state. Theta waves, 4 to 7 Hz, rise during mental stress or drowsiness. And delta waves, below 3.5 Hz, occur during sleep. In Brainball, once the signals are picked up by the electrode helmet, they are sent to a multimodal eight-channel device that monitors EEG, EMG, temperature, pulse, and skin conductance. This machine then interprets the signals and sends messages to the game table by serial communication. These signals in turn power a magnetic strip mounted on the table that controls the movement of the ball. Less thinking wins the game.

The Day That Nothing Mattered

As it turns out, on this day that nothing mattered, I overlooked a key element of human performance. I, like most losers in this game, mistakenly assumed that I could "think" the ball across the goal line. Analysis and reason, I had thought, begets victory. However, in Brainball—as is often the case in life—outlook is as important as intellect. Consider the impact of a leader's outlook on the performance of others. For example, imagine your boss observing as you play Brainball against a coworker. What influence would this have on your performance? Would you win or lose? Now imagine playing without your boss in the room. Would you do better or worse? A leader's outlook—even in silence—has a dramatic effect on the performance of the team. This is why hope matters.

Why a Leader's Beliefs Are like Dirt

In this age of spreadsheet bingo, meaning matters. Triumphant leaders—hopeful leaders—communicate meaning by virtue of their beliefs. Leaders' beliefs are the soil in which we plant our aspirations. In this way, your beliefs are like dirt. You've gotta dig 'em up now and then. As a leader, you must show those who look to you for leadership not only what you believe but also why you believe it. Because coincidentally, what we cannot see in our leaders, like what we cannot see in dirt, turns out to be what is most important. Just as most tree failures are caused by problems with the soil, too many team failures are the result of a leader's mismanagement of beliefs. When people fail to believe in their leaders or when leaders fail to believe in their followers, they lose not only games but hope as well. And when people lose hope, they leave. Therefore, to make things grow—dreams, people, earnings—you must tend to your outlook as much as your intellect. You must believe as much as you think.

The Return on Hope

The great irony of intelligence is this: While we may tolerate those who appeal to our intellect, we follow those who appeal to our beliefs. However, we are hesitant to talk about beliefs in light of physical evidence. After all, how do you measure the return on investment (ROI) of a leader's beliefs? Is it possible? Is it even necessary? What good would be had in weighing the dream of Martin Luther King Jr. or creating a pro forma statement to forecast the patience of Mahatma Gandhi? What value would be had in attributing the free cash flow generated from Ty Cobb's relentless gamesmanship to the price of a bleacher seat? Isn't the role of hope to encourage us to do it even when we cannot prove it?

However distracted we have become by fuzzy math and homespun statistics, we continue to follow people who believe—the hopeful, the willful, and the courageous. Although attempting to measure a person's beliefs is filled with irony, as it turns out, hope yields above-average returns. Consider the "return on hope" (ROH) in the following cases.

Nuns and Cigarettes

In the 1930s, a group of young Catholic nuns were asked to write short, personal essays about their lives. They described their childhood, schools attended, religious experiences, and events that led them to the convent. Their essays were meant to help assess their career paths as sisters. More than sixty years later, the nuns' essays surfaced again when three psychologists at the University of Kentucky reviewed them as part of a study on Alzheimer's disease. David Snowdon, Deborah Danner, and Wallace Friesen read the essays and scored them for positive emotional content. The nuns who expressed the most positive emotions lived up to ten years longer than those who expressed the fewest indicators of hope. This gain in life expectancy is larger than the gain achieved by those who quit smoking (typically two to eight years, depending on age).

Oncology's Mystery

In an article he wrote for the *Western Journal of Medicine* in 1988, Dr. William Buchholz made the following observation after his attendance at a national meeting of the American Society of Clinical Oncologists:

> As I was eating breakfast one morning I overheard two oncologists discussing the papers they were to present that day. One was complaining bitterly: "You know, Bob, I just don't understand it. We used the same drugs, the same dosage, the same schedule, and the same entry criteria. Yet I got a 22 percent response rate and you got a 74 percent. That's unheard of for metastatic lung cancer. How do you do it?" Bob responded, "We're both using Etoposide, Platinol, Oncovin, and Hydroxyurea. You call yours EPOH. I tell my patients I'm giving them HOPE. Sure, I tell them this is experimental, and we go over the long list of side effects together. But I emphasize that we have a chance. As dismal as the statistics are for non–small cell, there are always a few percent who do really well."

Dr. Buchholz's observation is shared by many in the medical community—among them Dr. Toshihiko Maruta, a psychiatrist at the Mayo Clinic in Rochester, Minnesota. Maruta and his colleagues reviewed the psychological tests of more than 800 people done in the 1960s and, based on their responses, classified 197 of them as pessimistic. He then checked to see how long they lived. Pessimists' risk of death was 19 percent higher than average in any given year. In addition, in 1975, researchers asked 660 people about their attitudes on aging. They were asked whether they agreed or disagreed with statements such as "Things keep getting worse as I get older" and "I'm as happy now as I was when I was younger." In 1998, researchers then checked to see which participants were still living and noted when others had died. On average, those who viewed aging as a positive experience lived 7.5 years longer.

Hope and School Performance

In a six-year study of two hundred University of Kansas students, psychologist Rick Snyder discovered that a student's level of hope was a better predictor of his or her ability to make it through a university than ACT scores or high school grade point averages. According to Snyder, "The higher a student scores on the test [Snyder's Hope Scale], the more likely the student will not drop out, the better his or her grade point average, and the more likely he or she will graduate." High-hope students posted GPAs one-half point higher than low-hope students.

Hope for the Bottom Line

Hope's power goes straight to the bottom line—from ROH to ROI. In an exploratory study of fast-food restaurant managers, researchers Suzanne Peterson of Arizona State University and Fred Luthans of the University of Nebraska discovered that stores run by hopeful managers were more profitable and experienced lower employee turnover than those run by their lower-hope counterparts. The researchers also discovered that hopeful managers beget more satisfied subordinates.

The Convergence of Greatness

Although the psychological evidence is not yet as compelling as lung capacity, physical strength, and body mass, elite athletes are increasingly investing in the psychology of sport, but why? It's simple, really. The law of diminishing returns is in effect. The body has approached its limits. Enter better equipment to make up the small margin that remains. Like elite athletes, leaders face the same challenge of convergence and respond in kind. We recruit the same graduates from the same schools, mimic each other's strategies, and thus achieve the same results. All attempts to corner the market on intellect and information have reached their limits. Therefore, it should come as no surprise that the sun is slowly setting on Louis Terman's IQ test, surely to rise on the unorthodox assets of leadership. Enter hope.

Silence Its Greatest Presence

If hope works for nuns, students, and athletes, there must be an application to leadership. While oncologists and theologians have long studied the power of hope over cancer and congregations, very little has been done in the field of leadership. Although we continue to feed our infatuation with statistical reasoning and other forms of high math, hope remains. It is perhaps the single greatest character attribute of successful people.

As Mannie Jackson told me regarding the advice of his lifelong mentor, his high school basketball coach Joe Lucco, who said to him as a young player, "I cannot tell you what to think. All I know is that sometimes in life, you've gotta believe." But this is not the entire story. Belief and desire alone will not get you there. Hope is a way of acting as much as it is a state of mind. One such action discussed later in the book is wayfinding, a method of navigating uncertainty based on experience, observation, and intuition. In the interim, consider how hopeful you are right now. How would you expect to perform in the following situations? What would you do?

Rejoice or Cry?

In 1914, when his laboratory burned to the ground, America's most prolific inventor, Thomas Edison, walked quietly among the ashes and was reported to have said, "There is great value in disaster. All our mistakes are burned up. Thank God we can start anew." This, of course, is somewhat paradoxical considering that this author of 1,093 patents is most often quoted for what would appear to be a myopic devotion to hard work, noting dryly that in percentage terms, hard work is a lot more important than inspiration. Edison's "1 percent inspiration" must have been highly concentrated. Among the hopeful, starting anew is a welcomed task because it allows them to escape their greatest competitor, their own success. However, using hope to your advantage requires more than inspiration and hard work. As you will learn, it involves emancipating conventional beliefs about success, failure, possibility, and communication.

Like Edison, Jack Cakebread—founder of the Cakebread Cellars winery in Napa Valley—welcomes the opportunity to escape the past in exchange for the future. During the course of our conversations, we spoke about how he managed through phylloxera—a disease that was predicted to wreak havoc on the Napa Valley grape-growing region and ultimately did. However, Jack's response was not what I expected. Whereas others saw but doom and gloom, Cakebread saw opportunity. He said, "We knew it was coming. It was going to be the best thing that ever happened to this valley." What could Jack see that others could not? And what role did his outlook play in the moment of uncertainty? Stay tuned. Given his outlook and his wayfinding skills, Jack Cakebread, like Thomas Edison, was not just hopeful in a time of uncertainty; he was jubilant. And not only did he *see* the bright side, he *acted* on it. As owner of one of the most requested wine brands at the nation's top fifty restaurants, Jack knows of what he speaks, as you'll soon learn.

Sink or Swim?

In 1941, Sir Lawrence Holt had a problem. At the beginning of World War II, German U-boats frequently torpedoed his commercial ships, crippling not only his business but also his assumptions about success. The paradox of survival that followed each ship's demise piqued the British ship magnate's interest. Specifically, Holt could not explain why most of the drowned sailors were young while most of the surviving sailors were older. Having neither solution to his problem nor an answer to his question, Holt shared his observations with well-known pedagogue James Hogan in an attempt to understand why this had occurred. What they discovered would go on to affect generations of future leaders.

Holt and Hogan observed that young sailors perished because of what seemed like a perfectly logical thing to do when stranded at sea during a world war. They tried to save themselves. And there's the catch: the younger sailors perished because they tried to do it alone. Older sailors, by contrast, worked together and were more hopeful in their efforts, whether actively waiting for rescue or upon reaching shore. In a sense, younger sailors believed that hope was theirs to lose in the first place, as if it were some kind of material treasure. Once they had lost hope, they panicked and drowned.

Older sailors, having survived previous shipwrecks, used hope and each other to nourish their courage, patience, and will to fight. Therefore, they survived. What we now know, with advances in science, is that likely the older sailors' experience with sinking ships helped in the maturation of their neural networks. In other words, their brains were hardwired to maintain hope—a topic explored in depth later in this book. You could say that the older sailors had a greater physiological capacity to hope. Information, teamwork, and memory made them even more hopeful. As Harry Emerson Fosdick preached in "Procrastination," "How utterly bereft we all should be without that backreach of memory and that outreach of hope!" The backreach of memory, albeit filled with the horror of previous accidents, made the older sailors more hopeful and thus triumphant. However, the question remains, what could Holt have done to mitigate his problem—to help younger and inexperienced sailors succeed in the face of a challenge?

With their observations, Holt and Hogan, along with Kurt Hahn—the German educator, innovator, and founder of Britain's prestigious Gordonstoun School—created a program to help English sailors learn to survive. Inspired by Hahn's motto—central to Gordonstoun's ethos, *"Plus est en vous,"* French for "There is more in you than you think"—Holt named the program after a nautical term referring to the moment when a ship leaves its safe harbor for the unknown challenges of the open sea: Outward Bound.

In 1941, Hogan, Hahn, and Holt opened their first school in Aberdovy, Wales. Twenty youngsters enrolled in the twenty-eight-day program. The focus of their efforts included four objectives: physical fitness, compassion, support, and craftsmanship. Think about it. When was the last off-site leadership retreat you attended where you, along with your coworkers, worked on developing compassion? When was the last time you worked on courage and strength? When was the last time you worked on hope? Today, Outward Bound schools operate in thirty-two countries helping thousands of next-generation leaders learn "to serve, to strive, and not to yield." However, the question remains, if you were one of Holt's crew, what would you have done? What would your team have done? Most important, what can you do now to teach hope?

Create or Litigate?

In 1928, Walt Disney suffered a devastating setback. Because he had naively signed away his ownership rights to his distributor, the twenty-six-year-old animator lost his first successful cartoon, *Oswald the Lucky Rabbit*. "Alone with nothing," Walt recalled later, "I created Mortimer on the train ride home. My wife thought Mortimer was too pompous, so later she suggested Mickey." Disney, claiming he had nothing, overlooked his own creativity. As you'll soon learn, hope and creativity are good friends.

Fund or Fire?

Following the great stock market crash of 1929, Adolph Ochs, publisher of the *New York Times*, issued a memo to his staff: "We must set an example of optimism. Please urge every department to go ahead as if we thought the best year in the world is ahead of us." Although fifteen advertisers cancelled their contracts with Ochs in a single week, Ochs mitigated employee layoffs opting to use the $12 million surplus he had built during the roaring 1920s to pay salaries. And rather than spin the financial horror story of the day, at the end of the year, Ochs chose Admiral Richard Byrd's successful exploration of Antarctica as the most important news story of 1929. Once the Great Depression had ended, the *New York Times* had more readers than any other newspaper in the country. In the newspaper business, having more readers translates into premium advertising rates. Hope pays.

Enable or Avoid?

His dream is to eradicate world poverty by granting small loans to the poor—a group of people growing at five times the rate of the rest of the world. Considering that 2.5 billion people on this planet live on less than $2 per day, this goal is quite ambitious. Against all conventional banking wisdom, Muhammad Yunus has made loans to 4 million of the poorest people in Bangladesh. Because they have nothing to offer other than hope for a better life, he asks for no collateral. Amazingly, 99 percent of all the loans are paid back in full. How does Grameen Bank, a multimillion-dollar microlending institution, use hope to fight poverty at its 1,267 branches while contributing 1 percent to India's total gross domestic product? Moreover, how do leaders like Yunus find a way to make the impossible possible? It involves escaping the past. It involves beliefs. Yunus, like most triumphant leaders, is a *belief manager*, the topic of an upcoming chapter.

Your Test Results

So how did you do? Did you rejoice or cry? Sink or swim? Create or litigate? Fund or fire? Enable or avoid? If you sank—not to worry—so did I. In part, that is why I chose to write this book. I was not satisfied with merely being inspired. Although I generally like to feel good, I would prefer to *succeed* while feeling good. As you will learn, Edison, Ochs, Holt, Disney, and Yunus shared an approach to leadership that gave rise to their unusual success. They not only thought about hope but also used it. They regarded hope as a form of planning. And mysteriously, it works. Consider the following:

- When two fighter pilots are in similar hopeless situations, why does one bail out while the other finds a way to save himself and his very expensive aircraft?

- When two companies are in similar dire straits, what enables one leader to turn it around while the other fails?

- When the Napa Valley was brought to its knees by a root louse destroying its valuable vines, why did one leader not only survive but thrive?

- When stranded on the space station for five months as it spiraled out of control, what role did a forgotten Russian scientist's research play in saving the life of one of America's greatest astronauts?

- Under communism, what role did jazz and a required university class on the "science of atheism" play in brainwashing an entire society? Why didn't it work?

- What did a group of pioneering neuroscientists and Buddhist monks discover recently in the shadows of the Himalayas that sheds new light on the role of outlook and human performance?

As you will soon learn, hope is an active participant in each of these scenarios. For now, consider the reason to believe. Consider the need for hope.

3

A REASON TO BELIEVE

*The audacity of hope! In the end, that is God's
greatest gift to us, the bedrock of this nation. A
belief in things not seen. A belief that there are
better days ahead.*

—*Barack Obama*

If time could be branded, Georg Wilhelm Friedrich Hegel would be
its advertising agency. Time's slogan? "Zeitgeist." It is a German word
meaning "spirit of the age." Zeitgeist is shaped by, reflected in, and
communicated through our cultural institutions—music, movies, literature, and philosophy. German philosopher Hegel coined the term
in the nineteenth century to describe the inescapable moral tone that
defines each era, making each not only unique but influencing all
those who live in it. Like responsibility, you cannot escape it. Zeitgeist represents our insatiable search for meaning. We like to brand
time, and we have Hegel to thank for it. The capacity to arrive at a
worldview is not only a philosophical skill but also one of leadership.
Of great value is the mind that travels along the arc of history—the
one that can see the "big picture." And when the spirit of the age can
be summed up in a single word, we are even happier. After all, isn't
that the goal of a great brand, brevity in communicating a message?

Antiestablishment was the Zeitgeist of the 1960s, when Edwin
Starr sang, "War! . . . What is it good for? Absolutely nothin'!" Flash
forward to the 1980s. People who once chanted Starr's lyrics bought
themselves shiny new Beemers, selfishness replaced the greater good,
and world peace took a back seat to *my* peace. Michael Douglas's portrayal of the obsessively money-centered workaholic trader Gordon

Gekko in the film *Wall Street* was one such piece of evidence of the 1980s Zeitgeist. His mantra: "Greed is good." All the while, the catchy New Wave sound of Nena's 99 *Luftballons* eclipsed her sociopolitical commentary on the coming nuclear devastation. Greed got better ink. From decade to decade, we've embraced Hegel's time-branding strategy. It's fashionable. We find comfort knowing that we are wearing the right shoes while standing on the right side of the issues. So what is the Zeitgeist of our age today? What are its implications for twenty-first-century leaders? And why is hope a particularly relevant antidote?

The Zeitgeist of Our Age

According to the Bureau of Labor Statistics, the average twenty-five- to thirty-four-year-old puts in 2.9 years before moving on to the next job. This is one-third the time that their parents invest in a job. As one would expect, people in the fifty-five to sixty-four age bracket are more loyal to their current employers, investing 9.6 years, on average, before looking for greener pastures. Commitment has become passé. One wonders, what do people lose first? Interest or hope? And who is responsible for our commitment-phobic culture? According to a wealth of research on employee turnover and job satisfaction, employees often cite a lack of leadership as one of the primary reasons for a premature departure—hence the axiom that "people don't leave companies; they leave people." Confusing the issue even further is that most leaders and their followers disagree about what matters in a job. Leigh Branham's analysis of nearly twenty thousand exit surveys from companies in seventeen industries illustrates that 89 percent of managers believe that retaining good employees is about the money, while 88 percent of employees cite reasons *other than pay* for leaving. Although leaders and followers typically look for the light at the end of the tunnel together, they often see it through very different lenses. Their divergent opinions about what matters makes the future more difficult to see. And when people cannot see light at the end of the tunnel, they have two options: stop and subsequently get hit by oncoming traffic, or turn around and get the hell out of the tunnel. In the absence of leadership, people are left waffling, spinning their wheels, and ultimately out of control. "Turnover" isn't the only title on the soundtrack of our age. If entertainment is any indicator, powerlessness is pervasive. Consider this: the best-selling video game of all time is one that allows gamers to create and manage the lives of a simulated family. The Sims (*Sim* is gamer-speak for "simulated person") actually lets players "play God."

Playing God

Unlike a majority of video games, whose sales peak in the first six months, after which they retreat like a cowardly army, The Sims, originated by Will Wright and now owned by gaming giant Electronic Arts, continues to sell in record numbers year after year. Equally telling is the game's broad appeal. When released in 2000, The Sims not only appealed to hard-core gamers but also to non-gamers and the most unorthodox game demographic—girls. More than half of Sims gamers are girls.

Gamers determine every aspect, from chin length to hairstyle, of the Sims they create, who may resemble anything from beauty pageant hotties to mutant man-children. You'd think, given the stress associated with managing one's own life, that the last thing we'd want to do is worry about looking after the lives of others. However, like the escape promised by romantic comedies and U2 concerts, we stand in line to do so. The Sims is more than a fun game. Its extraordinary success suggests a craving for control; a want of a better life. If you consider the greatest *weakness* of this simulated game of life, the reason for its extraordinary success becomes instantly apparent. As with most things in life, details reveal meaning.

Many gamers of the original version cited a single reason for their discontinued use—boredom. However, it is why they were bored that is most telling: there was no goal. In the original version, although you could create a "perfect" or "imperfect" family, there was no option for the creation of *life aspirations* for the simulated family. Therefore, playing the original game is a bit like eating Chinese food—at first, you feel full, but thirty minutes later, you're hungry again. Without meaning—in simulation as in life—we get bored. Therefore, in the newer edition, The Sims 2, when a player creates a Sim, the player also chooses a life's aspiration for the being. From getting a job to marrying rich, when each daily task is successfully completed, "aspiration points" are awarded to the Sim. (And here is where simulation becomes reality.) Aspiration points, in turn, lift a Sim's mood. As my favorite London tube station billboard reads, with double entendre, THERAPY IS WORKING. With mood lifted, the points allow the Sim to buy things such as trees that grow money, "fountain of youth" water coolers, and sunglasses that make the Sim more popular in the neighborhood.

However, where there is simulated bliss, there is simulated violence. Just look at other popular gaming titles: Doom, Grand Theft Auto, Mortal Combat. Violence is not only a fact of *simulated* life but also of the real variety—suggesting yet another indicator of the spirit of our age. The Bureau of Labor Statistics' census of fatal occupational injuries ranks murder as the number two cause of workplace deaths among women and the fourth killer of males—so much for happy hour. And if not at risk of death, we face an equally devastating blow to organization sustainability—apathy. According to the Walker Information National Employee Benchmarking Study, only 20 percent of all U.S. employees want to be with their current employer in two years. (No wonder the risk of heart attack is 20 percent higher on Mondays.) For those of you keeping score at home, the songs on the soundtrack of our age thus far include "Job Churn," "A Yearning for Control," and "Workplace Violence." Add a dash of corporate corruption and a smidgen of geopolitical turbulence, and leaders today face what could be construed as a nearly impossible challenge.

Our Disposable Age

In an age when we trade in and trade up everything from jobs to cell phones, CEOs to coaches, and vintage homes for McMansions, the Zeitgeist of our age seems increasingly apparent: *disposability*. We'll just get another one—another car, another cell phone, another coach, another CEO, another customer, another employee, another soldier. We have responded to the Zeitgeist of our age with a single solution for all that ails us: a giant recycling program for everything.

Why We Love to Fire Leaders

At this disposable moment in the arc of history, soulfulness is as important as mindfulness. The human spirit is thirsty—and so are stockholders, customers, students, fans, and citizens. Now is a time for greatness. The good news is this: each and every day, you have the opportunity to influence the future. The bad news is that you have less time. The doors most commonly installed on executive offices are of the revolving variety.

According to Burson-Marsteller, average CEO tenure has shrunk to five years from ten. More telling is Wall Street's reaction to leadership turnover. It rejoices! Consider this: Hewlett-Packard's stock price shot up 7 percent the day after its controversial CEO was forced out the door. Sara Lee's stock jumped 4 percent on the announcement of a change in leadership. The average increase in stock price at the announcement of a departing CEO is 1 percent, and if the change is forced by the company's board of directors and an outsider is brought in to change the game, the stock shoots up even higher—3.5 percent. Hope springs eternal—particularly when the board plays musical chairs with incumbent leaders.

According to Leslie Gaines-Ross, chief knowledge and research officer at Burson-Marsteller, "If CEOs aren't able to deliver quickly, investors view a new CEO as their only hope of keeping the company competitive. Every four to five years, companies must reinvent themselves. Some CEOs lose steam." Unfortunately, the business world suffers from EDD—earnings deficit disorder. We measure our hopes and dreams based on quarterly returns. If earnings don't meet expectations, neither does our hope in the future. And when hope isn't apparent, a new leader becomes that hope. We fire leaders in exchange for hope. The question is, why wait until your departure to communicate hope? The sacrificial CEO is not the only option for communicating hope. It would behoove boards to teach their leaders about expectations management and communication. Teach them about hope. Because whether deliberately or inadvertently, when leaders fail to communicate hope, their employees, owners, and directors lose faith not only in them but in the future.

Rewriting the Future

In the spirit of our age, hope is the opportunity to rewrite the future. From shrinking product life cycles to binge-and-purge hiring and firing, the world isn't going to get easier to manage. We need hope not only to cure what ails us but also for its performance benefits. When used appropriately, hope yields tangible benefits, from enhancing creativity to improving problem-solving skills. However, hope's primary benefit is its ability to give meaning in meaningless moments. Hope carries the burdens of failure but also of success. Hope carries meaning.

Becoming a *Porteur de Sens*

A management trend is afoot in Europe, likely a response to the Zeitgeist of our age. It is called *porteur de sens* (French for "bearer of meaning"). In a keynote presentation I gave for TAP Pharmaceuticals, the French-born vice president for research and development, Xavier Frapaise, introduced the day's events by calling on each of his directors and managers as a *porteur de sens*, a bearer of meaning. Triumphant leaders engage not only the heads but also the hearts of those who look to them for leadership. Therefore, becoming a *porteur de sens* involves sharing not just the objective but the meaning of the journey as well.

In this particular pharmaceutical business, which is focused on treating 3.5 million people with gout and 350,000 women who have had hysterectomies, meaning motivates. However, you do not need to be in the business of saving lives or improving health to be a *porteur de sens*. For example, the leadership and employees of semiconductor manufacturer Advanced Micro Devices believe that they are "making technology affordable to the world." This is a far more inspirational battle cry—far more meaningful—than "manufacturing and selling semiconductors." Triumphant leaders give meaning to work by working on meaning.

People crave meaning and leaders who offer it. The role of *porteur de sens*—although a fashionably French term—is not recognized only by the French. Germans share this philosophy, translating it directly into German as *Sinnträger*. We all want to know *why* we are doing what we are doing. Sure, we want to be happy, but we fundamentally want to *believe*—in possibility, in our work, and in ourselves.

Xavier told me, "I have found that most people in this world, myself included, struggle with the meaning of life. As leaders, the least we can do is help people find meaning in their work." Xavier's words are particularly profound when you consider his self-proclaimed skepticism: "I am French and a scientist," he notes. "I am born and trained to be skeptical." Although Xavier may be skeptical, he is hopeful. His unique combination of intellect, curiosity, and compassion afford him the benefits of hopeful leadership. Hope sets objectives, ignites will, focuses the organization in turbulent times, renews energy, displaces boredom as it succeeds, fosters creativity and innovation, and inspires people to want to do the right thing. By giving meaning to life, hope lets us live, play, and work in a world outside the lines. Hope reduces inhibitions, and reduced inhibitions unleash creativity.

A World Outside the Lines

Thinking creatively involves a number of things, not the least of which is curiosity, inspiration, time, and intellectual courage. Scientific evidence suggests that fallen inhibitions (a symptom of a hopeful outlook) gives way to greater creativity. Fear not, and ye shall create with greater vigor.

Ulrich Kraft recounts a story of a San Francisco art teacher whose creativity was enhanced following a chance illness. Jancy Chang had been painting since she was a child. From Western-style watercolors to classical Chinese brushstrokes, she always strove for realism—to paint landscapes as realistically as she could—literal, not abstract, depictions. Then, at the age of forty-three, something happened. Everything she had trained herself to do, from lesson planning to grading, she could no longer do. By age fifty-two, she could no longer remember her students' names and was ultimately forced to retire.

Shortly after her retirement, Chang met Bruce Miller, clinical director of the Memory and Aging Center at the University of California at San Francisco. Miller diagnosed Chang with frontotemporal dementia, in which regions of the brain that control speech and social behavior are selectively damaged. Patients who suffer from this rare form of dementia, among other things, lose their inhibitions, often becoming introverted and awkward in social settings. However, what Miller also observed in Chang was an exponential growth in her creativity. According to Miller, "The more she lost her social and language abilities, the wilder and freer her art became." The same lack of inhibition that caused embarrassing moments in public allowed her to be increasingly more impressionistic and abstract. She began to paint outside the lines.

Miller was dumbfounded. How could a person whose brain was deteriorating become more talented? Miller later identified others who exhibited similar behavior, including a stockbroker who traded his conservative suits for outlandish styles, became intrigued with painting, and went on to win several prizes for his work and yet another who invented a sophisticated chemical detector while only able to recall one in fifteen words on a memory test. Although scientific understanding of creativity is in its infancy, creativity is not necessarily an innate gift. We can enlist it through encouragement.

As Steven Smith, professor of psychology at the Institute for Applied Creativity at Texas A&M University, explains, "Many people believe that only a handful of geniuses are capable of making creative contributions to humanity. It just isn't true. Creative thinking is the norm in human beings and can be observed in almost all mental activities." The question is, why is creative inspiration more prevalent in some people versus others? Outlook may play a role.

Whereas fear and inhibition draw boundaries around possibility, making impossible situations even more unworkable, hope opens pathways in the mind, thereby allowing creativity to flourish. Hope and creativity form a reinforcing loop. A hopeful mind sees more possibilities—more ways to solve, attain, and win. Similarly, our outlook, not necessarily what we know, can enhance our ability to solve problems. Consider people who have mastered the art of messy situations. Consider hope and the problem-solving skills of fighter pilots.

The Art of Bailing Out

During World War II, the U.S. Air Force commissioned a study to understand how pilots get out of seemingly hopeless situations. The question was simple: when in battle, why do some pilots bail out while others find a way to save themselves and their very expensive aircraft? At first, the researchers used intelligence tests. However, they soon realized that IQ was insignificant. This could be explained in part by the relatively small variance in pilots' IQ scores, reflecting the fact that officers chosen to train as pilots generally had high IQs (after all, why put a multimillion-dollar aircraft in the hands of someone south of brilliant?). Although in practice, intelligence was not a predictor of performance, the investigators maintained their assumption that superior pilots somehow thought differently. It turned out that they thought very differently. Step inside the minds of the world's greatest fighter pilots.

The answer to the Air Force's question emerged from research conducted by psychologist Joy Paul Guilford at the University of Southern California. Guilford's job was to think about thinking. From her studies, she had developed a model for human intellect. In it, she made distinctions between what she called *convergent* and *divergent* thinking. Whereas convergent thinking seeks to find a single correct solution to a problem, divergent thinking involves generating many possible solutions to the same problem. Those who bailed out were convergent thinkers; the exceptional pilots were divergent thinkers. Because IQ tests test only convergent thinking, it came as no surprise to the Air Force that there was no correlation between intelligence and superior flying ability. In its own tests, IQ didn't sync up, and Guilford's work helped explain why. Enter hope. Hope promotes divergent thinking, and divergent thinking promotes hope. When solving problems, simply knowing that many solutions could exist makes us better prepared to solve them. In hindsight, the idea of divergent thinking seems quite obvious. However, this is precisely the brilliance of Guilford's insight. Most great ideas elicit the same reaction: why didn't I think of that?

The Psychobiology of Cliff Clavin

Divergent thinking is not the sole domain of fighter pilots. Odds are you know a divergent thinker, if not in real life, then on TV. Consider one of the most memorable episodes of the popular sitcom *Cheers,* in which John Ratzenberger's character, Cliff Clavin, trivia mastermind and postal carrier, was selected to compete on the TV game show *Jeopardy* (*Cheers* episode 182, "What Is . . . Cliff Clavin?" which first aired on NBC on January 18, 1990). With a huge lead over the other contestants and having successfully answered questions in categories including civil servants, stamps from around the world, mothers and sons, beer, bar trivia, and celibacy, Cliff decides to wager all his winnings in Final Jeopardy. The Final Jeopardy question involved giving the real names of three Hollywood celebrities known popularly by their stage names. The clue was "Archibald Leach, Bernard Schwartz, and Lucille LeSueur." Cliff responds with "Who are three people who have never been in my kitchen?" at which point, the show's host, Alex Trebek, answers, "I'm sorry. That is wrong." Cliff retorts, "Wait a minute, Alex. I can offer conclusive proof that those three people have never been in my kitchen." Although Cliff's answer was not right, it was not wrong. Cliff Clavin could have been Guilford's poster child.

Like gamers, fighter pilots, and trivia masterminds, triumphant leaders use hope to solve problems, unleash creativity, and give meaning to the task at hand. When applied, hope is a form of extrinsic motivation, used to motivate others. However, hope is also a form of *intrinsic* motivation, used to motivate oneself. In both applications, hope involves believing—in yourself, in others, and in an unrealized future.

Think about believing. Recall the last time someone believed in you—I mean really believed in you, so much that they put you in a situation that even *you* thought was beyond your capacity. Perhaps it was a coach, a teacher, or an old boss. How did it make you feel knowing that someone thought you could walk on water and run through walls? How did you perform?

Believers are the best leaders. They are convinced beyond a reasonable doubt that the human spirit is capable of anything once it can persuade the rational mind that it's worth making the trip. Recent scientific findings on beliefs contribute to the mounting evidence in support of the power of hope as a leadership tool. There is "new news" regarding the self-fulfilling prophecy. Consider the stigma of a pretty woman.

[By the way, if you are still wondering what response Alex Trebek was expecting Cliff Clavin to give, it's "Who are Cary Grant, Tony Curtis, and Joan Crawford?"]

4

THE STIGMA OF
A PRETTY WOMAN

Fear less, hope more; eat less, chew more; whine
less, breathe more; talk less, say more; love more,
and all good things will be yours.

—*Swedish proverb*

Vaclav Havel, playwright and former president of the Czech Republic, once wrote in a secret letter to writer Karel Hvizdala about his source of hope, "I think that the deepest and most important form of hope, the only one that can keep us above water and urge us to good works, and the only true source of the breathtaking dimension of the human spirit and its efforts, is something we get, as it were, from elsewhere."

Triumphant leaders often acknowledge another person's hope as the reason for their own. The belief that the leader had in others—or for that matter the belief that the leader had in *anything*—was so fervent that it caused observers to believe in the impossible, in others, and fundamentally in themselves. From God to grandmothers and from coaches to college professors, triumphant leaders often cite others for their outlook and their own success. When people look to leaders, they are looking for hope. The question remains, are they getting what they need?

A Call for Consciousness

"Deeper consciousness among leaders is what we need in this world. Not only will it affect the way organizations are managed, but it also has the potential to give the nation a reason to believe." These were Mannie Jackson's words to me very early in the course of writing this book. As former senior vice president of Honeywell, director of six Fortune 500 companies, and corporate turnaround CEO, Mannie knows a thing or two about leadership. He understands that the most important things in leadership (as in life) you cannot see—beliefs, expectations, aspirations, desire, fear, and hope. Therefore, Mannie, like most triumphant leaders, has created unconventional techniques for managing the unknown. He has a different relationship with hope.

Inspired by Mannie's words, I turned to the world's reigning consciousness guru for insight, Dr. Deepak Chopra. "Andrew," the doctor told me, "you will have to forgive me for some of my ideas, but I come from a very Eastern perspective. I am a student of consciousness. I have always believed that if you can *see* something, touch it, and experience it through the senses, it is just an illusion. It is only an expression of something that you *cannot* see. That is consciousness. I use the words *consciousness, spirit,* and *awareness* synonymously. Without it, you cannot see, touch, taste, smell, perceive, think, or feel. My whole grounding and teaching is that you believe in something only when you can really experience it and when you understand how it is created. If you really follow the process that consciousness is the ground from which everything else comes, then only invisible things are real. Everything else comes and goes. Love is real. Compassion is real. Healing is real. Our connection to nature is real. If you focus on all things that are real, your beliefs will be an expression of your experience rather than a cover-up for insecurity." To underscore his enthusiasm for his work and his own beliefs, Chopra continued, "I don't have to believe in gravity. I can prove it."

Chopra's words suggest that we must work harder to believe in those things that we cannot see and, as leaders, to encourage others to believe as well. If something is obvious or tangible, there is no need to believe in it. You can prove it. After all, what is courageous about believing in electricity? Turn on the lights. Since leaders are dealers in the most intangible things—an ambiguous future, a lofty mission, stretch goals, heartfelt aspirations, and the fervent and col-

THE STIGMA OF A PRETTY WOMAN   39

lective desire of a team, leaders must be the greatest believers. As Chopra continued, "If invisible things are real, you [as a leader] should have a theoretical understanding of them. You should be able to experience them. You should be able to replicate them for others if they don't believe in them themselves. If they believe, then you [the leader] shouldn't have to convince them." Isn't this the goal of most leaders—and almost everyone else—not having to convince others that what we see is worthy of our attention and hard work? Followers work harder for leaders when they truly believe not only in the leader's vision but also in the leader's beliefs and the leader's hope for the future. Consider the fervent followership of one of the most hopeful leaders on the planet, the fourteenth Dalai Lama.

Getting What They Need

Dr. Nawang Rabgyal is the representative of the Dalai Lama to the Americas and director of the Office of Tibet in Exile in New York. "When entertaining the wife of French President François Mitterrand in Dharamsala (the Dalai Lama's home in exile)," Rabgyal told me, "the Dalai Lama took her on a tour, pointing out various antiquities on the grounds. When they approached a statue of the Buddha, His Holiness stopped, pointed to the statue, turned to Madame Mitterrand, and said, 'My boss.' The Dalai Lama has a wonderful sense of humor." With increasing enthusiasm in his voice, Rabgyal continued, "People want to be like him. He is a real leader. He does not seek power. He does not want to rule Tibet once we have our freedom. He wants to follow in the footsteps of Mahatma Gandhi. Although Mahatma Gandhi led the struggle for freedom, once the nation achieved it, he did not take part in the administration. His Holiness wants to do the same. He wants us to lead ourselves."

The Dalai Lama is such a fervent believer in those who look to him for leadership that he wrote a clause into the constitution allowing for his removal with two-thirds vote in parliament. You may be asking, why would he want to do that? As Rabgyal explains, "He is such a down-to-earth leader. He is a symbol of our hope and unity.

And he knows this to be the case. His Holiness believed that it is possible to have too much faith in a leader and therefore wanted to provide us with a way to amend or even delete his role if we deemed it no longer necessary." How many leaders do you know who would do this? For that matter, how many leaders do you know who would do just the opposite? What happened next is the greatest testament to the Dalai Lama's beliefs and his efficacy as a leader.

Shortly after the clause was discovered, the Tibetan people called for its immediate removal from the constitution. They so believe in their leader that they didn't even want the option to remove him from office. And so in a unanimous vote, the clause was removed. Several years later, in 1969, the Dalai Lama made yet another plea to his people to consider removing the office of Dalai Lama if Tibetan society was not benefiting from it.

The fourteenth Dalai Lama believes so much in the capacity of his people that he encourages them to lead themselves. As a result, he commands not only their admiration but their dedication. The Dalai Lama has achieved what every leader secretly desires—the people aspire to be as good, as compassionate, as thoughtful, and as hopeful as he is. However, not only do Tibetans benefit from the Dalai Lama's belief in them; the Dalai Lama also benefits from their belief in him. What people believe about you has the capacity to affect your performance. Beliefs are more than perception.

The Psychology of Believing

A team of psychologists at Iowa State University recently found that the contention that a person's beliefs can affect the fate of another person has a scientific basis, causing researchers around the globe to revisit the validity of the self-fulfilling prophecy. To understand the power of a belief over behavior, try this. Put down this book. If you are able, stand up and walk around the room. While walking, envision yourself tripping. Go ahead. I'll wait. Do it now. What happened? If you tripped, you have just experienced a self-fulfilling prophecy. A false belief led to its own fulfillment. If you didn't, I suggest you consider a career as either a tight end or a ballet dancer. You decide.

Columbia University professor and sociologist Robert Merton coined the term *self-fulfilling prophecy* in his 1957 work *Social Theory and Social Structure*. He proposed that self-fulfilling prophecies had the potential to wreak havoc on society by materializing into unfair labor practices and discriminatory policies. He even went so far as to suggest that the phenomenon could perpetuate economic downturns.

The phenomenon is also known as the Pygmalion effect, a name inspired by playwright George Bernard Shaw's incarnation of phonetics professor Henry Higgins and his pet project, Eliza Doolittle. Pygmalion was a king of Cyprus who fell in love with a statue of his own making. In Shaw's *Pygmalion,* Professor Higgins insists that he can take a Cockney flower girl, Eliza Doolittle, and pass her off as a duchess by refining her speech and manner. However, as Doolittle suggests to Higgins's friend Pickering, "You see, really and truly, apart from the things anyone can pick up (the dressing and the proper way of speaking and so on), the difference between a lady and a flower girl is not how she *behaves* but how she is *treated*. I shall always be a flower girl to Professor Higgins, because he always treats me as a flower girl, and always will, but I know I can be a lady to you because you always treat me as a lady, and always will."

If Shaw's words invoke images from the musical *My Fair Lady* (adapted from *Pygmalion*) or Julia Roberts pumping her fist into the air, yes, this is the same story as *Pretty Woman*. For you Freddie Prinze Jr. and Rachel Leigh Cook fans, *She's All That* is the 1999 continuation of the Pygmalion myth. You can blame Hollywood for its lack of creativity, but you can't blame it for its ability to recognize a great story.

"Not How She Behaves, but How She Is Treated"

Shaw captured the self-fulfilling prophecy in nine words: "Not how she behaves, but how she is treated." Shaw's words remind me of those of the founder of a multigenerational family business who, in response to a question about preparing his kids to take over the leadership reins, responded by saying, "I don't think they are ready to lead just yet, but I'm mentoring my kids each and every day." Mind you, at the time, his kids were fifty-six, fifty-nine, and sixty-three. Dad was eighty-nine. We are always our parents' children. We treat people as we see (believe in) them regardless of how they may have grown or changed. As a leader, are you more like Shaw's Higgins or Pickering? Have you ever asked those who look to you for leadership, "Do you believe that I believe in you?" Try it. You'll know if they're telling the truth. It takes courage to answer this question, but it also takes courage to ask it. Further, it requires even greater confidence to show, not just say, that you believe.

Consider Chicago White Sox manager Ozzie Guillen. In game two of the 2005 World Series, in the top of the ninth inning, one of his star pitchers, Bobby Jenks, nearly blew the save by permitting a two-run single that tied the game. Fortunately, in the bottom of the inning, Chicago's Scott Podsednik hit a walk-off home run to win the game and was subsequently mobbed by his teammates in a party at the plate. Guillen opted out of the celebration. Here's why. As Guillen recalls, "I was looking for the guy who fell. I didn't care about Podsednik. He did his job. I was looking for Jenks. When a guy falls, that's when you show him some love and let him know you still believe in him." Guillen found Jenks. And when he did, he hugged him. As Jenks recalls, "He lets you know things will be all right no matter what happens." In game four, once again, Guillen tapped Jenks to close. And that he did. Guillen believed in Jenks, and therefore so too did Jenks and the 2005 Chicago White Sox believe in Guillen. The morning after they were crowned the World Series champions, ending an eighty-eight-year losing streak, the *Chicago Tribune* headline read simply, "Believe it!" That they did. Believers are the best leaders.

Shedding New Light on an Ancient Myth

Although we intuitively know that believers, like Ozzie Guillen and Bernard Shaw's Pickering, are the best leaders, the Pygmalion effect has historically been dismissed as conjecture more than theory due to a low statistical correlation. In other words, the evidence that a person's beliefs could have a material affect on another person's performance was theoretical—until recently.

The Iowa State researchers discovered that the *false beliefs* that two or more people have of another person, when shared, can influence that person's behavior. However, the inherent challenge we face, according to this research, is that although negative beliefs equate to negative outcomes, positive beliefs don't necessarily affect a more positive outcome. So then, you may be asking, why be hopeful? We must seek to be actively positive if for no other reason than to hedge the downside risk of our natural predisposition for negativity.

The Iowa State study examined whether the false beliefs of mothers and fathers could predict how much alcohol their child would drink over the course of a year. The results illustrated that parents' beliefs predicted their children's alcohol use beyond the risk factors. Kids drank more when their parents thought they would drink more ("Not how she behaves, but how she is treated"). This effect was strongest when *both* parents overestimated their child's alcohol use; hence the *accumulated* effect. On the other hand, there was no accumulative effect for positive beliefs. In other words, convincing your spouse that together you can will your child's grade point average into the stratosphere won't work. However, *failure* for your child could be in the cards if you both believe he or she will fail and share those beliefs with each other.

The implications for you are this: if shared, your negative beliefs can impede the performance of those who look to you for leadership. You must therefore seek to be actively hopeful. This does not mean living in denial, nor does it mean giving pep talks. It means that you must recognize the saliency of negativity and manage it through your decisions, actions, and communication. Use hope. However, also know that being actively positive is not as easy as it may seem. Believing requires courage, and courage requires hope. Here's why.

A Three-Day Walk for Hopeful Leaders

Miserable people have company, but what do hopeful people have other than themselves? Odd as it may seem, living with hope is like living with an undiagnosed disease. There is a stigma attached to it. What will I tell people back at the office? Will they really believe me, or will they think I'm crazy? Do I really admit that I have this dream or think that this problem can be solved? Unfortunately, we often exchange our hopes for the quiet comfort of avoiding the comebacks—"You must be joking" or the maddeningly popular "Whatever." Ideas quiver in the turbulence of our minds. Therefore, triumphant leaders manage beliefs as much as objectives. They manage "why" as much as "what." They are belief managers—the topic of Chapter Nine.

Although almost everyone wants to believe in the possibility of a new day, a better life, and a more profitable future, it seems that we humans are a grumpy bunch. We have an insatiable appetite for all things negative. Consider the fact that more people are drawn to Dante's *Inferno* than his *Purgatory* or *Paradiso*. After passing through the depths of hell, one would think that most people would want to follow Dante and his guide Virgil as they ascend the mountain of purgatory. Nonetheless, this doesn't seem to be the case. For many people, living in the *Inferno* is a more familiar, if less desirable, life than living in *Paradiso*. We are predisposed to live with known hells rather than to search for unknown heavens. After all, dreams take far too much work, and who doesn't like to complain now and then or take pleasure in the tribulations of perfect strangers? It feels good. Given our sullen predisposition, to use hope to your advantage, you must first understand what you're up against. Consider the competitive advantage of negative emotions.

5

LIFE'S SHORT–
WHY SO NEGATIVE?

Although the press is often accused of having a
liberal bias, its real bias is a preference for the
negative.

—*Thomas Patterson*

In the 1960 presidential race between John F. Kennedy and Richard
M. Nixon, 75 percent of media coverage was favorable in tone and
only 25 percent was unfavorable. By the 1980 campaign between
Ronald Reagan and Jimmy Carter, negative had edged out positive,
exceeding 50 percent. Since then, no major party presidential nominee has received more positive than negative coverage.

In a project titled "The Vanishing Voter," conducted at Harvard
University, researchers interviewed nearly one hundred thousand
Americans during the course of the 2000 presidential campaign in
order to discover why potential voters were not voting. Among their
findings were that although negative news coverage is not the only
reason that Americans stay home on election day, as dissatisfaction
from negative news increases, so does a voter's inclination to hug the
couch. As ABC newscaster Peter Jennings once observed, "Forget
about the issues. . . . There is enough mud being tossed around to
keep a health spa supplied for a lifetime."

Pollsters for the Gallup Organization present similar conclusions. According to Gallup, between 1936 and 1968, Barry Goldwater
was the only major party presidential nominee whose public image

was construed as more negative than positive at the end of the campaign (that was in 1964). Since 1968, a third of all presidential nominees have been perceived unfavorably. This should come as no surprise. In our Jerry Springer pop culture, we as a species seem to have an insatiable obsession with negativity.

Never to Have Loved

Negative information is perceived as more salient than positive information. For example, when making decisions, whether we are aware of it or not, many of us weigh the costs of losing (a negative event) more than the rewards of winning (a positive event). Consider gambling. When wagering, the pain associated with losing the $100 we have just won is often more severe than the positive feelings associated with the possibility of winning another $100. This phenomenon is called aversion to losses and is partly responsible for at least one Nobel Prize in economics. By integrating insights from psychological research into economic science, Daniel Kahneman's work in the area of behavioral economics puts a hole in the logic supporting the contention that it is better to have loved and lost than never to have loved at all. In fact, it's a hole so large that you could drive a truck through it.

As depressing as it may seem, you would be better off to have never known love than to get dumped. One need not look further than reality television to witness this phenomenon in action. As contestants are voted off a show week by week, the stakes increase for each remaining contender, thereby increasing the level of anxiety. There is simply more to lose. This also explains why, following the Olympic Games, silver medalists exhibit higher levels of disappointment than bronze medalists. Amos Tversky and Daniel Kahneman's research concluded that if we can easily simulate something mentally, we think it is very likely to be true or to occur. So in the case of Olympic medals, as a silver medalist, it is relatively easy to identify that "one small thing" that you could have done differently to win the gold. On the other hand, as a bronze medalist, several things would have needed to go your way to garner the gold, while only "one small thing" could have resulted in no medal at all. Therefore, counterintuitive as it may seem, Olympians are generally happier to win the bronze ("to have medaled") than to win silver ("to have almost won the gold"). Like the dark horse nominee on the red carpet at the Academy Awards who smiles into the camera and says, "I'm just happy to be nominated"—only later that night to drink herself silly—we hate to lose. But we also suffer from "almost winning" ("I could have been a contender!"). In addition to our fascination with negativity and our aversion to losing (and almost winning), as it turns out, our obsession with the negative is a bit more complicated. Let's examine why we love misery.

The Effect-Cause Relationship

With most things in life, causes precede effects. However, with hope, effects precede the cause. In his book *Hope and Despair,* Anthony Reading, professor emeritus of the Department of Psychiatry at the University of South Florida and medical director of the Bay Medical Behavioral Health Center in Panama City, Florida, notes, "One of the reasons science has had such a difficult time coming to grips with hope is that doing so requires understanding how something merely imagined and yet to occur can cause something else to happen." For example, hoping to win a game, hoping to turn around a company, or hoping to get promoted are acts for which the cause (our hope in some desired future) follows the effect of our actions in time. By contrast, if you do something and then "hope it works out," this is not hope but merely wishful thinking, otherwise known as false hope. Reading continues, "Even more puzzling, not only can something that has not yet happened act as a cause, but so too can something that may never happen, provided that a person believes it is likely to happen." If you think you have no chance of succeeding, you probably won't; if you think you have every chance of succeeding, it is far more likely that you will.

The implication for you is this: in matters of the mind, physics isn't as relevant. That's why it's called physics. You must accept that effects (your actions) *precede* cause (your hope) in order to use hope as a tool. Otherwise, you risk leading with false hope ("hoping it works out"). In addition to the unconventional nature of hope's effect-cause relationship, our predisposition for the negative has a lot to do with marketing. Negativity has a better publicist.

Negative Trumps Positive

Barbara Fredrickson, director of the Positive Emotions and Psychophysiology Laboratory at the University of Michigan, offers three reasons why negative emotions receive a disproportionate share of our attention. First, it appears that negative emotions outnumber positive ones. Anger comes in more colors than joy. Second, positive emotions exhibit very little variation in the human facial musculature. If Mama ain't happy, it's obvious. If she's content, it's not so easy to tell. And third, positive emotions, unlike their negative counterparts, lack obvious and measurable autonomic responses (such as increased blood flow to the legs when scared). Add to this the scientific community's lack of models for studying positive emotions, and *voilà*—negativity wins the day. Like the physical sciences, negativity is more observable.

Down in the Mouth

Robert Schrauf, an anthropologist and associate professor of applied linguistics at Pennsylvania State University, asked study participants in Mexico City and Chicago to write down as many words as they could that describe human emotion. He then asked them to characterize each word as positive, negative, or neutral. "I found this surprising result," Schrauf recalls. "Half of all the words that people produce from their working vocabulary to express emotion are negative. And 30 percent are positive and 20 percent are neutral." The question is, why so negative?

As Schrauf explains, when dealing with negative information, "there's a tendency to slow down our processing and to think more carefully, while positive emotions tend to tell us that things are benign or safe. . . . So processing of those emotions is more scriptlike. Things are going OK, so you don't do a lot of word processing." "But if you feel guilty," Lee Dye observes, "it may take a little more effort—and more thought—to figure out why and what to do about it." In this regard, we use language to cope. And since it is more difficult to cope with anger than with joy, we create more specific words for negative emotions so that we can better focus on them. Schrauf's findings appear to contradict a widely accepted contention by psychologist Robert Zajonc in the late 1960s that there is a preponderance of positive words over negative words in the English language. However, there is one very important difference: Schrauf analyzed oral expressions, whereas Zajonc studied written language.

Using the 1944 Thorndike-Lorge Word Count, which contains 4.5 million words from a variety of mass-circulation publications, Zajonc discovered that

> the word "happiness" occurs 761 times, "unhappiness" occurs only 49 times. "Beauty" is to be found at least 41 times as often as "ugliness," and "wealth" outdoes "poverty" by a factor of 1.6. We "laugh" 2.4 times as often as we "cry"; we "love" almost 7 times more often than we "hate." We are "in" at least 5 times more often than we are "out"; "up" twice as often as we are "down"; much more often "successful" than "unsuccessful"; and we "find" things 4.5 times more often than we "lose" them—all because most of us are "lucky" (220) rather than "unlucky" (17). We have all the reasons in the world to be "happy" (1,449) and "gay" (418) rather than "sad" (202) and "gloomy" (72), for things are 5 times more often "good" than "bad," almost 3 times more often "possible" than "impossible," and about 5 times more "profitable" than "unprofitable."

What does this suggest? Do we speak in negative terms and write in positive terms? Or might this suggest that we are better able to communicate our positive emotions in writing than in speech? And what effect does language have over perception? According to Zajonc and many other studies, the more we are exposed to something, the more we like it. Zajonc's groundbreaking work is referred to as the *mere exposure effect*. Among other things, this effect helps explain why we are so drawn to advertising logos. After all, if you really think about it, the Nike "swoosh" is a bit of an odd-looking thing. But we love it! Now imagine the effect of your words on those who look to you for leadership.

Since Zajonc's work dates back to the 1960s and although I am not a linguist, I do have access, like you, to the world's largest and most contemporary "word count," Google. To satisfy my curiosity and also to see if the 1944 Thorndike-Lorge Word Count is still relevant, I put my faith in Larry Page and Sergey Brin's iconoclastic Internet search technology. And guess what: Thorndike-Lorge stands. My Google search turned up 403 million instances of *hope* but only 20.5 million of *despair*, 77.8 million instances of *joy* versus 45.5 million of *anger*. If you juxtapose Zajonc with Google and Harvard's Vanishing Voter findings, it seems our predisposition for "reporting" the negative in conversation is, in fact, a choice. Consider the headline ABC News used for the report of Schrauf's findings: "Negative Words Dominate Language." Now *that's* a headline that gets our attention!

While these studies provide compelling if not contradictory findings, it seems the one thing that neither Zajonc's nor Schrauf's studies accounted for is context. In other words, it is perhaps telling to observe that many of the positive words—in Google at least—are used in the context of phrases such as "the pursuit of" (for example, finding happiness at work), while the negative words are typically associated with "management of" (as in anger management). Although it seems that some linguists may have their tongues tied about the preponderance of positive and negative words, it is generally agreed among scientists that positive emotions are fewer than their negative counterparts, making them more difficult to study. After all, scientists like to study things in petri dishes, on slides, and in isolation. This is where positive emotions become a bit of a sticky wicket. They tend to blend. Is she thrilled or satisfied? Joyful or proud? Giddy or flat-out drunk? Not only does this present a scientific challenge, but it presents a significant leadership challenge as well.

Specifically, in the din of negativity, how do you rally your team around a desired outcome without falling prey to cliché—"think positive" or "be happy"? How do you communicate hope? The easy answer would be to create more positive words than negative ones. However, as Pablo Picasso is said to have remarked, "Every positive value has its price in negative terms. The genius of Einstein leads to Hiroshima." No doubt we would follow suit with words. Therefore, communicating hope requires unconventional methods, one of which is storytelling, the focus of Chapter Thirteen.

Eyes in Disguise

Anger. When was the last time you saw it? If you are a frequent flyer, you needn't think past your last flight. The myriad of contorted faces, furrowed brows, and pursed lips attributed to the airline industry would make even Salvador Dalí blush with envy. Now consider the last time you saw hope. What did it look like? Psychologists refer to outward expressions of emotions as "signals." Whereas it is hard to *see* hope, it is relatively easy to see anger, fear, and sadness. Negative emotions have historically provided greater signal value than the positive variety.

Try this, but first make sure no one is watching. Make a sad face. Good job. Now make an angry face. (You've done that before, haven't you?) Now, make a hopeful face. I'm waiting. I'm ready when you are. There you have it—the universal "feel good" sign otherwise known as the Duchenne smile. Lacking any differentiating features, all positive emotions share a similar look: the corners of the lips curl upward, and the muscles contract around the eyes, thereby raising the cheeks.

French neurophysiologist Guillaume Benjamin Amand Duchenne de Boulogne began studying facial expressions more than 150 years ago. In his experiments, Duchenne photographed his subjects experiencing a variety of emotional states. He stimulated their expressions

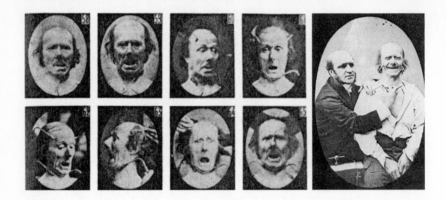

by sending small jolts of electric current to specific facial muscle groups. The images are reminiscent of the artificially uplifted faces found in the pages of *People* magazine. Duchenne's principal subject, "The Old Man," was ideally cast, as he was afflicted with total facial anesthesia. (He couldn't feel the pain of Duchenne's electrical jolts.)

In 1862, Duchenne published his findings in *The Mechanism of Human Facial Expression*, the predecessor to Charles Darwin's *Expressions of the Emotions in Man and Animals*. Duchenne discovered that genuine and fake smiles involve entirely different groups of facial muscles. To the clinically trained observer, among them Paul Ekman, the world's contemporary guru of facial expressions, the "true" smile involves a complex series of facial muscles; however, for your purposes, focus on the eyes. The next time you are disembarking an aircraft, look closely at the flight attendant's eyes as she says, "Thank you. B'bye now." If her eyes crinkle at the corners, she's *truly* smiling and genuinely pleased that you chose to fly the friendly skies. However, if her eyes remain unchanged, odds are she's faking it. Generally, when faking a smile, the person's mouth performs a cappella. Politicians and supermodels are master smile fakers. Their eyebrows (and "eye cover," the skin between the eyebrow and eyelid) are rarely engaged, but their pearly whites shine brightly (odds are they're fake too). Unlike a thin disguise of a fake smile, most intriguing about the Duchenne smile—the real smile—is that you cannot will it into existence because a real smile is partly controlled by your subconscious.

To probe this phenomenon, as Steven Johnson explains in *Mind Wide Open*, scientists have studied stroke victims who suffer from central facial paralysis, a condition whereby one side of the face cannot be voluntarily moved. When these people are asked to smile, only one side of the face turns upward. However, when told a joke causing "real laughter," the same person's face breaks into a full smile—both sides. This explains why it is difficult to cover up a real smile. Your smile has two drivers at the wheel. Imagine that one day a coworker whom you don't like walks into the office and announces that he has accepted a job offer at another company and will be leaving soon. It feels good, doesn't it? Involuntarily, the tiny voice inside your head throws a kegger in celebration, and your face subsequently bursts into a Duchenne smile. Suddenly aware of this, you spring into action; seeking to maintain a minimal level of tact and composure, like stifling a sneeze at the symphony, you mount a cover-up. You bite your lip. This is a classic case of your conscious and subconscious voluntarily and involuntarily battling for the wheel to your face.

Although positive emotions have historically exhibited very little external signal value, with advances in technology, using MRI technology, scientists have identified internal signals of positive emotions. When the pleasure centers in your brain light up, synapses shoot off like fireworks on the Fourth of July, even when the external signal of a smile is covered up. However, short of walking around with your head in a scanner so that those who look to you for leadership can see your hope in the future, this presents a significant leadership challenge.

Namely, how do you communicate your hope in a desired future, particularly when you, as a leader, may be more aware than others of negative information (a key executive is about to announce her resignation; you're about to lose a major customer; your Chinese outsourcing partner is on the verge of bankruptcy)? Ignorance is bliss. However, leaders aren't ignorant—yet another reason for the lonely nature of leadership. Therefore, learning to communicate hope in the presence of negative information without coming off as a fake requires a new way of thinking. It involves believing. While you may be able to fake how you feel, it is virtually impossible to fake what you believe. You either believe it or you don't. If you do not believe, short of a visit to a plastic surgeon for a few Botox injections, neither will anyone else. The only way to take control of your face is to take control of what you believe. If you believe, even fiction can be truth— the topic of Chapter Nine.

Explosive Bosses and Other Threats

A third reason why positive emotions have been overlooked is that they have no distinguishable autonomic response. In other words, whereas negative emotions trigger noticeable changes in digestion and breathing, for example, there is no obvious connection with positive emotions (unless hope triggers excitement, which in turn triggers an increase in heart rate). Negative emotions deal direct. Consider the uncontrollable urge.

When angry, we have an urge to attack. When scared, we have an urge to escape—"fight or flight." So when organizations hit the skids, particularly in the absence of leadership, people run scared— figuratively and literally. Or worse yet, people stay and work out of paranoia, believing that someone is "out to get them." Psychologists refer to this phenomenon as automatic vigilance. Randy Larsen, chairman of the Psychology Department at Washington University in Saint Louis, illustrates automatic vigilance by citing a journal entry made by Captain Meriwether Lewis, of Lewis and Clark fame. The explorer was scouting alone one day in search of the best route for his expedition.

> Suddenly [Clark is] surprised by an aggressive grizzly bear charging at him from out of the bush. Lewis narrowly escapes by jumping into a river. After the bear withdraws, Lewis makes his way back to his troops, a distance of about 12 miles. Along the way, he notices a variety of other animals, most of which he perceives as threatening and several of which he shoots preemptively. In his journal he describes feeling surrounded by danger: "It now seemed to me that all the beasts of the neighborhood had made a league to destroy me." The editor

of the Lewis and Clark journals, in a footnote to this passage, notes that the animals Lewis encountered along the way were not typically considered aggressive or dangerous, and opines that Lewis was probably nervous after his frightening encounter with the grizzly.

Once bitten, twice shy. This is automatic vigilance. Teams and organizations experience the same thing. Layoffs, reengineering, and explosive bosses leave a mark. Although we know this to be true anecdotally, with advances in technology, there is growing evidence that suggests a more explicit biological connection between positive emotions and human performance. Most notable is the recent tantalizing work of a group of neuroscientists who, in the shadow of the Himalayas, have made a startling and historic discovery into the power of the human mind. Why the Himalayas? The nearness of Buddhist monks. To satisfy one's curiosity about the power of hope and other positive emotions, who better to study than people for whom the mind is more than simply a manifestation of the brain?

Monks in a Magnet

He was born on July 6, 1935, in the village of Taktser in northeastern Tibet. Born to a peasant family, Tenzin Gyatso, His Holiness the fourteenth Dalai Lama, was recognized at the age of two, in accordance with Tibetan tradition, as the reincarnation of his predecessor, the thirteenth Dalai Lama. He is a leader times three: the head of the Tibetan government in exile, the leader of Tibetan Buddhism, and a spiritual leader beloved worldwide. Like his thirteen predecessors, the fourteenth Dalai Lama is the manifestation of the Buddha of Compassion, who chose to reincarnate for the purpose of relieving suffering. Recognized universally as the publicist for the compassionate and nonviolent resolution of human conflict, he was awarded the Nobel Peace Prize in 1989. In corporate-speak, the Dalai Lama has exceeded expectations.

In addition to his formal leadership roles, the Dalai Lama has a keen personal interest in the sciences, manifested in his strong mechanical aptitude. As a youth in Lhasa, Tibet's capital city, the Dalai Lama taught himself to fix broken machinery, from clocks to movie projectors to cars. He has said that if he were not a monk, he would have been an engineer. Imagine the Dalai Lama running a fix-it shop. He would undoubtedly take "full service" to a much higher level. "Check your oil today? Tires? Level of compassion?"

The fourteenth Dalai Lama believes that science and Buddhism share a common objective: to serve humanity and create a better understanding of the world. He believes that science provides powerful tools for understanding the interconnectedness of all life and that such understanding provides an essential rationale for ethical behavior and the protection of the environment. It should therefore come as no surprise that in October 2004, the Dalai Lama would invite a group of neuroscientists to his home in Dharamsala, India. The event was organized by the Mind and Life Institute, whose avowed purpose is "to promote the creation of a contemplative, compassionate, and rigorous experimental and experiential science of the mind that can guide and inform medicine, neuroscience, psychology, education, and human development."

Major themes for this historic meeting read, as one would expect, like topics from an advanced text on neuroscience: "an overview of the cellular and synaptic substrates of plasticity; the nature of practice and skill development to address issues of how mental skills can best be acquired; the role of preexisting individual differences and their impact on methods of skills development; Buddhist perspectives on learning and transformation; and developmental issues and the importance of early experience." In laymen's terms, they came to study the effect of mind over matter. They published their findings in the *Proceedings of the National Academy of Sciences*. Needless to say, this was not your conventional science fair.

Imagine: like plaintiff and defendant, on one side, representing the brain, five neuroscientists beholden to biology and no slaves to fashion; on the other, representing the mind, a dozen Tibetan Buddhist monks, dressed in flowing burgundy and saffron robes, who are, as Sharon Begley of the *Wall Street Journal* suggests, united beyond a reasonable doubt that one of them is the reincarnation of the thirteenth Dalai Lama and another is the reincarnation of a twelfth-century monk. At either end of the room, large screens are aglow with brain scans—theirs. However different their opinions about the afterlife, they convened in the shadows of the Himalayas with a shared interest: neuroplasticity.

In the field of brain science, neuroplasticity is the place to be. Neuroplasticity refers to the ability of the brain to change, both structurally and functionally, based on experiences. As Begley suggests, "In pianists who play many arpeggios, brain regions that control the index finger and middle finger become fused. . . . When one finger hits a key in one of these fast-tempo movements, the other does so almost simultaneously, fooling the brain into thinking the two fingers are one. As a result of the fused brain regions, the pianist can no longer move those fingers independently of one another." The mind, influenced by outside experiences, changes the brain. However, the monk study provided even more promising, if not endlessly intriguing, findings.

Until the monk study, neuroplasticity concerned itself primarily with the relationship between *outside* experiences, such as piano playing, and the structure of the brain. So why study monks? To explore whether or not there is a relationship between *internal* forces and the brain. In other words, can we affect our performance from the inside? (After all, it takes years to learn to play the piano.) There is arguably no single group of people on the planet better equipped for this type of experiment than those for whom meditation is a centuries-old tradition. Buddhist monks have long believed in the power of the mind and its independence from the brain. We Western intellectuals are the ones who have the insatiable need to see in order to believe. However, given these findings, even skeptics can now be convinced. We can now see what believing looks like.

The experiment pitted amateur meditators against Buddhist monks with more than ten thousand hours of cumulative meditation to their credit. Their task was to "generate loving kindness toward all beings"—what is known as compassion meditation. Sure beats Coke versus Pepsi. According to Buddhist monk Matthieu Ricard, who, incidentally, also holds a Ph.D. in genetics, "We tried to generate a mental state in which compassion permeates the whole mind with no other thoughts." The neuroscientists' objective was to observe the relationship between the mind (thoughts) and the body (brain). Do our thoughts alone, independent of outside influence, have a material effect on our brain structure and function? The short answer is yes. However, no one could have imagined how strong the correlation would be. The monks blew the neuroscientists' minds. They swept the novices. They cleaned up. In fact, according to Richard Davidson, one of the study designers and facilitators, "most monks showed extremely large increases of a sort that has never been reported before in the neuroscience literature." Here's what happened.

Activity in the left prefrontal cortex (the home of positive emotions) cast a shadow higher than the surrounding Himalayas on the right prefrontal cortex (the home of negative emotions and anxiety). This had never before been seen based solely on internal activity. The monks were literally able to control their level of consciousness. Stunned were the neuroscientists. Happy was the Dalai Lama. I do wonder if the Dalai Lama had to work to restrain himself from shouting, "I told you so!"

While this discovery in and of itself is of historic proportions, it's not all that the neuroscientists discovered. What they observed next confirms the impact of a leader's outlook on his or her performance.

The Uncontrollable Urge to Help

A region in the brain triggered by the sight of suffering showed a spike in activity, as did a region that manages planned movement. It is as if the monks' brains were moved beyond rest to restlessness. Their hope was not passive but urgently active. Their brains were nearly uncontrollable in their wanting to go to the aid of those suffering. As one of the monks reflected, "It feels like a total readiness to act, to help." In other words, the result of the deliberate action of the mind (a hopeful outlook) caused a physical reaction in the brains (a need to act). Isn't this the goal of leadership—to encourage others to act? Imagine if all those who looked to you for leadership had an uncontrollable urge to help. These findings suggest that there is a very real connection that has gone unobserved until now. As the reincarnated Buddha of Compassion and a group of pioneering neuroscientists have taught us, hope creates action.

As science continues to advance, our knowledge of positive emotions will continue to evolve. Leaders take note. The monk study sheds new light on hope. No longer does fear have a monopoly on the urge to act. Hopeful urges do exist. When in sight, we do what's right.

The Positive Urge

Given this new evidence, when there is a preponderance of negativity—the economy is in the tank, a star player has been traded, you've been through a bottomless round of layoffs, or geopolitical turbulence continues to hang heavy on the hearts of citizens of the world—be aware of the power of the urge, both positive and negative. Know that positive urges do exist. You need only work harder to recognize them in others due to the explicit and overbearing nature of negative emotions.

Just as you should understand the power of negativity in order to apply hope effectively, you must also understand the power of fear, because like hope, fear works. Take a step inside the anatomy of fear.

6

BOHEMIAN OPTIMISM AND FEARMONGERING

Dictators are perishable. Russia is eternal. The
misery of the countries we come from lies in the
utter absence of hope.

—*Milan Kundera*

Do yourself a favor. Before you go to bed tonight, put your shoes outside, take out the garbage, and throw that Matterhorn-shaped pile of
clothes into the washing machine. If you don't, after you slip into
your favorite pajamas, crawl under your down-filled comforter, and
snuggle up for a good night's sleep, from the bottoms of your shoes,
from that used newspaper you took from the office,
and from that mountain of dirty laundry, tiny creatures
will awaken in your room. While you sleep, creepy-
crawly critters will emerge and begin their journey. Slowly,
yet with the ambition of second-string quarterbacks, they will
begin their march. Spiders. Their destination? Your mouth. Don't
worry. Only the strongest survive. Among the dozens found in most
bedrooms in the wee hours of the night, only four, on average, will
make it to their destination. However, do not fret. The average person falls asleep seven minutes after turning off the lights. At least you
won't be awake to taste them.

How does this make you feel? Has your pulse increased? Do you
feel slightly short of breath? Not to worry, the stealthy spider story is a
myth—an urban legend. Here is why I shared it with you. If you have
a *real* fear of spiders (arachnophobia) or if you are very good at visual-
izing, simply reading the preceding paragraph would have changed the

temperature of your skin. "False evidence appearing real" (FEAR) can have the same effect as real fear. Do this. Rub your forefinger and thumb together. Do they feel a bit clammy? If so, you've just experienced fear in action. Fear, like hope, works. Here's what happens.

If, before you began reading this chapter, I were to have placed your finger in a meter designed to record skin moisture, the meter would have recorded a reaction immediately after you saw the drawing on the opening page. Contrary to popular opinion, our minds do not wander haphazardly. Our thoughts are carefully orchestrated electrochemical events that register inputs sourced by our senses. When you begin thinking about spiders, your body, like a regular at the neighborhood bar, orders a neurochemical cocktail to manage feeling fearful. Fear creates a reaction. And although arachnophobia will likely not impede your ability to lead, allodoxaphobia will. That is the fear of other people's opinions. "What if I make a fool of myself? What will they think?"

Allodoxaphobia explains why the fear of public speaking ranks higher than the fear of dying—a phenomenon lending itself not only to intrigue but also to comedy. Jerry Seinfeld once purportedly joked that if that's true, most people at a funeral would rather be in the coffin than delivering the eulogy. Fearing other people's opinions is the greatest threat to hope. However, only people who are afraid of their own opinions suffer the fate of others'. Triumphant leaders respect the power of fear and therefore choose hope. Here's why.

A Leadership Choice

Hope, like fear, is a leadership choice. Both can be used to influence human behavior. However, in an absurd twist of reality, unlike hope and more like celebrity scandal, fear causes an immediate reaction. It is why some leaders use it as a motivator. It works. However, fear is like Listerine. It stings on contact, and eventually we spit it out. Over time, fear self-destructs. Although we stand frozen in fear, once we've got our wits about us, we run like hell and eventually burn out. After all, who can run that far? Hope, on the other hand, is the most sustainable form of human motivation, although it requires infinite patience as the object of our desire takes time to realize. Therefore, it is a leader's responsibility to create the conditions under which hope can manifest itself among a team. Otherwise, if fear is allowed to persist, it becomes desperation. Desperation is the silent killer responsible for the ABCs of team underperformance: apathy, burnout, and carelessness. Therefore, the leadership challenge is to learn to use hope not in the absence of fear and desperation but in its presence.

Creating a Hopeful Climate

Desperation occurs in organizations when people do not understand the objective and do not feel that they have the appropriate influence to affect outcomes. Desperate people make hasty decisions simply because they do not know what else to do. This begs a debate: are we afraid to act because we do not see hope in the future, or do we not see hope in the future because we are afraid to act? If, as a leader, you believe that organization rigor mortis is a result of the lack of clarity about the organization's objectives, your natural inclination may be to share your vision with your team, have them memorize the organization's mission, or open the kimono that is your organization's strategic plan. The likely result? Desperation becomes frustration. Why? Because even though they now know exactly what you want them to do, they still feel powerless. This is much like the feeling I have on airplanes. I know precisely what I want to occur (I want the plane to land); however, I have no control over the aircraft. Therefore, I am a frequently frustrated flier.

If, on the other hand, you believe that your team's desperation is a result of their fear of making a decision and taking a chance, your natural inclination may be to give them a pep talk. The likely result? Desperation becomes unbridled confidence, even arrogance. Although they will run through walls for you, they will likely never look for open doors. Why? They remain directionless and will therefore eventually succumb to fear once the pain sets in. Drywall leaves a nasty mark.

These widely used leadership approaches rarely suffice in achieving leaders' objectives. In fact, over the long term, they often do more harm than good. Harm, in this case, comes in two flavors: unrealistic expectations and powerlessness. Hope is the only appropriate solution that deals with both. Hope manifests itself among teams only when people truly understand their leaders' desired objectives and feel that they have real authority to affect outcomes. This requires faith in both directions. A shared vision will not work in the absence of distributed authority, and vice versa. You need both to create the future. In the absence of either condition, fear will win the day. Fear has derailed many dreams throughout history. Therefore, if you wish to use hope to your advantage, you must become a student of fear. You must understand it intimately.

Turning Retreat into Advance

The trappings of fear were most famously described by Franklin Delano Roosevelt in his first inaugural address on March 4, 1933, when he proclaimed, "The only thing we have to fear is fear itself." Roosevelt didn't stop there; he elaborated on the theme. But history left Roosevelt's larger message on the cutting-room floor. This is the unfortunate reality of living in our sound-bite society. We prefer life in its concentrated form, shrink-wrapped for our receding attention spans and miniaturized to fit our cellular phone screens. Consider love. It was once expressed poetically in the nineteenth century by Elizabeth Barrett Browning: "How do I love thee? Let me count the ways. I love thee to the depth and breadth and height my soul can reach, when feeling out of sight." If Browning were alive today, she'd undoubtedly write the same as "xoxo;-)." Unfortunately, in brevity, we've lost meaning. In fact, even the pope has to work to keep our attention today. In June 2005, the Vatican announced the introduction of an abridged version of the Catechism. Only those who command inordinate attention are afforded the creative freedom of detail. More light casts a longer shadow.

What followed Roosevelt's often quoted one-liner is the punch line to his inspirational prelude: "Nameless, unreasoning, unjustified terror paralyzes needed efforts to convert retreat into advance." Converting retreat into advance, paralysis into movement, and passivity into action is the role of hope. Roosevelt's intent was not merely to bring our attention to the fear of fear but to give us explicit instructions. He issued a call to action. Move forward. Choose courage in place of cowardice and hope in place of fear.

As Roosevelt suggested and as the Founders of the United States intended it to be, democracy is the wallboard that hangs on hope's frame. However, although hope is the most effective scaffold on which to build a nation, it does have competitors, not the least of which is fear. Although fear is a self-inflicted wound, consider the effect of fear when dealt by leaders of large groups of people.

Hope in the Shadows of Fear

Twenty-first-century humans are awash in choices. The smorgasbord of governance options available to us include theocracy, totalitarianism, democracy, and communism. Among them, democracy is the only form of governance that extends, uses, and distributes hope to all who believe in freedom and wish to pursue the dreams they create versus the ones assigned to them. For example, any child of the appropriate age born in the United States can apply for the job of president. This is hope in action. However, hope is not only a nation builder but also a freedom builder. Consider the role of hope in dismantling fear.

Eureka College's most famous alumnus, Ronald Reagan, knew that the Soviet Union—and communism's stranglehold over it—would "end up on the ash heap of history" years before the idea became widely accepted. In hindsight, the demise of communism seems preordained. However, triumphant leaders do not deal in hindsight; they focus on foresight. Consider the foresightedness of Ronald Reagan. Consider his hope.

Remember the made-for-TV movie *The Day After*, a chilling film about the devastation of a small Kansas town following a nuclear holocaust? It aired in 1983. I, for one, thought the Russians were coming. Reagan, on the other hand, made his "ash heap" remarks in a speech to Britain's Parliament in June 1982. The question is, what did Reagan see that I and my frightened fellow Americans had overlooked? Where did Reagan find his hope?

Peter Schweizer, a research fellow with the Hoover Institution, offers one of the best analyses of Reagan's foresightedness. In response to the question of the origin of Reagan's vision, Schweizer wrote:

It is difficult to say with complete certainty. There were external influences over the course of the Cold War that directed and focused his thinking, as well as concepts and ideas that he developed on his own. But far from being a simple conduit for presidential aides and others who believed only they knew the proper course of action, Reagan embraced many of these ideas before he was president. He was himself once asked how he figured all this out, and he gave an interesting answer. Rather than claiming superior intellect, he simply pointed out that everyone knew the Soviet Union was evil, expansionist, and in trouble but that no one wanted to say it. Courage, it seems, made all the difference, an important lesson in an age when supreme importance seems to be placed on the intelligence of our leaders rather than their courage.

Reagan had hope. However, for a leader to be hopeful in silence is insufficient. The expression "unsung hero" is an oxymoron. Communication matters. And so on June 12, 1987, in a speech delivered to the people of West Berlin that was audible to residents on the eastern side of the wall, Reagan spoke of hope and triumph:

To those listening throughout Eastern Europe, a special word: Although I cannot be with you, I address my remarks to you just as surely as to those standing here before me. For I join you, as I join your fellow countrymen in the West, in this firm, this unalterable be-

lief: *Es gibt nur ein Berlin* [There is only one Berlin]. Behind me stands
a wall that encircles the free sectors of this city, part of a vast system
of barriers that divides the entire continent of Europe. From the
Baltic south, those barriers cut across Germany in a gash of barbed
wire, concrete, dog runs, and guard towers. Farther south, there may
be no visible, no obvious wall. But there remain armed guards and
checkpoints all the same—still a restriction on the right to travel,
still an instrument to impose upon ordinary men and women the will
of a totalitarian state. Yet it is here in Berlin where the wall emerges
most clearly, here, cutting across your city, where the news photo and
the television screen have imprinted this brutal division of a continent upon the mind of the world. Standing before the Brandenburg
Gate, every man is a German, separated from his fellow men. Every
man is a Berliner, forced to look upon a scar. [West German] President von Weizsacker has said, "The German question is open as long
as the Brandenburg Gate is closed." Today I say, as long as the gate is
closed, as long as this scar of a wall is permitted to stand, it is not the
German question alone that remains open, but the question of freedom for all mankind. Yet I do not come here to lament. For I find in
Berlin a message of hope, even in the shadow of this wall, a message
of triumph. . . . General Secretary Gorbachev [of the Soviet Union],
if you seek peace, if you seek prosperity for the Soviet Union and
Eastern Europe, if you seek liberalization: come here to this gate! Mr.
Gorbachev, open this gate! Mr. Gorbachev, tear down this wall!

Reagan saw the promise of hope "even in the shadows" of fear.
He realized, before most others, that hope is abundant even in silence. It takes a leader to shine light on that hope—to make it visible. It takes a leader to make hope actionable. Reagan understood
that having hope was not enough. A leader's hope must be communicated, particularly in times of uncertainty. In the United States,
hope is not a partisan issue. It is an American issue. In addition to
Reagan, consider how other U.S. presidents have managed the most
extreme form of uncertainty—crisis.

Hope's Quid Pro Quo

Bill Clinton is literally the man from Hope (Arkansas). Clinton's "I feel your pain" empathy not only helped heal the nation after the Midwest's Great Flood in 1993, but it also became instrumental in the comeback of the Democratic party. In the 1994 midterm elections, Clinton's party lost its power in Congress. This marked a low point for the party and Clinton's first term. And then another tragedy hit—the bombing of the federal building in Oklahoma City. Clinton's "on the ground" presence in Oklahoma—his outreach, his empathy, and his ability to connect with people—helped boost his approval ratings over 50 percent, ultimately setting the table for his reelection in 1996. Triumphant leaders use hope in place of fear, and when they do, those who look to them for leadership stand in ovation. People will forgive a leader for his weaknesses but never for his lack of hope.

Like Clinton, Reagan rose to the occasion in the immediacy of a crisis. Consider Reagan's words following the space shuttle *Challenger* explosion in 1986: "The future doesn't belong to the fainthearted, it belongs to the brave." Triumphant leaders believe in the future, and therefore we believe in them. Simply, they give us hope and so we give them ours.

Hope in Place of Fear

Fear is a great teacher. Ironically, the best way to learn how to use hope to your advantage is to study fear. The fearmongers of Central Europe could have held master classes on how to motivate people. Although perhaps not in theory, fear was central to the practice of communism. Their strategy of fear, deployed during the latter half of the twentieth century, would make today's viral marketers green with envy. It was beyond cunning. And although communism failed, imagine what it would be like if we, as leaders of nations, corporations, athletic teams, and nonprofit organizations, were as deliberate about hope as the communists were about fear. What could we achieve? To help you envision the extent to which I am suggesting that you use, communicate, and promote hope as a tool in your leadership role, consider the strategy of fear designed and promulgated by the rulers of Central and Eastern Europe between 1945 and 1989. Where, when, and how they used fear, imagine substituting hope. Welcome to Prague.

Bohemian Optimism Marinated in Fear

The sky was the color of wet cement, and the air was so cold you could smell it. Peering from the airplane window, I thought to myself, "I guess this is what newborn countries are supposed to look like." On the surface, the Czech Republic was everything that I had imagined it to be—cold, complicated, and recently communist. This is my distinct memory of January 23, 1993.

I had come to Prague to teach a course in international financial management at Vysoká Škola Economická, the University of Economics, Prague—Central Europe's leading business school. Prior to arriving, I armed myself with the requisite knowledge intended to ease my apprehension, namely, that $3 would buy a round of beers for me and twelve of my closest friends, $30 would cover the monthly rent, and $75 a week in salary would allow an American professor to live the high life. I must admit, my apprehension lifted like a San Francisco fog the moment my lips met Pilsner Urquell. I was prepared to provoke, to pontificate, and of course to party. After all, the Communist party may have ended, but the celebration of freedom had just begun.

Although the soot of four decades of failed politics still covered the country's capital city, who can't find beauty in a nation whose cultural envoy was Frank Zappa and whose U.S. ambassador at one time rode in on the "Good Ship Lollipop," none other than Shirley Temple Black. Add to this a president, Vaclav Havel, who began as a dissident playwright and enjoyed the company of the Velvet Underground and Lou Reed. Bill Clinton, eat your heart out. Although I had been hired to teach international finance to a class of Central and Eastern European college students, I quickly became a student myself. I began to study Bohemian optimism.

Bohemia is a region of the Czech Republic considered the nation's cultural and political epicenter. However, the word *Bohemian* has also come to describe a person with artistic or literary interests who disregards conventional standards of behavior. And so I adopted the expression "Bohemian optimism" while living in Prague to describe a unique form of hope the Czech people used to defeat communism, a cautious and deliberate conviction that things will improve.

Czechs display eternal patience. What makes their particular variety of hope unique—what makes it Bohemian—is its absence in everyday life. It is not an absence in the sense that people are hopeless; rather it is an absence in the form of public displays or communication of hope. However, shyness is not a Czech trait. In fact, if you've ever had the opportunity to use public transportation in Prague, you will certainly be familiar with Czechs' penchant for public displays of affection. So why then were public displays of hope frowned on?

Hope implies that the current reality does not reflect a desired future. Hope implies room for improvement. And hope implies change—a dirty word to Communist party bigwigs. Therefore, communism discouraged hope by promoting fear. Hope was not for public consumption. However, what held the country together during its four decades of darkness was a shared, almost subliminal social understanding that politics would capitulate to patience. In the calm of communism, hope simmered silently. Although the country appeared calm, it was frozen in fear. As Vaclav Havel observed, "True enough, the country is calm. Calm as a morgue or a grave, would you not say?" Communism marinated everything in fear. Fear detained hope, but never was the nation hopeless.

A Nation Learning to Forget

Many things changed just days before my arrival. At midnight on January 1, 1993, the Czech Republic was born, a separate nation from Slovakia, to which it had been wed since the end of World

War I. Hope was alive and well in Prague, the new and former capital; however, those who were celebrating it were not Czech. They were tourists, cultural anthropologists, and hippies who'd grown tired of San Francisco's Haight and Paris's Saint Germain des Pres. Journalists wrote of Prague as the Paris of the 1920s and the San Francisco of the 1960s. If you were looking for a muse, it could be found in Prague.

In every passageway, around every corner, glimmers of hope were beginning to appear. Some courageous people began painting the balconies of their apartments in a sign of liberation. Now that land and property had been returned to their rightful owners, pride reappeared. Would-be novelists and screenwriters sat with pens in hand observing and writing for hours on end. Surely, they had come in search of the next *Atlas Shrugged* or *On the Road*. Musicians from around the world camped out on the Charles Bridge singing songs of freedom by Bob Marley and John Lennon. The "to do" list of Czech parliamentarians read like the instruction manual from the game Risk: draw new borders, issue new currency, tear down Stalin statue.

However, where were the Czech people? I had expected them to be celebrating into the night, but the only sounds in the streets were German beer-drinking songs. The Czechs, it turns out, were practicing Bohemian optimism—sitting at home, in silence, wondering how long freedom would last. Although the face of communism had changed dramatically during the course of its long tenure (it became more consumer friendly), its impact on the human spirit would take a bit longer to settle in. After all, the forgetting curve is relatively flat. Once you learn something, it is virtually impossible to forget it. For example, try to forget your name. Assuming that you are of sound mind, it's virtually impossible. In fact, most people immediately think of their name when asked to forget it. Now imagine the challenge of an entire country learning to forget its past in order to create its future.

For Czechs to exercise hope, moving down the forgetting curve was as important as moving up the learning curve. Overcoming fear requires learning to forget whatever it is you fear and why you fear it. Imagine if humans domesticated spiders instead of cats and dogs. We might not be as frightened of them. Fear, like a cruise ship attempting to stop suddenly, continues to drift, carrying its followers in its wake.

The Great Awakening

When I arrived, this three-week-old country had just begun the process of nursing a hangover from its forty-year binge with political and social dogma. Its doctrines promoted fear, encouraged blind faith in its leaders, and outlawed everything from travel to music. Communists all but destroyed hope on a national scale. Above the Jewish Quarter of Prague, where Stalin's statue once stood, was now a monstrous metronome methodically tapping out the passage of time. Ironically, a German food company sponsored the new mechanism. Goodbye socialism, hello advertising! Although time marched on, this remnant of the country formerly known as Czechoslovakia had not yet settled on its new name. It had a branding problem. In fact, the country was officially nameless from January 1, 1993, until June 7 of that year, when it underwent its cartographic christening as Çesko (Czech Republic in English). The country that ranked fifth among industrial world powers, was the sole democracy east of the Rhine, and was admired for its highly advanced social legislation under the leadership of Tomas Masaryk had fallen asleep at the wheel during its encounter with communism. Witnessing its reawakening was breathtaking.

Two weeks after I arrived, the Czechoslovak crown (its primary currency) ceased to exist. In April, a new currency was issued. People skipped work that day to stand in extremely long lines to exchange their now defunct currency for a new one. It was quite a sight. Since there was no such thing as a savings account, people were literally standing in line with bags full of cash. In February, the Czech Republic and Germany signed a treaty to help strengthen Czech borders—including the newly formed one with Slovakia—and had agreed to send more than one hundred thousand illegal immigrants back to their native lands, including Slovaks to Slovakia—talk about signing divorce papers! This affected me only insofar as my Slovak-manufactured refrigerator had broken on the day of my arrival. With the new border controls in place, getting it repaired wasn't easy. Thankfully, it was cold enough outside to keep my plastic bag-o'-milk (a Czech phenomenon) below room temperature.

Museums were being converted to banks, and banks were beginning to offer checking accounts. For forty years, everyone paid bills at the post office, in cash. What was once a cash economy had now hopped a ride on the merry-go-round that is revolving credit. (Perhaps convention should have been preserved in this regard.) One of the most prominent among the museum-cum-bank buildings was a building named for Czechoslovakia's first communist president, Klement Gottwald. Its grand staircase—now completed with state-of-the-art ATMs, led to a glorious mountain of money. Just down the street, ground had been broken for the creation of a shiny new stock exchange. Prague was in full bloom in the winter of 1993.

The Persistence of Old Habits

But what about Bohemian optimism? While the hearts of the new country's citizens were moving ahead with great speed, their minds lagged behind. They remained skeptical. After all, Russian tanks could roll on Wenceslas Square again, couldn't they? It was as if the country had fallen into a coma since World War II only to awaken to twenty thousand expatriate Americans preaching the merits of free markets and busloads of German tourists singing the praises of Czech beer. Urban planners and architects were engaged in vigorous debates, each vying for the opportunity to repair, resurface, and reinvent the city's aged infrastructure. As Gene Deitch, one of my twenty thousand fellow expatriates living in Prague, once commented, "For some reason dirty, crumbling buildings in Italy and Greece are charming, but in Prague, they somehow become the result of the evils of communism."

However poetic the buildings, they were falling down. And although Karl Marx's dream and a few buildings had crumbled, bureaucracy hadn't. Political dogma had succumbed; however, organization

convention was alive and well in the form of postcommunist bureaucracy. It is a nightmare only Kafka devotees can appreciate.
Bureaucracy was running naked through the streets of Prague. In fact,
it had made its way into every aspect of life, including simple mundane
tasks like grocery shopping. Old habits die hard. Fear remained, albeit
in a different form.

Possibility: The New Fear

In an effort to manage in-store traffic, grocery stores limited the
number of customers allowed to shop at any single point in time.
Fewer customers was the goal of any grocer worth his salt—or so it
seemed. Grocers controlled traffic by limiting the number of customers to the number of shopping carts. Once the shopping carts
were all taken, you had to wait your turn. As a result, long lines were
commonplace at even the largest stores. "Security," they called it. In
fact, you were forced at gunpoint (I'm not kidding; the security guard
was armed) to rent a grocery cart upon entering the store even if you
only planned to purchase a single item. On more than one occasion,
I felt that my manhood was being significantly compromised by having to parade a single package of cookies through empty aisles in a
large red shopping cart.

As fear dispersed, so did structure. With the rigidity of the party
system gone, it was as if the people attempted to reinstate structure in
the most obscure ways. And retail stores were not alone in their efforts
to create new rules. In a nation governed by fear, citizen-centricity was
uncommon. Although capitalism had arrived in Prague, customer
service didn't make the trip. In postcommunist Prague, customer service continued to mean *obey the signage, stand in line,* and *take what
you're given*—typically not very appealing. To the Czechs, it somehow
made sense. But I had grown accustomed to the finer things in life—
indulgences like toilet paper without splinters and cold milk in a plastic jug rather than warm milk in a plastic bag. You get the picture. To
this day, I still can't figure out why you could buy diapers at the sta-
tionery store. Prague was and continues to be a city of paradoxes. After

all, freedom was a foreign concept for most Czechs to grasp. To paraphrase Vaclav Havel, "You may be free, but you still have to pay to ride the train."

The Prague Paradox

The Prague paradox—driven by fear—extended not only to institutions but also to citizens. The social construct of communism had manifested itself in the way people communicated. Everyone living under communism had a split personality. One personality promoted the party line in public. The other silently fought it at home. Under communism, you were not only asked but *expected* to believe in things counter to your moral code. Your country didn't care if you agreed with its social doctrine or not. It just wanted to make sure you agreed in public. Come to the rallies. Show your support. Wave the party flag. This is the strategy of fear. (Sound familiar?)

The implications of fear on nations, as on organizations, are the same—silence, secrets, and duplicity. Organizations led by fearful leaders are staffed by split personalities. Truth comes in two flavors, public and private—a boardroom and a barroom version.

Split Personality: The Two-Faces of Communism

In America, two-faced individuals are frowned on. We expect people to tell the truth and share their true feelings. However, under communism, as under all forms of fearful leadership, it is the other way around. Everybody wears two faces, and everybody knows it. Your "home face" is *your* face. Your "street face" is *their* face. Under communism, *they* were the Communist party bosses, the ones who controlled not only the country but also your destiny. However, they mistakenly believed they could control hope by using fear. But why did fear work for so long?

Almost everyone went along with the split-persona phenomenon because wearing two faces came with lots of fringe benefits. The cost-benefit analysis was relatively easy for most people to compute. The cost of leading a two-faced life was your integrity. Show up. Attend the rallies. Support the government publicly. Like the costs, the benefits were easy to compute. If you played along, you were able to keep your job, your kids' education, and your freedom. Simply, you were granted a life. This sounds reasonable enough as long as you were willing to live in silent fear, suppress your opinions, and never travel outside of your country. This was the strategy of fear. Imagine the complexity. Imagine the nuance. Imagine the management required to pull it off for forty years.

The Strategy of Fear

In my observation of life under communism and from my experiences living in postcommunist Prague, I became very familiar with the country's controversial political dissident playwright president, Vaclav Havel. Havel attributed communism's tenure to this two-faced phenomenon, which was not the problem but rather a symptom of fear. Communism promoted fear and protected ideology by pitting individuals against one another in public. No one would dare speak out against the party for fear of persecution. Therefore, hope was contained. With hope contained, so were dreams and aspirations. The logic was simple: nothing will change if hope is kept in check (pun intended).

The suppression of hope explains why the country could move people but not ideas, protect its borders but not its freedom, and believe in community but not in God. If the people were not allowed to express patience with self (hope), expressing patience with God (faith) was strictly verboten. In fact, in an attempt to reason away the existence of God, all university students were required to enroll in a course called "The Science of Atheism." At the end of the course, students were required to take individual oral exams with their professors. Sitting face-to-face, each student was obligated to scientifically prove to their professor that God did not exist. Whether you believed in God or not was inconsequential. From education to music, the strategy of fear was deeply embedded in day-to-day life.

Imagine if we were as deliberate about hope as an organizational principle and leadership skill as the communists were about fear.

All That Jazz

God was not the only enemy of communist ideals; so was music, specifically jazz. Under communism, creativity was dangerous. You didn't dare express your creativity in an inappropriate written or musical context for fear of reprimand. The paranoia among party bosses was so thick that jazz was outlawed due to its improvisational nature—it allowed people to express themselves in ways contrary to the principles of communism. Plain and simple, jazz was too individualistic. Communists believed that like religion, music had the power to stir human emotion—it was, like Marx's description of religion, the opium of the people. If not controlled, it could lead to anarchy.

Therefore, in 1958, a set of regulations were posted to outlaw jazz altogether. These regulations are perhaps the best evidence of the complexity and sophistry of the strategy of fear favored by both the communists and the Nazis. An elaborate mandate appeared briefly in the Western world in 1966, before it was confiscated and destroyed. Czech author Josef Skvorecky recorded the mandate in his banned book, *Eine kleine Jazzmusic*. It read as follows:

1. Pieces in foxtrot rhythm (*so-called swing*) are not to exceed 20% of the repertoires of light orchestras and dance bands.

2. In this so-called jazz type repertoire, preference is to be given to compositions in a major key and to lyrics expressing joy in life rather than Jewishly gloomy lyrics.

3. As to tempo, preference is to be given to brisk compositions over slow ones (*so-called blues*); however, the pace must not exceed a certain degree of allegro, commensurate with the Aryan sense of discipline and moderation. On no account will Negroid excesses in tempo (*so-called hot jazz*) or in solo performances (*so-called breaks*) be tolerated.

4. So-called jazz compositions may contain at most 10% syncopation; the remainder must consist of a natural legato movement devoid of the hysterical rhythmic reverses characteristic of the music of the barbarian races and conducive to dark instincts alien to the German people (*so-called riffs*).

5. Strictly prohibited is the use of instruments alien to the German spirit (*so-called cowbells, flexatone, brushes, etc.*) also mutes which turn the noble sound of wind and brass instruments into a Jewish-Freemasonic yowl (*so-called wa-wa, hat, etc.*).

6. Also prohibited are so-called drum breaks longer than half a bar in four-quarter beat (*except in stylized military marches*).

7. The double bass must be played solely with the bow in so-called jazz compositions.

8. Plucking the strings is prohibited, since it is damaging to the instrument and detrimental to Aryan musicality; if a so-called pizzicato effect is absolutely desirable for the character of the composition, strict care must be taken lest the string be allowed to patter on the sordine, which is henceforth forbidden.

9. Musicians are likewise forbidden to make vocal improvisations (*so-called scat*).

10. All light orchestras and dance bands are advised to restrict the use of saxophones of all keys and to substitute for them the violoncello, the viola, or possibly a suitable folk instrument.

Amazing, isn't it? Although communism's grip was laid to rest in 1989, if you were to visit a jazz club in Prague today, you will likely find a tuba in lieu of an upright bass. Fear lingers. Fear was not only paid lip service in politics; rather, it was institutionalized in the educational system, consumer experiences, and even in this case in music. Fear was not only a state of mind; it was a state of the world. Like music, education was a victim of the strategy of fear. The last thing communists needed were mobs of hopeful students running around trying to change things. So they controlled the students too.

Hope Under Lock and Key

Although Western economic theory had been taught at the university since 1975, it was only offered to the party's chosen few. After all, good communists understood the value of keeping their friends close and their enemies closer. There was no room for Milton Friedman in the halls of academe, much less the minds of young communists. Well, actually there was a room—a very small one—designated for Western ideology. Know thine enemy. They had that one nailed.

Under lock and key, Central Europe's most prestigious business school maintained an archive of Western textbooks. These were maintained for limited consumption by the party elite. My students, historically, were not among the privileged. Hope, by virtue of knowledge, was secured with lock and key. Soon after I arrived, however, Western textbooks began to pop up in retail shop windows around Prague merchandised like Louis Vuitton's best bags. Small halogen lights shone on their covers like Monet at the Met. Considering their prices, the lighting was appropriate. Although communists attempted to stifle education and the free exchange of ideas, the muffler that hung from the country's educational chassis had holes. Students had hope in spite of their oppressors.

The Otto Principle

Back in the classroom, I maintained an acute awareness and great respect for the severity and clandestine nature of the postcommunist hangover. With this in mind, I stood before my first class with a hint of trepidation. After all, I had come to Prague to promote Western ideology. For my students to act differently, they would need to think differently. Therefore, over the course of the semester, I asked my students, who had come from countries including the nation-states of war-torn Yugoslavia, Poland, Hungary, Ukraine, Russia, Slovakia, and the Czech Republic, to challenge what they had learned and ask new questions. After all, I was an American in Prague. I was expected to be provocative—or so I thought.

I wanted my students to develop their own opinions as to the future of their country and their role in it. Therefore, I forced them to take sides on geopolitical, economic, and social issues. We had great debates. At the end of the semester, I asked each of my students what he or she had learned as a result of taking the course. Among the responses I received, there is one I have kept. It was submitted by a young man named Otto. He was Hungarian. In response to my question, he wrote, "That man can [have] two points of view on the same problem."

This twenty-year-old idealist had summarized in twelve words what I had attempted to teach in twelve weeks. Finding multiple answers to the same question, alternative solutions to the same challenge, and different paths to the same destination—that is the essence of hope. With hope, the Czech people just kept trying, looking for ways around, through, over, under, and in between en route to a desired goal—freedom. In his book *Ignorance: A Novel,* Milan Kundera wrote the words that opened this chapter: "Dictators are perishable. Russia is eternal. The misery of the countries we come from lies in the utter absence of hope." As fate would have it, the characters in Kundera's novel were wrong. Although, as Kundera himself writes two paragraphs later, "All predictions are wrong; that's one of the few certainties granted to mankind."

Imagine

Although the citizenry of Central and Eastern Europe ultimately defeated fear, imagine if those who governed this part of the world for over four decades had used hope in place of fear. Imagine if they mandated hope—in their music, literature, media, and social interactions. One wonders, where would they be now? Imagine what this former Central European outpost of democracy could have achieved under different leadership, hopeful leadership. Imagine if Czechs were only allowed to, well, *imagine.* Is it any wonder that today on Kampa Island in the middle of the Vltava River near Prague's Charles Bridge sits a shrine to the late John Lennon? Imagine.

Fear Management

The communists had no monopoly on fear. Imagine if we all lived and worked under a strategy of hope as deliberate, as orchestrated, and as profound as the communists' strategy of fear. Where would we be now? Imagine a fearless world. Unfortunately, fear is omnipresent. It exists not only on a geopolitical stage but also deep inside the human spirit. Consider social phobia.

Socially phobic individuals avoid large groups of people, and when in the presence of groups, they suffer from all sorts of nasty symptoms, not the least of which is a sensation of detachment from reality. Considering that 5.3 million American adults between the ages of eighteen and fifty-four have social phobia, it is a miracle that our organizations are as functional as they are. While phobias are based on specific situations, fear is more generalized.

Fear is the feeling that danger is imminent, that something bad is about to happen based on a known cause (for example, the house is on fire). However, when fear is *not* justified, we avoid all situations that may give rise to that fear. After all, we humans do not need the presence of a real threat in order to be scared. We are creative. Recall the myth of spiders and the automatic vigilance of Meriwether Lewis. As Tom McCoy of Advanced Micro Devices commented to me, "Fear is the most negative and most powerful force in the universe. It is a leader's responsibility to recognize it, manage it, and if possible, eliminate it from the organization." How? Enter behavior therapy.

Say a person is afraid to contribute new ideas because he fears his boss's opinion. If this fear becomes generalized, he will likely shut down entirely and resist the temptation to share new ideas with anyone ever again. Sound familiar? This problem is pandemic in most organizations. The challenge is not only in recognizing it but in managing it. To manage fear, behaviorists resort to an array of techniques, including exposure treatment, flooding, systematic desensitization, and modeling. Afraid to speak in public? Exposure treatment prescribes a controlled public-speaking experience. Flooding is a form of exposure treatment whereby the person is allowed to be afraid until the fear fades away. In other words, keep speaking in public until you are no longer afraid to speak in public. In some cases, this can be done using only your imagination. Rather than actually speaking, you would simply imagine yourself speaking in public. If your team is afraid to take chances or to make decisions or to do something new, flooding would suggest that you force the team members to create, make a decision, and take a chance. Since flooding can be too extreme for some people, behaviorists have developed an alternative technique called systematic desensitization.

Systematic desensitization involves three steps: trained relaxation, anxiety hierarchies, and counterconditioning. The first step involves putting people at ease—creating a safe environment. The second step involves identifying the reasons for the person's fear. This is known as creating an anxiety hierarchy. For example, if your team is afraid to introduce new ideas, ask why. The list of responses may include fear of cannibalizing current market share, risking one's personal reputation if the idea fails, or even being promoted if it succeeds. (I'll no longer be able to do what I love once I'm promoted.) Identify and prioritize this list. This requires patience on your behalf because you—like most leaders—are probably action oriented. You like to solve things quickly. Don't rush this step. Also know that you likely suffer from different fears than your team members. This list may surprise you. The third step, counterconditioning, involves dealing with each fear beginning with the least anxiety-producing one and working up the list. For example, if a person is afraid of flying, her hierarchy may include a generalized fear of airports, flight attendants, gate agents, the physical act of boarding the aircraft, and so forth. Counterconditioning involves working through each of these independently, starting with the least anxiety producing. In an organization setting, consider the innovation process—a thrilling journey into possibility. Everyone loves a great idea, but great ideas are like supermodels—never lonely and intimidating to most admirers. If your team members are afraid to consider new ideas, the most generalized fear is likely that they will lose their jobs if it fails. Deal with this first. Then move up the ladder until the entire hierarchy is discussed and plans are put in place to mitigate their concerns.

The last technique, modeling, was introduced by social learning theorists and involves observing others doing what the observer fears most. Consider again the fear of flying. Perhaps the person who is not afraid to fly listens to music, reads, or works on his laptop, whereas the person who is afraid to fly rings her hands and stares out the window while listening to air traffic control. The goal of the fearful flier would be to attempt to model the behavior of the fearless flier. Incidentally, this is why entrepreneurs are frequent readers of the biographies of successful people. They like to model their behavior. If it worked for these guys, perhaps it can work for me. If you are unable to facilitate "live observation," reading case studies is an effective modeling strategy as well.

The goods news is that the application of these fear management techniques—the hierarchy exercise, for example—can achieve results in a single application. It just takes the willingness to talk about something that many people would rather not discuss—fear.

If the Future Were Guaranteed

Finally, if you need a quick way to help your team overcome their fears, try this. Have each person picture success in his or her mind's eye—what does it look like? Describe it. Then ask what Tom Stat of IDEO asked of my students at Northwestern: "If the future were guaranteed, what would you do right now to make it happen? Do that."

7

DEBUNKING THE
MYTH OF WISHING

"I don't know what you mean by 'glory,'" Alice
said. Humpty Dumpty smiled contemptuously.
"Of course you don't; till I tell you. I meant 'there's
a nice knockdown argument for you!'" "But 'glory'
doesn't mean 'a nice knockdown argument,'" Alice
objected. "When I use a word," Humpty Dumpty
said, in rather a scornful tone, "it means just what
I choose it to mean; neither more nor less." "The
question is," said Alice, "whether you *can* make words
mean so many different things." "The question is,"
said Humpty Dumpty, "which is to be master; that's
all." "That's a great deal to make one word mean,"
Alice said in a thoughtful tone. "When I make a
word do a lot of work like that," said Humpty
Dumpty, "I always pay it extra."
—*Lewis Carroll*, Through the Looking Glass

According to the *Oxford English Dictionary*, *hope* can be used as a
noun or as a verb. As a noun, its first meaning is "a positive expecta-
tion and desire for something to happen." However, its second meaning is "a person or thing that gives cause for hope." Aha! You can be
hope. What I find even more compelling is that when used as a
verb, *hope* means "to intend, if possible, to do something." Hope is active, not passive. If we blend the definitions, we get "a person who
gives cause for hope by intending, if possible, to do something." Isn't
this the definition of a leader? Leaders therefore personify hope.

Although this definition resonated strongly with me, as one who favors Socratic teaching to preaching, I decided not to define *hope* during the course of interviewing those who have contributed to this book. Rather, I allowed the leaders to define it for themselves. And am I glad I did. As you'll soon learn, they see the world differently. As Christopher Columbus is said to have written of his journey to the New World, "Those who see the light before others are condemned to pursue it in spite of others." While we readily recognize that successful people *think* differently, how often do we ask whether they *believe* or *feel* differently? Could it be that they exploit intuition and emotional sentiments as creatively as logic and intellectual judgments? They must. How else could Pablo Picasso stare at an empty canvas and see a masterpiece? Or how could John Lennon sit in silence and hear a song that's never been written? As it turns out, in their lives as leaders, their thoughts on hope are unconventional. Then again, so is their success. Consider the seven myths about hope and how triumphant leaders define and use hope differently.

Myth 1: Hope Is the Same as Wishful Thinking

Language is important. Words matter. As Deepak Chopra explained to me, "I tell my patients not to keep using words unless they really know what they mean. I often see people in such despair using the word *hope*, but they do not really understand hope. They say, 'I am hoping to get better.' This statement is the result of a hopeless state of consciousness. I want them to really see that there is a field of possibilities. There are creative solutions. There is vision. There is inspiration. There is meaning. There is purpose." As Chopra suggests, hoping to get better, in the absence of action, is false hope, wishful thinking, or blind optimism. Herein is the difference between blind optimism and hope.

In Hebrew, there is no word for optimism. However, there is a word for hope. *Tikvah* means to twist or to twine around like strands in a rope. While you can find rare uses of the phrase *roeh shehorot* (meaning "to see black") and its antonym *roeh veradot* ("to see roses"), the phrase connotes naiveté. Optimism, among the leaders I've studied, is a passive activity. Twisting and twining requires work, as does hope. To hope is to ignite *action* toward a desired objective. Hope is active, not passive.

Aristotle warned us that expecting the best can get us into trouble. In his words, "Those who hope easily are easily deceived." However, he didn't stop there. He went on to say, "With all the failure and disappointment in life, it is possible to become 'positive in nothing' and thus to do all things much too feebly." Aristotle's counsel was to "expect life to be hard but still believe in the triumphs of good." Expect difficulty, but never let go of the triumphs of good. Aristotle's counsel is shared by Vaclav Havel, the dissident playwright, who in 1985, in forbidden communication with Karel Hvizdala through underground mail, wrote:

> Hope, in this deep and powerful sense, is not the same as joy that things are going well, or willingness to invest in enterprises that are obviously headed for early success, but, rather, an ability to work for something because it is good, not just because it stands a chance to succeed. The more propitious the situation in which we demonstrate hope, the deeper that hope is. Hope is definitely not the same thing as optimism. It is not the conviction that something will turn out well, but the certainty that something makes sense, regardless of how it turns out. It is also this hope, above all, which gives us strength to live and continually to try new things, even in conditions that seem as hopeless as ours do, here and now.

In your business—as in mine—wishful thinking will get you nowhere, but hopeful thinking will take you everywhere. It is why there is always hope, while wishes fade along with the shooting stars tethered to them. Deepak Chopra shares Vaclav Havel's wisdom. In Chopra's words, "Pursue excellence. Forget about success. That is real hope."

Wishful leadership is irresponsible and reckless. As Admiral Jim Stockdale, the highest-ranking U.S. military officer in the Hanoi prison camp, commented to Jim Collins on surviving imprisonment in Vietnam for eight years:

> The optimists were the ones who said, "We're going to be out by Christmas." And Christmas would come, and Christmas would go. Then they'd say, "We're going to be out by Easter." And Easter would come, and Easter would go. "And then Thanksgiving, and then it would be Christmas again. And then they died of a broken heart." He then turned to Collins and said, "You must never confuse faith that you will prevail in the end—which you can never afford to lose—with the discipline to confront the most brutal facts of your current reality, whatever they might be.

It is important not to get lost in Stockdale's reasoning. He did *not* suggest that actively hopeful prisoners cracked. In his assessment, he defined optimists as "the wishful." In his definition, the wishful lose energy by ignoring negative information, capitulating to time, and longing for things to turn around. Actively hopeful individuals, on the other hand, believe they will prevail but also willingly acknowledge the current negative reality and thus work diligently toward their desired goals. Hopeful leaders do not mistake windmills for evil giants or peasants for princesses. Unlike Don Quixote and very much like Admiral Stockdale, hopeful leaders recognize information as it is—both good and bad. Although it is worth noting that Cervantes's four-hundred-year-old tale of a mad idealist and his sidekick, Sancho Panza, is second only to the Bible in global readership. However idealistic Quixote and Sancho may be, we are all secretly attracted to the unbridled confidence of optimists. However you choose to define hope or optimism, give it action.

As a leader, managing false hope is easy. When you hear someone utter the words "I am hoping to . . . ," respond with "And what exactly are you doing to make that happen?" If no response is forthcoming, the person is living with false hope. Your job, as a leader, is to help such individuals put actions to their thoughts. Help them create a plan to make hope happen.

Myth 2: Hopeful Leaders
Are Happiness Promoters

Happiness is a good thing. In fact, according to the *Princeton Review*, I live only a few short blocks from the happiest college students in the nation, at DePaul University. I'm glad to have them around. Moreover, laughter is a good thing. Nothing beats hearing my son laugh. However, whereas kids smile and laugh up to four hundred times a day (adults only seven to fifteen times a day), neither success nor hope requires a good-natured disposition. In fact, in the course of writing this book, I have met very successful individuals who, while profoundly hopeful, are a bit forlorn in their disposition. Hence the common advice to "hope for the best but prepare for the worst." However, have you ever asked, "What if we were to hope for the best and actually prepare for it?" Assuming, of course, you also create the appropriate "worst-case scenario" plan, what could be possible? Nonetheless, hope does not require happiness. In some cases, the leaders I have met are in fact downright grumpy; in other cases, even paranoid.

Consider Paul Orfalea, an outrageously successful serial entrepreneur. Orfalea is a self-described hopeful pessimist. For him, the sky is perpetually falling. In our conversations, he remarked, "I'm worried most of the time. Ask my executives." At which point he called one of his executives into his office, and sure enough, she concurred. Talk about an open-door policy. However, later, during lunch and when her boss was not present, she admitted her fondness for his leadership style. As she said to me with admiration for him, "People loved working for Paul when he owned the company. People wanted to follow him because he believed in them." Her presence as an executive in his current ventures is the best testament to his leadership.

Large-scale social trends suggest that happiness is related to affluence and choice, at least indirectly. Assessments of well-being by social scientists David Myers of Hope College and Robert Lane of Yale University reveal that increased affluence has been accompanied by decreased well-being in the United States and most other affluent societies. Specifically, as gross domestic product in the United States more than doubled over the course of thirty years, the proportion of the population describing itself as "very happy" declined by approximately 5 percent. That's 14 million people. Myers and Lane found that among other factors, the overabundance of choice has contributed significantly to a net decrease in happiness. In the context of leadership, the implications are clear. Leaders fail when their followers do not know what to do. The choices are simply too daunting. Therefore, it is a leader's job to make decisions, not to promote happiness. In fact, if Bobby McFerrin were to write a song about hopeful leadership, I might suggest that he title it "Do Worry, Be Cautiously Optimistic." A decisive leader, it could be argued, creates a happier team environment because his or her people know what to do. A happy yet indecisive leader, on the other hand, will not necessarily beget a happy workforce, although who wouldn't like to work for a happy and decisive leader?

Jack Cakebread told me a story about one of his hopeful heroes, Winston Churchill. As Jack explained, Churchill "absolutely hated two things: surprises and photos. Finding a smiling Churchill [photograph] is no easy task." However, Churchill was hope. Consider his words about Dunkirk in the House of Commons on June 4, 1940: "We shall fight on the beaches. We shall fight on the landing grounds. We shall fight in the fields and in the streets; we shall fight in the hills. We shall never surrender!"

Cakebread told this story as we gazed at a photo of Churchill given to Jack by Churchill's grandson. Ironically, a grumpy-faced Churchill keeps a watchful eye on a giddy Cakebread. For Jack, an innocent smile seems to swim just below the surface of his face. He's an extremely good-natured guy. In fact, during our conversation, he was suffering from a few broken ribs due to a recent fall in his home garden. Yet you'd never know it from his attitude. Jack Cakebread is endlessly hopeful. However, so is Churchill, although, unlike Cakebread, you'd never know it from the look on his face. You don't need to look it to be it. However, you do need to believe it.

Myth 3: Hope Requires Great Leaps of Faith

Many people falsely believe that having hope means making a leap of faith. However, though triumphant leaders make mental leaps, their actions are more similar to stepping off a curb—the distance is not as daunting. Triumphant leaders translate their lofty vision of the future into very practical steps. I call it "curb stepping," the topic of Chapter Twelve. It is how they activate hope. As Charles Schwab once said to me, "I had just started working. I knew that San Francisco was a few miles from Wall Street. To be honest, while the weather is good in California and we are surrounded by three major universities, I hired anyone who would join me. I had to start somewhere." The only reason triumphant leaders' steps appear to be leaps of faith is that we see only the most recent ones they've taken. Look back through almost any leader's success, and you will find many footprints in the sand. It's a long road that begins by stepping off the curb.

Myth 4: Hope Is What You Have When You Have Nothing Else

Hope and fear do not distinguish between success and failure. In other words, losers maintain no jurisdiction over the feeling of hopelessness or fear. Consider hypersuccessful elite athletes who frequently suffer from bouts of anxiety and even severe depression. One such case is that of Terry Bradshaw—former Pittsburgh Steelers quarterback, four-time Super Bowl champion, member of the Football Hall of Fame, two-time Emmy winner as an "outstanding sports personality," and antidepressant spokesman. Although Bradshaw's despair is clinical, even in success, no one is immune from despair, not even heroes.

Despair goes well beyond the playing field and may in fact be the greatest impediment to your organization's productivity. According to the World Health Organization, depressive disorders are the single largest cause of disability in the world. According to WHO's yearly World Health Report titled *Mental Health: New Understanding, New Hope*, researchers discovered that over 36 percent of all years lost to disability are due to mental illness. This puts a significant burden on the health and productivity of your organization and the world at large. Although most leaders outside the health care profession are not responsible for curing illness, you are nevertheless partly responsible for the welfare of your employees. In this disposable world, tend to your team's aspirations. Be their hope.

Myth 5: All Leaders Are Hopeful

For the most part, we choose the jobs we have. We volunteer to walk into the factories, onto the elevators, and into the offices from which we do our work. Churchill had it right: "We shape our buildings, and afterwards our buildings shape us." However, we also shape our lives based on the decisions we make and the decisions we do not make. In so doing, we allocate our willingness to work based on our beliefs, our aspirations, and fundamentally our hope in our leaders. Having said this, hopeless leaders do exist. Although no one would admit to being a hopeless leader, such can often be found worshiping at the altar of the past. In fact, one could argue that hopelessness is much easier to exercise than hopefulness. Why? A known past is easier to critique than an unknown future.

In my conversations with the owner of a software company, I asked why the organization had failed to gain momentum under its original leadership. He responded simply by saying that he and his co-founder had different relationships with hope. To him, as the firm succeeded, his stress level decreased as his hope for the future increased. In the same situation, his cofounder reacted exactly the opposite way. His stress level increased as his hope for the future decreased. Why? Although both were reading the same financial statements and attending the same board meetings, they had vastly divergent reactions to success. While one leader saw how far they had come and the promise of the future, the other saw more to lose now that they had real customers, real money, and a real business. One looked forward; the other looked back. One was hopeful; the other was hopeless. Triumphant leaders glance in the rear-view mirror from time to time, but they keep their eyes on the road. Look forward.

Myth 6: You Are Born Either Hopeful or Fatalistic

Perhaps you know someone who seems to be perpetually hopeful. How does she do it? She must be hiding something. Even more likely, she must be *on* something. And if so, how can I get some of what she's taking? Odds are her hopeful outlook is self-inflicted. Could it be that she's brainwashed herself into a hopeful state of mind? Perhaps.

The term *brainwashing* was popularized by Edward Hunter in his 1951 book *Brainwashing in Red China* and later on the big screen by Angela Lansbury and Frank Sinatra in the 1962 cult classic *The Manchurian Candidate*. Brainwashing was Hunter's translation of the Chinese term *hsi-nao*, meaning "cleansing of the mind." During the Korean War, some U.S. prisoners of war renounced their citizenship in radio broadcasts. American officials widely believed that for Americans to abandon the ideals of their country, the communists must have devised some nefarious means of thought control. This in turn prompted the U.S. Army to conduct shipboard interviews with more than four thousand American soldiers upon their return to the United States.

Robert Jay Lifton, one of the psychiatrists involved in the interviews, has written extensively about the events in his 1961 book *Thought Reform and the Psychology of Totalism*. According to Lifton, Chinese interrogation techniques were time-honored methods of psychological coercion that involved isolation, humiliation, and the repetition of propaganda. And it worked. This then begs the question, can the human mind be brainwashed into having a hopeful outlook? Can you train your brain?

In the early 1900s, scientists discovered that nerve cells are a bit like an old married couple—they do not actually touch one another, yet they talk from time to time. This communication happens via tiny gaps between the cells called synapses. Across these synapses, powerful chemicals carry messages from one cell to the next. The chemicals are called neurotransmitters. Austrian scientist Otto Loewi discovered the first neurotransmitter in 1921, through an experiment involving two frog hearts that came to him in a dream. Like a person walking across a bridge, the neurotransmitter is released by an axon terminal, crosses the synapse, and attaches to a receptor on the other side, called a dendrite. Neuroscientists have learned in recent years that new dendrites actually sprout to make connections with other neurons. This is how learning takes place—in the connections be-tween the neurons. The more new experiences you have, the more likely you are to make new neural connections—even into old age. However, to make these connections occur, you have to continue to have new experiences; otherwise the connections diminish. Essen-tially, the brain, like a muscle, becomes stronger when exercised and weaker when not. Through such techniques as belief management, wayfinding, and curb stepping (discussed later in the book), you can learn to use hope as a tool. In the interim, know that we humans do not have to be stuck in our ways. We choose to do so.

Myth 7: Hope Never Ends

Theologically, hope is one of three Christian virtues. The other two are faith and charity (love). According to Christians, the object of all three virtues is God. As Father William Byron, a Jesuit priest, econ-omist, and former president of the Catholic University of America, writes in his book *Answers from Within*, "Your faith is directed toward God, your hope is grounded in God, and your charity (love) is aimed directly at God." In Paul's letters to the Colossians in the New Testa-ment, Paul states, "Hope begets faith and faith begets love." However, unlike love, which never ends, hope does. Whereas as a Christian, one's hope from God does not end, in a secular sense, from time to time, it certainly feels like it does. Once we have achieved what we had hoped for, hope becomes possession. This is why hypersuccessful people are never satisfied. However, hope ends only temporarily. Therefore, triumphant leaders are adept at sustaining hope even in success. Hopeful leaders cast their hook in the direction of the future even when their boat is full of fish.

Part Two

EXERCISING YOUR HOPE MUSCLES

I tell our kids that life is not a straight line. It is up and down.
And as leaders, we must either show them the light at the end
of the tunnel or give them a flashlight. They need to know
there is hope and how to act on that hope. Sure, it's easy to
have lots of hope for minor things, but then something
major happens. It is *then* that you must exercise your hope
muscles. Most of life is an exercise of your hope muscles.

–Geoffrey Canada, founder of the Harlem Children's Zone

With myths dispelled, the chapters in Parts Two and Three focus on
the beliefs and methods employed by triumphant leaders to put hope
to work. But first, I present a prelude to hope, a poem I wrote very
early one morning—1:30 A.M., to be precise—on the day that I made
the fantastically overwhelming transition from research to writing.
Inspired by an interview conducted by Tavis Smiley with the Harlem
Children's Zone founder and CEO Geoffrey Canada; surrounded by
stacks of books, academic papers, and transcripts from countless interviews; and with Lyle Lovett's "If I Had a Boat" playing through my

computer keyboard, I wrote "What Is Hope?" It is my attempt to coalesce all that I have learned during the journey of writing this book. If you are looking for the Cliffs Notes version of this book, this is it.

What Is Hope?

Blind faith to some; will to others—
Why is hope held under cover?
Groundless dreaming some would say,
But would you have it any other way?

Hope is a simple four-letter word
Like work and love, hope is a verb.
We hope to win; we hope to return;
We hope that we will always learn.

We hope for others; may they overcome
That which they fear, and then for some,
Hope can also be a noun,
Creating a smile from a frown.

Hope sees the future; hope conquers fear;
Hope moves us always from there to here.
Hope is outspoken in its beliefs.
Hope is willful; hope suffers defeat.

For us it does; it bears the brunt
Of our fears chanced on a hopeful hunch
That maybe, just maybe
We can leave this earth.
Even if just in our mind's eye we search
For possibility, progress,
And a shot at life's meaning.
Yes, this is the cause of hopeful dreaming.

But do not sit in idle reflection.
Grab hope by its wings; seek its direction.
Work you must to make it happen.
Hope is not passive; hope is action.

As for dreaming, heed its call;
Ask yourself, after all,
What has been accomplished tethered to this earth?
Dreams come not at night but at birth.

You can see them in a child's smile,
But in us hope lives in exile.
Our hopes exist behind our fears
Of risk, of failure, of too many years
Of attempting to know
when we begin
That the future is somehow predestined.

So rise up not on this land,
but inside yourself take a stand.

And harbor not guilt for the dreams you see;
Rather put them to work, and learn to believe,
To live, to love, to bring to others
A future so worthy, yet undiscovered.

With hope, seek, endure, and prevail,
Find your life's purpose and hoist the sail.
With hope, dream; take chances; embrace rejection;
Believe in yourself and seek not protection

From the desire that burns deep inside of you
Let it dance in this world; have hope and do.
Let your dreams, a wondrous power,
Live on this earth, not in the shower.

Now put hope to work
Like Aladdin:
Open the bottle;
Make it happen.

And fight with patience; wait it out;
All miracles begin with doubt.
Fight, I say; don't let things be.
Say it loud: "Hope begins with me."

—Andrew Razeghi

8

FIVE STONES

*If your hope has good reasons attached to it, then
maybe it's just a form of planning.*
　　　　　*—John Perry Barlow, Grateful Dead lyricist and
　　　　　founder of the Electronic Frontier Foundation*

I teach, and I love sushi. Every Tuesday night in the spring, after class, I
am a regular at Kabuki, a North Side sushi restaurant in Chicago's
Lincoln Park. I sit at the same table and place the same order with the
same waiter—one dragon roll, two *namesake,* and when in season,
toro. It is perhaps the only routine in my life. My waiter is as midwestern as they come—friendly, thoughtful, and harmless. As most wait-
ers are incognito, and considering his disposition, I suspected that he
is secretly an actor. Given our shared passion for raw fish, our brief conversations never moved beyond my order and our mutual praise of the
restaurant's chef—until one night near the end of the quarter, when I
teach a class on managing the organizational politics of new ideas.
In the class, we discuss how to mitigate the internal—often unpubli-
cized—challenges of introducing a new idea into an organization.
Ego, turf, coalition formation, reputation, and preparation are central
themes. My objective is to teach students to be *opportunistically aware.*
I open the class with a question: "How do you manage the inevitable?
Specifically, how do you manage individuals who will deem your idea
unfeasible, unattractive, and downright impossible?" Silence typically
follows. Perhaps the most challenging part of strategic innovation—
or life, for that matter—is enrolling others to believe in your dream.
We talk about how great leaders throughout history managed in the
face of uncertainty, including Martin Luther King Jr., Mahatma

Gandhi, Winston Churchill, and John F. Kennedy. We also discuss great ideas—from microlending to presliced bread—and how they made their way from conception to reality. Yes, even the most mundane products were once someone's dream.

Like many teachers, my lectures typically continue when class ends. Although I dismiss my classes, my thoughts remain. Therefore, I keep talking as I keep thinking. That is how I became a Kabuki regular. Teaching at night will make you an insomniac, even if you weren't one before. And since the need to continue sharing ideas requires an audience, this night, my lecture fell on my waiter's ears. However, rather unexpectedly, in a scene reminiscent of *The Karate Kid*, I became the student and he became the teacher. He said, "So, you're teaching them *mise en place*?" "What's that?" I asked. His veil lifted. "I'm training to be a chef," he said. "*Mise en place* is a French term meaning "putting in place." In cooking, it's all about preparation. *Mise en place* is the process and products we use to create dishes. *Mise en place* will typically consist of a variety of spices, cut vegetables, meats, and other food items. If you prepare your *mise en place* correctly, particularly if you are working in a restaurant that offers many different dishes, you will be prepared to handle any challenge that comes at you. If your *mise en place* is designed for only one dish, you will be able to make only that dish. So you want to make sure your *mise en place* is flexible." I tipped large that night.

The Art of Wakefulness

The value of preparation goes well beyond the kitchen. True or false? David killed Goliath with a single stone. True, but he took *five* with him just in case. Even David, with faith in God, understood the benefit of *mise en place*. In leadership, I call it *wakefulness*. Wakefulness is how triumphant leaders foster hope within themselves so that they may communicate it to others. In my research, I have identified what I call the Five Stones of Wakefulness. Mastering the Five Stones is the first step in exercising your hope muscles.

Wakefulness of Self: Character

In our schools, we teach leadership, but we dare not teach character. That's better left to the parents. However, we cannot speak of leadership independent of character. A leader's personal strengths and weaknesses are like product attributes—some confer benefits, and others have drawbacks. Wakefulness of self is a personal inventory and management of a leader's intellectual and emotional assets and liabilities. As Paul Orfalea told me, "When I owned the company, there were a lot of people a whole lot smarter than me. But I have always been good at numbers. I like numbers. So I would study the numbers, visit the stores doing well, ask them what they were doing that works, and then go to the other stores and tell them, 'Here's what they are doing. Why don't you try it and see if it works?'" Ironically, Orfalea's core strength was *copying*—literally and figuratively. He played to what he knew best—numbers and communication. Everything else he outsourced to other members of his team.

Do this. Create a list of your personal strengths and weaknesses. This list shouldn't read like your résumé; it should read like a good friend describing you to a perfect stranger. It should reflect your character. Get to know it. Invest in it. Recognize your weaknesses, and rather than attempt to overcome your weaknesses, find others who can fill in those gaps. Don't waste your time trying to learn everything. Leaders lose hope when they try to do it all on their own. Invest in your strengths. You are the leader. Delegate your weaknesses.

Wakefulness of Others: Relationships

The reason triumphant leaders do not lose hope in moments of uncertainty is that they seldom allow themselves to be alone. As Mannie Jackson explains, "Leaders get in trouble when they isolate themselves." Moreover, in these moments, hopeful leaders are attuned to "step changes" in people, when people rise to the occasion. As Charles Schwab reflects, "I admire anyone in the moment when they take their game to the next level." What surprised me most about this comment was that it was in response to my question "Whom do you most admire?" Thinking he would respond with someone like Abraham Lincoln, I got quite a surprise. Schwab's admiration is held out for *anyone* in the moment of ambiguity able to "turn it up a notch" in order to improve his or her performance, place, status, or game. Having just come off a round of golf with Phil Mickelson, Schwab invoked Mickelson's career performance as a case in point.

Mickelson's drive began when he was very young. At the age of four, approaching the eighteenth green of his first round of golf, he began crying—not because the green was located high on a hill but because he knew that the eighteenth hole meant that the round was about to end. That same spirit of not wanting the game to end led him to a phenomenal junior career. Mickelson would go on to win thirty-four San Diego County titles, followed by three NCAA championships, a U.S. amateur title, and a win on the PGA Tour's Northern Telecom Open as a collegian. To date, he is one of only a handful of players to capture more than twenty Tour victories, including the 2004 Masters, and to have played on five Ryder Cup and President's Cup teams. All the while, he commands a reputation on and off the Tour as a statesman of golf. Always the gentleman, Mickelson reflected on his performance in early 2005: "Unfortunately, I didn't win the Masters, but I did win three times at the FBR in Scottsdale, the AT&T at Pebble Beach, and the BellSouth in Atlanta, and it was fun to have my family there making memories we'll share for the rest of our lives." He then went on to win the 2005 PGA championship. Is it any wonder that Schwab admires Mickelson? While Tiger Woods is admired for his superior talent, Phil Mickelson is beloved for his *gamesmanship*. The Golf Channel's Peter Kessler—often called the "Voice of Golf"—once conjured up the scenario of Jack Nicklaus and Arnold Palmer standing before God. God says to Nicklaus, "You will be the one they all admire," and then turns to Palmer and says, "But you will be the one they love." Like Palmer, Mickelson has a relationship with the fans that is like no other. His relationship with fans transcends his game. People love to follow him.

Chris Lewis wrote the following for *Sports Illustrated* following Mickelson's 2005 PGA win:

> It wasn't eloquent, but it came from the heart. Or maybe from the bottom of the belly, sport's true emotional core. "Phil, you're one of us now," rang the voice from the grandstand as the winner of the 2005 PGA Championship, returning from the scorer's cottage, stepped back onto the 18th green at Baltusrol to collect the Wannamaker Trophy. "You gotta come down to the Shore for beers!" Golf doesn't spend much time thinking about loudmouths like him. Why should it? He'll never sponsor a PGA Tour event or rent a corporate tent at a major. He doesn't buy his kids $2,000 worth of golf equipment every year. Never mind the white-collar-or-blue-collar question—his shirt doesn't even have a collar. Yet, he was the most important guy at last week's PGA Championship. He lives for sports, and his interest level is what moves golf, on a week-to-week basis, from page C3 to C1. . . . It can make or break events.

In the relationship between a player and his fans, a leader and his followers, and a company and its customers, the awareness of others can make or break you. Mickelson's relationship with the fans is not unlike Schwab's relationship with his customers. The guy gets as much from them as they get from him.

Do this. Write down the half dozen or so individuals that you look to in moments of uncertainty—those who help you "figure things out." Like Schwab's admiration for Mickelson, these could be individuals you admire but interact with only occasionally. Regardless, you learn from them. For each person you identify, write down *how* this person makes you a better leader. What exactly does he or she do? For example, perhaps one helps you make sense of complex situations while another is adept at "reading other people." Once you have your list, go to each of these individuals and ask how he or she does what you admire most. For example, one may be adept at solving complex problems. Sit down with her and study how she thinks about information and how she arrives at insight. More often than not, she is following a methodology of sorts. Although it is likely a natural way for her to think, it may be completely foreign to you. Remember that your strengths as a leader include the strengths of those who make you a *better* leader. Your goal should not be to learn how to do what she does but rather to understand what it is that you do not know. Phil Mickelson makes Charles Schwab better. Do not overlook those who help you maintain hope. Keep your heroes close.

Wakefulness of Context: Situation

Triumphant leaders—hopeful leaders—are fundamentally nosy. Although leaders are often thought of as "big-picture people," triumphant leaders study situations in painstaking detail. To understand how hopeful leaders think, try this. Consider your current environment—the room in which you are sitting, the people around you, the sky above, and so forth. Now take a *closer* look around you—the coffee mug on the table, the cell phone on the desk, the carpet on the floor. Now I want you to look for something very specific. Identify everything around you that is brown. Go ahead, do it now. Now tell me, what did you see that was green? Don't look up. Does anything come to mind? Odds are your list of green things is considerably shorter than your list of brown things. As with most things in life, what we are asked to focus on commands our attention. However, hopeful leaders think a bit differently. While they study details and follow directions, they do not get lost in either.

Consider the work of Geoffrey Canada. As CEO of the Harlem Children's Zone, he knows the details of his situation, a sixty-block area in central Harlem that is home to sixty-five hundred of America's poorest children, more than 60 percent of whom live below the poverty line and 75 percent of whom score below grade level on New York State math and reading tests. However, he is able to rise from this seemingly impossible situation and create a vision and a plan. Like an aircraft taking flight, hopeful leaders are able to rise, quickly and high above the din of complexity, with an informed opinion and decision to act. Knowing the context and knowing it well reinforces their reason to believe that what they are doing is right.

As Charles Schwab explained to me:

> When I started in the business, the first thing that I did was study the industry inside and out. In the summer of 1960, although I was a failure as an insurance salesman, I got in and started to say to myself, "What is this crap that they are selling these people? My God!" I had to look at these mature people upstairs who are selling this junk to people. . . . I became suspicious about financial services. Therefore, I began to study it—to really study the products—how they were priced, what benefits they provided, what the margins were, and who was benefiting the most from the way the products were designed. It began my thinking that the old ways of doing things were wrought with all kinds of conflicts. I spent all my time thinking about it—every recipe about the financial services industry, the engineering of the stuff. I like to dig into the details. Out of that, I then had the courage to go into the discount brokerage business. There is nothing like education followed by a lot of good practical stuff. The more I learned about the dysfunction of the stuff, the more I realized we had a really important contribution to make—better prices, returns, and service.

Schwab, like Canada, arms himself with details. Details give rise to hope in himself, his vision, and ultimately his success. People lose hope when they lack information—when they don't know the details of a situation. After all, if you were caught in a fire and you didn't know where the exits were located, how would you feel? On the other hand, if you had studied the building prior to the fire and knew of at least three exits on your floor, you would likely be more hopeful, which would in turn help you find a way out. Hopeful leaders are enlightened leaders. Know the details. Write them down. Study them, but don't get lost. Then rise above it all and ask, "What does all this mean?" Then, and only then, make a decision to act.

Wakefulness of Cause: Contribution

More powerful than mission, more personal than purpose is a *cause*. Duties breed hope. As Michelangelo is said to have observed, "I saw the angel in the marble and carved until I set him free." It was his obligation. Consider the American Revolution and the wakefulness of cause of Thomas Paine. Not until Paine wrote *Common Sense* did the Americans' plight become a fight for independence and self-governance. Until Paine's published opinion in January 1776, the colonies were just that—colonies. Paine realized that they needed a common cause, particularly when, due to infighting, some colonial leaders began making an appeal to Britain to help resolve their conflicting opinions. Like a child threatening to "tell Mom," when tensions increased among the colonists, so did messages sent to the king of England asking, "What should we do with Vermont? And where exactly should Pennsylvania begin?" In the absence of a common cause, they fought for everything and thus achieved nothing.

By suggesting in plain English that "virtue and ability are not hereditary," Paine created a cause among the people. *Common Sense* sold no less than one hundred thousand copies, becoming an immediate bestseller. It was reprinted in newspapers, quoted in church services, praised in town meetings and taverns, and read by officers to their troops. Paine's *cause* united previously divided Americans in their fight. As Paine wrote in *The Crisis*, "These are the times that try men's souls." Paine's words moved people. They appealed not only to common farmers but to intellectuals as well. Although Paine's arguments were not original—they reflected the natural-rights tenets of British philosopher John Locke—Paine communicated them in a language accessible to the average American and with a passion that resonated with ordinary people. After all, Paine was one of them and therefore knew how to speak of their fate. His *Common Sense* gave meaning and focus by creating a common cause—independence.

To adopt wakefulness of cause, start by identifying what you do and, even more important, why you do it. Why does the organization exist? What is your cause? Promote *that* among your team. If you can't find a cause that describes your team's contribution to this world or if there are too many to get your head around (recall the happiness study—having too many choices causes stress), then do as Thomas Paine did: choose one and promote *that*. Causes breed hope.

Wakefulness of Effect: Outcomes

All leaders think in terms of objectives. In fact, we even have a concept to describe this type of thinking: management by objective. However, to hopeful leaders, objectives are insufficient. Objectives are like rocks thrown in a river. They sink as soon as they hit. However, the ripples remain. The ripples are the *effects* of a leader's objectives. Hopeful leaders foster and maintain hope in the future not only by thinking in terms of their objectives but also in terms of the effects of their actions on their team, competitors, customers, vendors, and themselves. They "manage by outcomes." As a leader, they ask, "How will *all* stakeholders respond to my actions? What are the implications? What will the effects be?" As Charles Schwab explained, "We'll never be as big as Merrill Lynch because we give it back to our customers. But I know we are doing the right thing on behalf of our customers." Schwab's awareness of the effects of his actions gives him the freedom to do the right thing and stay the course when the future would otherwise seek to derail him.

Geneticist Marshall Nirenberg shared the following story with me in response to the mixed reviews his work on deciphering the genetic code was receiving in 1962: In a conversation he had with Francis Crick, Nirenberg observed, "Everyone had an opinion. Some believed my work would result in the cure of cancer. Others thought it would cause cancer. Some thought it would lead to the end of mankind. Others thought I had identified the molecular structure of God. Well, it's all in a day's work." Nirenberg was aware of the possible outcomes of his work and was therefore able to maintain hope in his work, even under the scrutiny of onlookers. And thank God. Nirenberg's work has helped prevent disease and save lives. Nirenberg is an outcomes-based thinker.

This then begs the question: how can you move from objectives-focused thinking to outcomes-based thinking? Consider how physician Deepak Chopra works with his patients to translate desired outcomes into effects. He explained it to me this way:

> I ask patients first to describe their intended outcome. Very frequently, they will say, "I don't want to have cancer anymore" or "I want to get rid of my heart disease." Then I do my best to educate them on the idea that the *absence* of something is not a good way to describe an intended outcome. Therefore, I have them focus on what it means if the intended outcome were to occur. How would the intended outcome affect different expressions of reality, including your perception of the world around you, your cognition, your moods and emotions, your behavior, your biology, your environment, and your social interaction? Can you tell me what all those things would be like if you achieved the intended outcome? I have them write this down. If they can describe that state, I know they have a clear vision. If not, then I know they are focused on the wrong things. The second step I take them through is information gathering from every source that will help them achieve that outcome, whether it's books, scholarly work, experts in the area, and so forth. Third, I then have them analyze the information, looking for evidence to support their intended outcome. The fourth step is to let it all go. For an indefinite period of time, I have them engage in play, recreation, meditation, prayer, sports—anything that has nothing to do with the intended outcome. Then, at a certain point, they typically have a spontaneous creative insight. If that insight is genuine, they are inspired and moved to work toward the desired outcome.

To practice outcomes-based thinking, try this. Write down the top three objectives—personal or professional—that you are working toward at the present time. Now ask what the implications of each of these objectives are—for you, your family, your customers, vendors, employees, team, company, competitors, and the world at large. If you can't provide immediate answers, find them out, and then ask yourself if these effects are worthy of your attention. Are you working on the right objectives? And are these the intended outcomes you are seeking to create? Hopeful leaders manage effects. Think things through—all the way through.

Throwing Stones:
The Consistent Presence of Leadership

The Five Stones of Wakefulness—self, others, context, cause, and effect—work not in isolation but in tandem, together. So you must practice them together. There is no right or wrong time to exercise wakefulness. After all, being a leader is like managing a 7-Eleven: open all night and easy to access. As Jamey Rootes, president of Lone Star Sports and Entertainment and president of business operations for the Houston Texans, once said to me, "Leadership consists of a constant diet of lifting people's heads up. Hope is the essence of leadership." One of the best places in which to observe wakefulness in action, although not exclusive to it, is in the context of organization turnarounds.

John Rizzardi is the past international chair of the Turnaround Management Association, an association of professionals serving organizations in dire straits, financially and otherwise. In Rizzardi's twenty-two years' work in the field of turnaround management and twenty-six years as an attorney, he says, "I have seen the full range of personalities, from completely hopeless and suicidal to those who have prospered in the face of such difficult obstacles. From very large, well-publicized companies to very small privately owned enterprises, the most memorable, and perhaps most inspirational, situations are those that involve very few adversaries yet have the potential for tremendous personal loss as well as excellent success." One such memorable case involved a privately held company in the Pacific Northwest.

It was founded and operated by the family patriarch and had enjoyed decades of success in supplying products for aerospace manufacturers. Relationships with the company's lenders were fragile—and for good reason. Sales had plummeted from $40 million to $8 million in a mere two years. However, based on a combination of friendship and the fact that the patriarch had no problem adding capital to the company as desired by the lender, the lender relationship was held together. Then the inevitable happened. The patriarch died. According to plan, the company affairs were to be managed by three daughters, one of whom was identified as the successor to lead the company. For our purposes, we'll call her Ann. Prior to her father's death, Ann invested a considerable amount of time and energy grooming her abilities to oversee the company. Recognizing the inevitable decline of the business following her father's death, Ann persevered in the face of lender doubt by surrounding herself with the right tools in the form of various professionals and embarked to find a new CEO. All the while, she refused to sell, believing that the company had a market position and needed only to move through this difficult transition. Ann questioned everything and everyone. She demanded excellence, and she listened and implemented sound advice. She impressed the quality employees with her hope and her belief that a well-structured company could rebuild itself, find a new lender, and regain its presence.

Ann's mission has been accomplished. The company has recovered. Sales are strengthening, efficiencies are increasing, and morale is positive. So what makes Ann unique? Unlike her sisters, one of whom was often uninformed and the other who let her emotions get in the way of rationale decision making, Ann is wakeful. Hopeful leaders focus on the negative as much as the positive. "Think positive" is a red herring. In uncertain situations, followers stay with a leader when the overall experience—not a singular event—is net positive. This is the art of wakefulness in action. Now, hold on tight to what you believe because you are about to learn something that will surely astound you.

9

BELIEF MANAGEMENT

You can't convince a believer of anything; for their
belief is not based on evidence, it's based on a deep-
seated need to believe.

—*Carl Sagan*

They stood quizzically in the oddest of places—in front of a concrete
wall at the intersection of I-90/94 and Fullerton Avenue. They
brought candles, flowers, and chairs. In front of them, a yellowish
stain. Behind them, sawhorses and police tape helped form the walls
of a makeshift open-air museum.

In April 2005, just a few days after the death of Pope John Paul II,
a crowd gathered under one of the nation's busiest highways, known
locally among Chicagoans as the Kennedy. Although the yellowish
image, according to the Illinois Department of Transportation, was a
result of salt runoff from the winter roads, people continued to gather.
Why did they refuse to accept the science provided by IDOT? What
did they believe they were seeing? To some, like gapers on the highway, the curiosity of a growing crowd got the best of them. To others,
it was a miracle—the Virgin Mary. The alleged salt runoff appeared
in the form of the mother of Jesus. Or was it the other way around?
Regardless, they came.

They—both the pilgrims and the Illinois Department of Transportation—saw what they wanted to believe. However, religion and
road crews have no monopoly on belief. We believe in all sorts of
things, including the promise of fad diets and "Somebody's gonna
lotto; it might as well be you!" We also yearn to believe in the visions

of our leaders. Down deep, we all want to believe in a Baptist minister's dream, in the promise of a new idea, and most important of all, that our decisions will help us get to a desired future. We want to believe our hopes will be realized—assuming that we work at them.

Belief Versus Fact

In the minds of many people, including those who gather under Chicago's highways, belief trumps fact regardless of scientific reasoning. Consider this: how can you measure the love a parent has for a child? Ask any parent. You can't see unconditional love, but you can feel it. Or consider the frequent comments made by jury members soon after landmark cases—"The witness just wasn't believable." In moments of uncertainty, we want to believe even when our eyes tell us differently. However, there is more to believing than having a shared opinion. Beliefs affect outcomes. Consider the evidence.

Safety in Numbers

As when we seek shelter from a storm, groups provide a safe haven. They're cozy. We like to align ourselves with people who think like us, act like us, and—if we could have it our way—look like us. When a person shares your beliefs, you enjoy that person's company. In fact, we typically grant like-minded people greater freedom. In other words, the mistakes made by someone like us aren't as bad as the mistakes made by people who think differently than we do. It's OK to admit it. We're all human this way.

Groupthink and safety in numbers are anecdotal phenomena that have historically gone unproven—until recently. With advances in technology, scientists have confirmed that we do not need to see it in order to believe it. Depending on *who* believes it, we will see it. Literally. Therefore, as a leader managing an unknown future, you should rest assured knowing that you can enroll others to share in your vision by enrolling them to believe. They will see if you believe. This is no longer just an attractive cliché.

This once unexplained and now scientifically proven phenomenon—that human perception is biologically influenced by the beliefs of others—has enormous implications for leadership. You have the capability—not by sharing the organization's objectives but by sharing your beliefs—to influence the outcomes of your success. Objectives create markers, but beliefs create a shared vision. Consider the evidence.

Seeing with Your Eyes, Believing with Your Ears

In June 2005, the *New York Times* published an article headlined "What Other People Say May Change What You See." The article cites a celebrated series of experiments conducted in the 1950s by social psychologist Solomon Asch. The object of Asch's curiosity was social conformity. Asch had a penchant for perception. One experiment involved showing subjects two cards. On one card, Asch drew a vertical line. On the other, he drew three lines, one of which was exactly the same length as the single line drawn on the first card. The subjects were asked a simple question: which two lines are alike? This seems as straightforward as *Sesame Street*. Like all control groups in research environments, in isolation, there is nothing exciting about them, as was the case with this group. However, it was in Asch's experimental group that things really started to cook.

In this group, Asch planted seven actors. Each actor was assigned two duties: give your answers before the real respondents have a chance to answer and, when given the sign to do so, intentionally give the wrong answer. Each imposter responded individually; however, their answers were to be the same, even when intentionally incorrect. What happened next astounded Asch and would continue to puzzle him and the rest of the research community from that time onward: 75 percent of the genuine subjects agreed with the incorrect answers given by the bogus respondents at least once, and 25 percent agreed with them 50 percent of the time. Beliefs trumped sight. People traded their perception for the beliefs of others. They saw what others believed. Or did they?

Although Asch had discovered that beliefs can affect how people respond or at least what they claim to see, he remained puzzled about one question that he was never able to answer: Did the people who conformed to the imposters do so knowing that their answers were incorrect? Or did the pressure of the group's beliefs actually change their perception of what they saw? In other words, did they actually see differently based on the shared beliefs of others? As is the case and eternal beauty of science and academic discovery, although Asch has since passed away, his curiosity lives on. With advances in technology, researchers have since put Asch's question to rest. We have answers. And they have far-reaching implications, not only for leadership but also for society at large.

The Neuroscience of Believing

According to Gregory Berns, a psychiatrist and neuroscientist at Emory University in Atlanta who led the first study of perception using functional MRI technology, "We like to think that seeing is believing." However, as Berns and his team have discovered, seeing is believing what the group tells you to believe. Berns's findings immediately reminded me of a conversation I had with entrepreneur Paul Orfalea about leadership and vision. He made the following observation: "The problem with vision is that we believe with our ears regardless of what we see." What is most stunning about Orfalea's observation and Berns's findings is that the two have never met. Paul Orfalea reached this conclusion anecdotally after decades spent leading people. Gregory Berns observed it biologically in the laboratory. Berns's findings provide leaders with a challenge of enormous proportion (say nothing of the jury system).

In his study, Berns invited thirty-two participants, each of whom was told by the recruiters, "You will be doing the same task, but you're the only one who will be in the scanner." In the same vein as Asch's experiments, Berns asked the participants to determine similarities or differences in images. In Berns's study, he used two three-dimensional objects instead of Asch's lines. Two cards. Two objects. Two different points of view. Like Asch, Berns also involved actors. Berns even went one step further by encouraging interaction between the imposter group and the authentic respondent in the waiting room—they practiced together, took photos of one another, and traded small talk. Once inside the study room, study facilitators put the real participant into an MRI machine. As planned, the participant was told that the group outside the machine would look at the objects first and then announce whether they were the same or different. In some cases, wrong answers were given. In others, the right answers were given. And in other cases still, the participant was told that a computer had made the decision. Next, the MRI machine participant—the real subject—was shown the objects and asked whether they were the same or different. Recall that at this point, the real participant in the machine knew how the imposters outside the machine had responded. Their answers had been divulged and recorded. Here is what Berns discovered: on average, MRI participants agreed with the group 41 percent of the time, even when the imposters' responses were wrong. This is interesting; however, what Berns saw physically—something Asch couldn't see—is what makes these findings so compelling. Berns saw the brain.

If conformity to the group was a result of a conscious decision, changes in activity in the forebrain should register. The forebrain deals with things such as planning, conflict management, and other higher-order activities ("peer pressure" would register here). On the other hand, if conformity was the result of an actual change in perception—what the MRI participant was actually seeing—changes in activity should register in the posterior brain. This is the area of the brain that deals with spatial perception and—you guessed it—vision. So, you may be asking, did the real participants make a conscious decision to cave in to the group—to give what they knew was a wrong answer just to "fit in"—or did they actually see what the bogus respondents claimed they saw? Answer: the authentic participants did *not* make a conscious decision to cave into the group. They actually perceived the objects as the group had labeled them. As recorded by the activity in the posterior brain, they saw what the group believed. Equally astonishing, in cases where the MRI participants went against the group, when they thought independently, areas of the brain associated with emotional salience registered changes in activity. In other words, sticking to one's own beliefs when the beliefs of the group would suggest otherwise is not only emotionally difficult but also goes against the way our minds function. It's as if we want to go along with the group despite "knowing better." We feel compelled to want to believe.

Although the scientific community continues to debate whether one can draw conclusions based on MRI measurements, many early studies from the field of cognitive neuroscience suggest profound implications for the study of human behavior and the subsequent training of future leaders. The suggestion, and now the evidence supporting it, that groups can actually influence what others see as "truth" cannot be managed by simply encouraging independent thinking. Outlook and emotion come into play. Given Berns's findings, your beliefs may be the most important leadership tool you have. Get to know them and those of your team. Become a belief manager.

Belief Management

Belief management is a skill of triumphant leaders. As Geoff Canada told me, we leaders "have to be prepared to believe at a deeper level than others if we're going to get stuff done. I think there is plenty of reason for people to give up on anything that is important because it is much easier to figure out why things can't happen than why they can." Belief management involves recognizing those beliefs that both hinder and promote the advancement of a leader's vision. This includes the leader's beliefs as well as those of the team.

Ask yourself, "Are the members of my team unable to see the future as clearly as I do, or do they simply not believe in what I see?" Then ask your team the same question. In moments of ambiguity, it is vital not to mix lack of foresight with incongruent beliefs. Moreover, even if your team does see what you see, it is important to recognize that seeing does not always equate to believing. "Seeing" the hard evidence, financial or otherwise, is not always the most effective way in which to persuade, cajole, convince, or sell followers on the dreams and aspirations of the leader. Recall Paul Orfalea's "seeing ears." This, of course, can work for or against you as a leader. If your team believes you—*really* believes you—anything is possible. If it doesn't, no data or material evidence will convince them. Save your breath. As Orfalea suggests, although the hard evidence may prove the obvious, the power of belief is more persuasive. This philosophy is shared by many great leaders in addition to Paul Orfalea—a man who knows a thing or two about vision and success.

Beauty in the Ear of the Beholder

As the founder of a successful retail chain and a number of other profitable enterprises, Paul Orfalea has triumphed over a number of challenges on the road to success. In fact, his high school counselor once suggested to his mother that due to his repeated academic failures, she should enroll him in a trade school to learn to be something useful, like a carpet layer. At that point, Mrs. Orfalea took Paul from the counselor's office, looked him straight in the eye, and said to her son, "The A students work for the B students. The C students run the businesses. And the D and F students dedicate the buildings." Mom was right. Over twelve hundred stores now bear his college nickname—Kinko. Gotta love Mom!

What makes Paul Orfalea's success that much more unorthodox is that he, like Richard Branson, Albert Einstein, Thomas Edison, David Boies, Tommy Hilfiger, Pablo Picasso, Henry Ford, Ted Turner, and George S. Patton, has the gift of dyslexia. When Orfalea speaks of vision, he speaks both literally and figuratively. Therefore, he has learned to lead by promoting his beliefs more than his "vision"—his strategy and plans. In fact, as he said to me, "While at Kinko's, I'd create a plan every six weeks, and then I'd throw it away. Don't get me wrong; it was a useful exercise to think through, but my strategy was simple: find out what customers want and give it to them; serve the people in the field offices—they are our customers; and have a philosophy, not a mission statement." This all took the form of belief statements Orfalea often communicated to his employees. And although the man describes himself as "impatiently paranoid," he says, "My voice-mails were always hopeful."

What Paul Orfalea and leaders like him have in common is an understanding of and appreciation for the power of belief. After all, we humans are naturally inclined to align ourselves with those who share our beliefs, not necessarily those who know the same things we know. We want to fit in (preferably with people like ourselves). Rather than giving thought to the many disparate beliefs held across the team, lesser leaders surround themselves with people who think, feel, and act just like them. On the other hand, hopeful leaders explore, manage, emancipate, and communicate beliefs so that the team, as a whole, arrives at a desired goal. They curb dogma.

Curb Your Dogma: The Art of Belief Emancipation

Beliefs cut both ways. They can help, but when they become dogmatic, they can hinder human performance. For example, consider the annual performance review as contested by management theorist W. Edwards Deming. Deming attempted to teach us—and when we didn't listen, he taught the Japanese—that "people get rewarded for conforming." That's why U.S. industry was declining. To remedy the situation, Deming suggested that organizations abolish the annual performance appraisal. He was convinced that it robs workers of their pride in workmanship and, as he pointed out, "What do you have without pride of workmanship—just a job to get some money? There's no joy in that." Deming later summarized his point with a simple mathematical equation that illustrates that it is virtually impossible to measure the performance of an individual in the context of a team. Deming therefore concluded that we are ill-advised to do that, no less attempt to create a system of rewards based on such reasoning.

Mathematically, Deming wrote

$$x + y + xy = 8$$

If x is the individual's contribution, y is the system's contribution, and xy is the contribution made by the interaction between the individual and the system, how do you honestly and accurately extract the x component, the individual's contribution? Mathematically, it is impossible. Yet through creative compensation schemes, we continue to try and continue to compromise morale.

Deming's logic—his *belief*—is shared by those who oppose the so-called great man theory: that leaders are born, not made. Ironically, among those who oppose the great man theory is the father of the wealthiest man on the planet, William H. Gates Sr. Deming's principle helps explain why the senior Gates so adamantly opposed the repeal of the estate tax. Arguing that wealth is not solely the result of an individual's contributions but also that of the nation in which the person builds his or her business—its tax code, labor laws, and so forth—Gates makes a similar argument to Deming.

For example, imagine if Microsoft were founded in a nation with a less educated and less experienced workforce. Microsoft's performance would almost certainly not be what it is today. Therefore, if assessing an individual's performance in the context of a group is highly dependent on the group in which that performance occurs, this begs the question as to why we continue with the demoralizing exercise known as the performance review. The most likely answer is "because that's the way we've always done it." Ineffective as it is, this is our shared belief, one that's difficult to challenge. Therefore, hopeful leadership requires guts. It takes courage to go against what has "always been done." And to have the courage to challenge conventional wisdom, it takes hope. Hope sets the objective independent of the current reality or rules of the games. Therefore, in their bid to win, hopeful leaders often stand alone with their beliefs. However, they do not stand in silence. They emancipate old beliefs and communicate new beliefs in their bid for a desired future. I call it the art of belief emancipation.

The Great Emancipator

One of the greatest leaders—and therefore greatest belief emancipators—I have met in the course of writing this book is Charles Schwab. Curiously, the best believers seem to see the world differently—and I mean this quite literally. Like Paul Orfalea, Charles Schwab is also dyslexic. In a twist of counterbalance, both Orfalea and Schwab seem to have overcompensated for their vision with their beliefs. Could it be that they have learned to believe more deeply in order to see more clearly?

I have given Schwab a second nickname for his creativity and his courage. I refer to him as the Great Emancipator. (His other nickname, as you may know, is Chuck.) His success is predicated in his approach to belief management—the principle-centered identification, emancipation, eradication, and communication of beliefs. When Schwab founded his brokerage firm, he challenged, penetrated, and shattered the prevailing beliefs that barred the average American from the world of Wall Street. He figured out how to lower the fees charged for buying and selling stock. Take a step inside the heart and mind of the man named Chuck.

Off to See the Wizard

The office building at 120 Kearny Street in San Francisco looks like most urban high-rises. Its lobby is clad in granite, houses multiple elevator banks, and is staffed by the requisite team of security guards. However conventional the building may appear, the tenants of 120 Kearny are anything but conventional. This is the home office of Charles Schwab, the man and the company.

Upon my arrival, after I had checked in at the lobby reception, the security guard escorted me to a special elevator with no buttons in it. After swiping his badge in front of a small black box on the wall, he proceeded to program the floor into a panel where up and down buttons would normally be. He then said to me in a rather direct tone, "Get on the elevator. It will take you directly to the executive offices. Get off when the door opens." OK then. Images of *The Wizard of Oz* accompanied my trip upward. Several seconds later, I arrived.

Entering the lobby of Charles Schwab's personal office, I was immediately taken by the warmth of the room. With its expansive views of San Francisco, the office is decorated in colors, fabrics, and artwork that reflect the beauty of the surrounding Bay Area, from the cream hues of the Oakland hills to the pale blue of the Pacific Ocean. The office says class. It is pristine. Everything is in its place. If it is possible to feel quality by simply stepping into a room, this is the place. I had clearly arrived in a space of not only success but also great wealth.

At the oversized reception desk sat a man dressed all in black. His size was of equal proportion to the desk. He was as eloquent, poised, and professional as the room in which he sat. At first blush, he appeared to be the receptionist. However, once standing, and at a sudden second blush, I realized that although he was working as a receptionist, he was most likely much more than that. I had the distinct feeling that he was packing heat under his tailored sport coat. This, of course, I never confirmed; it's mere speculation. Some things in life are better left undiscovered.

As I approached the spotless reception desk, I noticed a single piece of paper. It was the only thing on the eight-foot-long desk. On it, in what must have been a 36-point font, was "3:00 P.M.—RAZEGHI." After I had enjoyed a few welcome moments of lounging on a handsomely tailored chair, the founder of the company that bears his name came out to greet me. Schwab's gait is that of a man who has achieved a stratospheric level of success. Successful people are allowed to walk more slowly. He has the poise of a professional golfer—his other passion. With shoulders back and looking straight ahead, Schwab greeted me with a smile, saying, "It's the man with hope." We then walked to his office.

Inside, I was again taken by its tailored yet unpretentious style. There is something about Bay Area light. We began our conversation with a question that I like to ask of all outrageously successful people: "Why are you here?" As he reflected, I couldn't help but think, shouldn't he be enjoying the good life in some exotic port of call accessible only to those who arrive in Gulfstream G550 executive aircraft? Although I've heard the answer to this question thousands of times, I never tire of hearing it. It is salt-of-the-earth stuff.

Schwab responded, "I guess—not guess, I know—that we help a lot of people. People who use our services get a lot of benefits. Some are almost utilities. This investing thing is crucially important, particularly in America." The drumroll was going just as I had expected. His words alone made my heart rate speed up. Schwab continued, "It goes to the essence of capitalism. After all, two-thirds of the word *capitalism* is *capital*." At this point in our conversation, and leaning forward in his chair, Schwab said the following while softly tapping out each and every word with his finger on the table in a subconscious yet subtle expression of his passion: "The world believes today in this word called *independence*. Independence in our business means objectivity and looking out for my interest, not being conflicted. And this is not only affecting financial services; it applies to everything from software to humanity. We live in an open-source world."

As I would soon learn, words hold a lot of meaning for Schwab. He discusses, chooses, and uses words very deliberately. He'll say things such as "that's a great word, a powerful word, a word I will have to remember to use more often in the future." In response to how he thinks about and uses *hope* to his advantage, Schwab responded, "Faith, hope, and charity is what first come to mind for me. *Hope* is a great word. It is a powerful word. It is a word that I relied on a lot in my career. . . . I always tended to convert the concept of hope into something more tangible—something people could feel, touch, and smell. Did I work on hope? I sure did."

Again, I am reminded of the courage required to be hopeful. In Schwab's case, his beliefs helped him foster the courage to put his hope to work. How does he do it? How does he maintain his beliefs and use them to his advantage? Schwab continued, "The fact that I was out here and scrambling around as a little entrepreneur with no resources was fortuitous. I wasn't encumbered by those old guys telling me what to do." Unencumbered by conventional beliefs about how to succeed in the brokerage business, Schwab's unconventional insight fueled his hope in the moment of uncertainty. In fact, his unconventional beliefs are precisely what he used to build his empire. However, you needn't move to San Francisco and work out of your garage to emancipate yourself from the beliefs that thwart growth. Start by recognizing what they are. Write them down. Then look for ways to change things, make things better, or create something new.

Shared Passion for a Shared Vision

Speaking of beliefs, Schwab continued, "I like to think in terms of giving people an understanding of why they should have the same passion as I do—why their life has purpose working here and why they should believe as much as I believe. I want them to seek a higher level of satisfaction above just making a salary. And so the better I can do that, the better I have been as a leader. The best way that I have found to do this is to help others understand why it is that we are here and how we fit in the financial services business—how it is that we got here and why it is so important." Recall the concept of *porteur de sens*? Schwab assimilated it naturally.

"When I started in this business, it was pretty crude, to say the least. I had little or no resources. I have one favorite example of a guy who came in to complain about something. He was from Chicago and had an accounting background. And I said, well, if you're so damn smart, come out of accounting and start working here. So he came around and started helping me out. It was very difficult. We were mavericks at best. Some people would call us unethical because we were selling stocks at a substantially lower price at the time. In 1975, the ethical standard of a broker was that a broker was to be polite and sell it at a given price. It was a gentleman's deal. On the other hand, we were sort of crass guys selling the stuff below somebody's cost. It was not easy, although I have to say that people were looking for jobs in 1975 and we were just coming out of a recession. Unemployment was high. We were in California—a nice place to live. We also sit in the middle of three or four major universities and so we were able to get smart kids." At which point, looking outward as if he had an epiphany, he said, "All right, Andrew, actually, I took *anybody*." He laughed and then continued, "They were a full collection of people. They took risks in their careers. Some were misfits at other places. I took a lot of misfits in. There were some strange people. Anybody who was a reasonable person and communicated well, I hired. I was one of the first businesses to hire women. Go to Wall Street, it was 99 percent male; we were 40 percent female." Schwab continued, "I feel good every day about helping people invest; helping them achieve financial independence." Then, while pausing and looking out the window over the city of San Francisco, his eyes cast somewhere on the horizon, Schwab said, in a quiet yet deliberate tone, "It's about the American dream." It worked. Like the many times before, my skin stood at attention, and like the many other times I have raised this question among successful leaders, I wanted to drop everything I was doing and help him fight the good fight. Hopeful leaders have objectives, but even more, they have beliefs—many of which are unorthodox. Schwab then continued, "Don't get me wrong; I'm also motivated because I like to succeed. I like to play a great round of golf. I was just skiing this weekend. I love to go down a ski run flawlessly. It's fun. You name it. I'm not a nut about being a perfectionist, but I love doing it well."

Belief Branding

At this point, it all became clear to me—the lobby, the professionalism, the furniture. This building is anything but conventional. It is Schwab, the man, his beliefs. Beliefs are the bedrock of leader branding. Schwab's beliefs pervade everything the company does. How it looks. How it communicates. How it helps its customers. Schwab believes. Therefore, so do others.

Like Schwab, Katrina Markoff leads with beliefs. As the founder and owner of artisan chocolate maker Vosges Haut-Chocolat, Katrina once said to me in response to why she does what she does, "I want to bring peace to the world through chocolate." Is it any wonder that she is one of *Inc.* magazine's "most fascinating entrepreneurs" and also owns one of the most desirable new brands in her industry? Her calling isn't just a marketing gimmick. Markoff believes that what she is doing provides a personal sense of peace by increasing awareness to other cultures. By way of example, she sponsors international trips for her customers and sells not only her products but also the stories of the people and the cultures that inspire her work. She has even built a yoga studio in her manufacturing facility for her employees to use in the spirit of what she believes. Markoff lives out her leadership brand. She lives out her beliefs. She is not only in the chocolate business, just as Schwab is not only in the financial services business. They both lead with beliefs.

Is it any wonder that leaders who really believe in their work don't like to retire? As Schwab says, "It's fun." Like Schwab and Markoff, the president and CEO of one of the largest association forums in the country, the Association Forum of Chicagoland, is also a belief manager. Meet Chicago's bobble-headed believer.

A Bobble-Headed Believer

When Gary LaBranche took the reigns of the Association Forum of Chicagoland in 2003, he immediately studied the organization's membership. As he recalls, "When I got here, the first thing that I saw was a flat line." In the decade 1993–2003, membership grew only 6 percent. LaBranche continued, "While many people were saying, '[Our business] could be worse,' I was saying, 'Yes, but it could be a lot better.'

"So I approached our director of membership, Sheri Jacobs, and asked her to share with me what we had been doing to attract new members over the past ten years. The Forum primarily used two recruitment strategies common to member organizations of its type: direct mail and 'member-get-a-member' campaigns. The typical direct mail campaign cost $16,300 per year and resulted in approximately twenty new members, for an average customer acquisition cost of $815." In the year of LaBranche's arrival, the organization ran a "member-get-a-member" campaign that cost $22,400 and yielded 120 new members. Better, but still less than stellar. In sum, in the year he arrived, these two campaigns cost the organization a total of $38,700 and yielded only 140 members, or an 8 percent increase in membership. Mind you: prior to this, membership had grown only 6 percent in the entire decade. So 8 percent in one year didn't look so bad. However, LaBranche wasn't satisfied. Now think about this for a moment. It's less than two years after the fateful events of September 11, 2001, which amazingly had very little effect on the membership size of this organization, which relies heavily on trade shows and meetings, and this new CEO walks in and says, "We could do better." Knowing the facts, LaBranche believes in the power of human ingenuity, but he also understands how beliefs can help as well as hinder an organization's growth. And so he did what nearly all triumphant leaders do: he launched a belief emancipation campaign inside his organization—starting with Sheri Jacobs.

"After Sheri shared these plans with me, I simply said, 'OK. That's good. Now stop doing that and do anything else. I don't care what you do; just do anything but what we've been doing.'" LaBranche had realized that the organization, not just Sheri, had succumbed to its beliefs about "what works"—in this case, about how to recruit new members. Do it like we've always done it, but with a twist, was the mantra. Having *emancipated* the organization from the past—manifested in his request to his director of membership to "do anything but . . . ," Gary LaBranche led the organization to a record-setting result. Given her boss's directive, Sheri Jacobs did what most human beings are able to do when challenged—she got creative. She found another way to get things done. It involved bobble heads. At one-quarter of the cost of a conventional campaign and through the creation and execution of a creative "buzz campaign" that targeted only thirty-five people (influencers) with thirty-five bobble-head doll recruiting kits (or, as LaBranche prefers to call them, "action figures"), versus sending twelve thousand pieces of junk mail with a 0.5 percent response rate, the organization's membership grew not by 6 percent, not by 8 percent, not even by 10 percent but by 34 percent in a single year! For $10,000 versus $38,700, the campaign delivered a 34 percent increase versus 8 percent. And it did more than increase membership, LaBranche noted. "In some cases, the buzz campaign opened the door to more than just one new member. In a few cases, an entire association staff joined the Forum. One organization went from 15 members to 385, another from 6 to 60."

Although LaBranche is neither a dragon slayer nor a hero by conventional standards, his story illustrates the effect of a leader's beliefs on the performance of a team. This relatively small campaign is simply one example of the type of results that hopeful leaders yield through belief management. In this case, Gary LaBranche is a leader who liberated his staff from their very own success. He did not tell his staff how to get the job done. He simply said, "Do anything but what you're used to doing." These words in isolation may not seem filled with profundity; however, coming from a leader, they are. Think about it: how many CEOs would have had this much faith in their staff, in themselves, and in the power of creativity to do this? How many CEOs, given the surprising health of a business even in turbulent times, would have taken an 8 percent increase to the bank happy, if not dancing with glee? Not this one.

Gary LaBranche, like other hopeful leaders, is a great belief manager. He recognizes beliefs, emancipates them, and uses them to make things happen. "In the larger sense," he observed, "the bobblehead and buzz campaign supported and enhanced our efforts to reposition and revitalize our brand. It emphasized new ways of thinking about the Forum around such brand qualities as innovation, experimentation, and freshness. It was also a very visible and unique break with the past, something entirely unexpected."

Perhaps most telling of this leader's commitment to his staff's calculated risk taking, Sheri Jacobs had the bobble head made in Gary LaBranche's image. And he agreed! Figuratively—and literally—this CEO's head was on the line. Schwab, Markoff, and LaBranche share the gift of belief management. But there is more to the story of believing. You must enroll others to believe as much as—if not more than—you. To understand how to enroll others in your beliefs, let's take a trip. (This would be a good point in the book to pour a glass of your favorite wine. And if you don't have a favorite, I have one for you to consider. We're going to the Napa Valley.)

Enrolling Others to Believe

WINE IS BOTTLED POETRY. So reads the sign as you enter the Napa Valley. It's heaven on earth, but not without its challenges. Jack Cakebread recalled, "There used to be fourteen wine distributors in California. Now there are three. The same thing happened in the automobile parts business. You had to learn to tiptoe through the tulips. You have to know what customer loyalty means to your customers—not to you. You have to get others to believe. It's *their* customers that make the difference. I don't care if you're fixing cars, cutting hair, or running a winery. You get that customer loyalty." This is one of Jack Cakebread's principles of success: loyalty, loyalty, loyalty. However, getting loyalty, unlike getting a bottle of his award-winning sauvignon blanc, is not as easy as asking for it. As Cakebread suggests, you must get others to believe.

On over three hundred acres, Cakebread Cellars yields ninety-five thousand cases of wine, earning this well-managed and privately held family firm an estimated $30 million each year and growing. With 60 percent wholesale profit margins and more than 75 percent on bottles sold at the winery, life is good in the Cakebread household. If that weren't sufficient, Cakebread's sauvignon blanc ranked number one and Cakebread Cellars ranked number two overall in *Wine and Spirits* magazine's sixteenth annual poll of the best-selling wines at fifty of the finest restaurants in the nation. However, things haven't always been this rosy for Jack Cakebread.

"The challenge early on was to get people to *believe*—particularly to get them to believe in my name," Jack recalled. "All the marketing people I talked to said, 'My God! Don't put that crazy name on there.' And I thought, You know, at Cakebread's Garage," one of his other businesses that he has since sold, "we fix cars, and we're darn proud of it. Why would we change that? And so I put Cakebread Cellars" on the wine. In 1973, Jack Cakebread understood that a brand was not a name but the meaning behind the name. Once his customers believed, others followed. Success has a hundred fathers. Like most hopeful leaders, Cakebread's beliefs and therefore his dreams seem so much more attainable than the average leader's vanilla-flavored objectives. His beliefs are contagious. Just take a look at his board. Cakebread reflected, "I've got the best people on earth working here now. You should see my board. I have an outside board of directors. These guys are good. They are enthused. They believe in what we are doing. Given their experience, I'd be crazy not to listen to them—P&G, AT&T, Williams-Sonoma, Pottery Barn, UC-Davis School of Management." To underscore his enthusiasm, he repeated, "These guys are good." Surrounded by the world's greatest marketers, yet as comfortable with his beliefs as he is in his own skin, Jack Cakebread is a hopeful leader. He is the kind of leader—like Charles Schwab—that you want to hitch your wagon to and say, "Wherever you're headed is fine by me." This is just a taste of Jack Cakebread and his award-winning wines. You'll hear much more from him throughout the remainder of the book; however, in the interim, meet one of the most hopeful believers I know—owner of the "Ambassadors of Goodwill," Mr. Illinois Basketball himself, Mannie Jackson.

"You've Gotta Believe!"

Edwardsville, Illinois, is a small, affluent community twenty miles east of Saint Louis, Missouri. It is best known for its German farmers, trial lawyers, and aggressive jury awards. It is one of those quaint towns where people know each other and have known each other for generations. They have a farmer's market every Saturday in the summer, a Halloween parade, and an independently owned coffee shop on Main Street, called Sacred Grounds, where locals drink coffee from brown mugs and share the news and gossip of the day. The town even has its own mascot, known locally by a single name—Preach. He's an elderly man who keeps a watchful eye over Main Street during his daily walks. His behavior begets his name. Against the backdrop of this unassuming and fantastically midwestern town shines the career of the man known affectionately as Mr. Illinois Basketball. Mannie Jackson is an active humanitarian, philanthropist, and owner of the beloved Harlem Globetrotters basketball team.

Jackson's career reads like the American dream. Born in a railway boxcar in Illmo, Missouri, Jackson would rise from his humble beginnings to become one of America's richest men only to return to claim his midwestern roots as the anchor of his success. Upon graduating from Edwardsville High School, Jackson attended the University of Illinois, where he became the first black All-American and captain of the Illini basketball team. All the while, he couldn't get a haircut or eat at most restaurants in Champaign-Urbana due to discrimination.

Upon graduating, Jackson joined the world-famous Harlem Globetrotters as a player and traveled the world as one of America's "Ambassadors of Goodwill," to quote President Gerald Ford. After hanging up his high-tops, Jackson launched into a fast-track career at Honeywell, where he rose to president and general manager of the telecommunications division and ultimately retired as a corporate officer and a senior vice president of Honeywell, Inc. He is one of the nation's most influential black corporate executives and has been listed as one of the top twenty African American high-net-worth entrepreneurs. Jackson has served on the board of directors of six Fortune 500 companies and is the director, vice chairman, and member of the nomination committee of the Basketball Hall of Fame. He was among twelve distinguished nominees for the Archbishop Desmond Tutu Award for Human Rights in recognition of his work in South Africa. No doubt about it—Mannie Jackson is outrageously successful, yet his story doesn't stop with his riches. Polished, poised, and extremely serious on the outside, Jackson has a heart of gold. Since 1993, his efforts have attracted over $10 million in charitable donations to foundations around the globe, from Nelson Mandela's Children's Foundation to the Lincoln School Alumni Foundation in his hometown.

Mannie Jackson and I share one thing in common. We both played basketball for the celebrated Edwardsville High School basketball coach Joe Lucco. However, this is where our stories diverge. While Jackson played on the team, I played in the alley. Jackson's most memorable coach was my neighbor. As kids, we would play outside all day and night waiting for Coach Lucco to drive by and witness our previously undiscovered talents. Well, that didn't happen. Coach Lucco drove by all right, but he never had the chance to witness the awe of my left hook. Jackson, on other hand, was one of Coach Lucco's rising stars, taking him to chicken dinners where he was a frequent speaker, whether at the local Kiwanis or church group gathering. Some forty years later, Jackson still speaks highly of his favorite coach. After all, as you'll soon learn, he has used Coach Lucco's wisdom throughout his own career.

Mannie Jackson's voice engages the ear. It's melodic. It's soft. It's reminiscent of Jimmy Stewart in his portrayal of George Bailey in *It's a Wonderful Life*. And his voice has that Saint Louis–area twang to it, replacing the sound "or" with "ar"—so "former player of the Harlem Globetrotters organization" becomes "*far*mer player of the Harlem Globetrotters *ar*ganization." He gracefully moves from sentence to sentence much like you would expect from a man of his stature, size, and eloquence. "My definition of hope," Jackson explained, "is a kind of a belief system. It embodies understanding, commitment, and the ability to submit to beliefs. And then hope is the engine that propels us through belief and passion to get it done. I got this thinking from an old coach of mine," he paused a moment to reflect and then continued with a self-effacing tone. "I was a pretty good basketball player in high school. I also admired leaders. I thought I wanted to be a leader. It was an intention I set up early in my life. My coach, Joe Lucco, was an inspirational leader. But beyond that, he was a true person, a good person. He used to talk to me a lot. But he never talked about objectives, about getting this done or that done. He talked about things he *believed* in. It wasn't a religious or spiritual conversation. It was, I believe a person should behave this way or that way; I believe life should go this way—he would talk in those terms. One weekend, his son Billy and I went to a talk he gave at a local Kiwanis group. His message was always the same: 'You've got to believe!' No surprise—that was his message on that night. However many times I heard him give that talk, I never grew tired of it. That speech and those words—'I believe'—stuck with me through high school and college. In fact, they're with me today. When I don't have an answer to something, I always brace myself with this thing—*I believe*. So my belief system thinking started when I was fifteen years old with Joe Lucco."

Jackson starts all his comments with these words: "I believe." He explained, "You don't need to have a great vision. You don't even need to have a great strategy. But you've got to believe. If you do not believe, people will drift and go somewhere else." There is something about how Jackson speaks the words—*I believe*—that makes you feel as if no one has ever spoken them before. His tone is deliberate yet welcoming. At times, I felt like jumping out of my chair and saying, "Amen!"

Chief Belief Officer

"Managing beliefs has become part and parcel of my operating procedure," Jackson explained. "So when people come to work for me, I share what I believe are the success factors. We talk about them. Once we agree on what we need to do to get it done, my whole conversation with them changes. I then challenge them so that I can understand the extent to which they are committed to the goal, the extent to which they really believe in it, and the extent to which I can count on their passion for getting it done. If I sense any hesitation or any reason that they wouldn't charge as hard as I would charge, either I replace them or I spend a lot of time with them on this whole belief system thing, helping them build the kind of passion and commitment I have for what's ahead. It all starts with assumptions.

"As a leader, you have to make some assumptions about what it will take to succeed. Vision, experience, and good research help you believe. Every business I get into, from marketing to engineering to operations, I always want to know what it will take to be best in class. I don't have the answers—I seldom do—but I work on getting enough answers until I reach the point that I can say to myself, now I can believe in it—this idea, this business, these people. And once I apply the success factors and set goals, I do not revisit the goals. At that point, I revisit each team member's attitudes. Because I think it is possible to have marginal goals and still be great if you have great people with the right attitudes, beliefs, and passion. I also believe that it is possible to have great objectives, but if you have marginal attitudes, you are probably going to fail. I have to have people around me who share in a belief system—both attitude and passion for what we are doing."

What makes Jackson's beliefs so particularly salient is that he is a "save the store" leader. He has turned around many organizations. In fact, my interest in speaking with Jackson was piqued by his success in turning things around—specifically a decades-old brand called the Harlem Globetrotters.

Contagious Passion

I asked Jackson how he felt at the moment he acquired this once great but all but forgotten brand. "I felt like I was going to drown at first," he admitted. "But I spent many years doing the impossible and overcoming obstacles by fixing things and rebuilding businesses. I knew that this organization had once filled a market niche, and that need hadn't gone away. But I also looked around, and I believed I had a feeling for what it would take to be successful in the business. The extreme success we achieved I never fully thought we could attain, but the entry-level success would have been acceptable to me. My philosophy is, we may not always hit home runs, but if you can be happy with a single or a double, then it would be worth the effort. I knew there was at least enough in that brand for a double or a triple. In the moment, that's what I thought. So I tried to keep things really simple—two or three initiatives that everyone could rally around and believe in. I needed everyone's attention, focus, and passion. Mostly, I needed them to believe. I then tested the attitudes of those I had chosen and who had chosen me. I finally found the right blend of chemistry and compassion from people I didn't have to watch."

He continued, "Beliefs matter because passion is contagious. I think all of us have the need to commit to something. We want to belong. The key to life is finding the thing you can get committed to. Most successful people recognize this early in their lives. I think we all have the capacity for commitment and a need to believe in something and somebody. So if people are operating at 60 or 70 percent, I'll allow time for them—to nurture their shared hopes—but after a while, I become intolerant. I'm wasting their time, and they are wasting mine. They need to be somewhere else, doing something they can believe in. It is always a challenge to get a diverse group of people to believe in the same thing. Because the great thing about high-performing teams is that no one has to be the same, but eventually you must share the same beliefs. The day I know more about finance than my CFO is the day I've got to close the doors."

"Have you ever lost hope?" I asked. Jackson's response: "I have never felt like there was no hope. The feeling is always—*what's next?* The reason I was good in sales is that I never took it personally when someone told me no. I felt like I just didn't do it well enough. Andrew, let me share a story with you." As a writer, these are my favorite words.

A Brand-New Suit

"Ed Spencer was the former chairman of Honeywell. He was a mentor of mine. He once invited me to a board of directors meeting to give a presentation on an acquisition. I had worked around the clock for two days to get ready for this presentation. After all, I was asking the company to spend a lot of money. And it wasn't only the money. I was asking the company to go into an entirely different area of business than it had been into. I think Ed Spencer felt that I was prepared and he believed that I was prepared, but I don't think he appreciated the depth of my presentation—and by that I mean it wasn't very deep." Jackson laughed and then continued, "Because I was a one-man show with an idea, I didn't have the staff. And so I went into that board meeting with an idea, a brand-new suit, and a brand-new tie. Man, I looked great, and I thought that my presentation was on target. And so did Ed. In fact, he spent a lot of time introducing me to the group—probably too much time. I had twenty minutes. Well, I got two-thirds of the way through the presentation—I was asking for $100 million—and they began to ask me questions. First I stumbled on the technical questions. Then I stumbled on the research dollars required to really think the project through. Finally, I made errors on some logistics stuff. After three stumbles, I was down on my knees. We weren't even at twenty minutes yet when the meeting quickly turned into lack of confidence. However, I kept battling through what I thought I knew and what I wanted to have happen. I wanted to convince them that they were looking at the wrong things. And then everything stopped. Ed stood up. They excused me from the room.

"I went in the hallway and packed up my stuff. Ed came out and said, 'Are you OK?' I said, 'What do you mean?' 'I have never seen anybody get beat up like that in my twenty-five years with this company. Don't worry,' Ed said. I looked at Ed and said, 'I'm not worried. When can I come back?' Ed just stared at me and then said, 'I'll talk to you later.' In that moment, all that I could think about was how to get a team together to get this right. Later Ed told me that he couldn't have taken that beating. But I honestly cannot remember feeling down. It was always—*what's next?* Let's get going."

"So what did you do?" I asked. Mannie continued, "I went back and got a committee of experts together. A few months later, I went back into that room again."

"And what did they do?" I asked with anticipation. "They stood up and applauded. First and foremost, they couldn't believe I was back. I then told them that I wasn't going to do the whole presentation again. I was only going to answer the questions they had asked me the last time. In the end, they signed off on it. This is how the business venture started.

"I don't tackle things I don't believe in because people want leaders to believe. I believed, and my belief overcame my lack of preparation and drove me to achieve. The complex matrix of relationships and beliefs has been grossly overlooked. And I know that it's not only genetic. People can learn. There are so many potentially great leaders out there. It's a shame—all the stuff you read in the paper about corruption in corporate America. I'd be willing to bet that 99 percent of the people working each and every day are hardworking, honest folks that want to do something great. And we spend so much time talking about two or three leaders who have done wrong. We should be focused on the value that great leadership brings to this society. It is overwhelming."

It should come as no surprise that once Mannie Jackson left Honeywell, he would achieve the greatest success of his career. With the Harlem Globetrotters, Jackson accomplished one of the most dramatic corporate turnarounds ever while simultaneously stepping into the history books to lead the purchase of the team in 1993. As the first African American to own a major international sports and entertainment organization, Jackson revived the near-bankrupt organization into one of the most admired and publicized teams in the world. (Brands are like plants—you've got to tend to their ever-changing needs.) He increased revenue fivefold and rebuilt the fan base to record levels. The team dramatically demonstrated that its resurrection was not limited to the financial arena; the Globetrotters confirmed their return as one of the best and most influential basketball teams in the world when on September 27, 2002, Jackson's Globetrotters (he owns 100 percent of the team) were only the fifth team inducted into the Naismith Basketball Hall of Fame. Jackson has also amassed an impressive list of national sponsors (they believed as well), expanded countries visited to 117 with attendance of two million annually, and garnered year 1999, 2000, and 2002 Sports Q ratings as the most liked and most recognized team in the world. The Globetrotters have since partnered with FUBU to create a collection of clothes based on the team. It has also created its own merchandising and licensing company, landing sponsorship, licensing, and promotion agreements that will gross over $50 million in sales.

As one would expect from an actively hopeful leader, Mannie Jackson's future plans include a vision of building a $250 million licensing business, coproducing a Broadway musical, writing a book on the history of the Globetrotter organization, coproducing a full-length feature film with Columbia Pictures, returning the team to its roots as one of the top professional basketball teams in the world, and securing the team's philanthropic legacy as "Ambassadors of Goodwill" around the world. And it all started with a chicken din-ner and a high school coach who believed.

Create a Belief Branding Campaign

Much like the promise of a company's stock price or the state of the economy, the future is up for grabs, depending largely on what peo-ple choose to believe. Truth is at play. As a leader, to create the fu-ture, you must be aware that this phenomenon is alive and well within your organization. You must therefore seek to give those who look to you for leadership a reason to believe in you beyond the mere fact that they work for you. Try this. Imagine if those who look to you for leadership were volunteers. Would you treat them differ-ently? If so, how? If you were they, why would you want to follow you? Create a culture of believers, and you will create an organiza-tion more resilient, more courageous, and more ably equipped to manage through ambiguity, around fear, and into the future.

Creating a Belief System

Start with yourself. Focus on a situation at hand—a challenge or op-portunity. Write down what you believe are the success factors, the things that will help solve the problem or make the opportunity pos-sible. Inventory your beliefs. Now consider, given these success factors, why should you do this? Get to know your beliefs. Write them down. Look after them. From this list, create belief statements. Start with "I believe . . ." and complete the thought. Focus especially on answering *why*—why does it matter that you succeed? Also, think about what you believe about yourself, about the people who look to you for leadership, and about your organization's place in the future. Think of your belief statements as an internal "leadership branding campaign" that succinctly communicates why all who look to you for leadership should sign up for yet another day.

Sponsoring a Belief Shop

Once your leadership branding campaign is in place, bring your next-generation leaders together in a room and ask them the following questions: What do you believe in? And why are you here—on this team, at this organization, in this career? Talk about their beliefs, not their jobs. Talk about their aspirations, not your expectations. Start a new conversation. People may report to bosses with expectations, but they work for people with aspirations. Give your team a reason to believe in you.

10

WAYFINDING

He made his own breaks.

—*An umpire's opinion of Ty Cobb*

Where there's a will, there's a way. Though appealing, this is misleading. Like most clichés, it's the mother of another—*beating a dead horse*. On one-way streets, unbridled confidence becomes hopelessness. It is why triumphant leaders think in portfolio terms: where there's a will and multiple ways, there is hope. This is the art of *wayfinding*.

The Art of Wayfinding

Imagine sailing on the open seas from Maui to Tahiti, a distance of twenty-five hundred miles, without a sextant, compass, clock, radio, or global positioning device. Oh, and one last thing: imagine doing it in an open canoe. Pacific Islanders traveled in this way for thousands of years. In nautical terms, wayfinding is a method of navigation controlled largely by one's observation of the sun, stars, ocean swells, and other signs from nature to find the path to a desired destination. Wayfinding is still practiced in some parts of Micronesia, although technology has put it on the endangered-skills list.

This ancient art involves three fundamental tasks: (1) setting course strategy, (2) holding this course while keeping track of one's position during the journey, and (3) finding land after reaching the general vicinity of one's destination (within four hundred miles of your target). Getting to the general vicinity is called getting "in the box." The basic idea is that when you are twenty-five hundred miles away from your objective, you cannot say with 100 percent certainty that you will hit it precisely; however, certainty increases as you approach the "box," which in turn makes the box smaller and more accessible. Wayfinders maintain hope by dealing with reasonable targets. They think inside the box. After all, when you are twenty-five hundred miles from your desired destination, odds are you are already outside the box!

As a voyager on the open seas, the key to mastering the art of wayfinding is observation. The stars will not tell you where you are or where you are headed unless you know from whence you came. In the absence of technology, wayfinding becomes an intense game of memorization. You must constantly know, remember, and recall your speed, time, and direction every moment you speed up, slow down, and change course. Here's why.

In the open waters, the weather doesn't always cooperate. When the sky is dark and wayfinders cannot rely on the flight patterns of birds to determine direction, they read the stars. When storms approach and clouds block out the stars, they read ocean swells. And when the ocean is dark, they read the movement of the canoe to determine where they are, where they have been, and where they are going. Observation begets experience, experience begets intuition, intuition begets multiple possibilities, and the recognition of possibilities breeds hope. Like the art of nautical wayfinding, leadership wayfinding involves a similar process.

Triumphant leaders identify multiple paths to a desired goal; check themselves based on logic, experience, and information available to them about the future; make a decision; and move forward. In this regard, wayfinding mitigates risk. It's a form of educated guessing. Like games of chance—craps, roulette, poker—the future is random. However, an informed opinion is always an option. The question is, what is the best way to formulate an educated guess? Consider a throw of the dice.

When you roll a single die, you can be 100 percent certain that a 1, 2, 3, 4, 5, or 6 will come up. This, of course, is why Vegas does not pay out based solely on the appearance of random numbers. To win, you need the right number at the right time. However, here is the hook—you have absolutely no idea which number will appear or in what order. This is why it's called gambling. Like the future and life, it involves uncertainty and risk. This randomness applies to all situations where there are a range of values possible but an uncertain value for a specific time or event—inventory required, phone calls per minute, interest rates, and so forth. Therefore, in moments of ambiguity, we turn to simulation to "think things through" for us.

Simulating the Future

One such simulation is named after the sun-drenched principality on the French Riviera ruled by the Grimaldi family for over four hundred years. Monte Carlo simulation is a technique used to quantify uncertainty and to provide a "best guess" answer to very complex problems, those with many variables at play. Think of it as the extreme version of getting a second opinion. Since its introduction, Monte Carlo has been used to solve a wide range of problems, from nuclear reactor design to stock market forecasting and even stellar evolution. Although Enrico Fermi used random methods of computation when calculating the properties of the neutron in the 1930s, Monte Carlo methods are most often attributed to the work of Stanislaw Ulam, a Polish-born mathematician who worked on the Manhattan Project during World War II; in 1951, he worked with Edward Teller designing the hydrogen bomb. Five years earlier, in 1946, while recovering from an illness, playing cards, and attempting to determine the probabilities of winning a game of solitaire, he formalized Monte Carlo simulation.

His question was simple: "What are the chances that a Canfield solitaire laid out with fifty-two cards will come out successfully?" Ulam first attempted to estimate based on combinatorial calculations; however, he soon realized that there must be a more practical method. After all, imagine sitting at a table with a fifty-two-card deck and attempting to compute all the possible combinations of cards leading to successful plays. Nightfall, not to mention boredom, would surely visit you soon.

Monte Carlo, while requiring the computational power of computers, is actually a very simple concept, a system of observing random outcomes over a multiplicity of scenarios. When scenarios are repeated, say, ten thousand or more times, the average solution provides an approximate answer to the problem. Thus computers help. Like getting a second opinion from a physician, accuracy is improved by running more scenarios. Monte Carlo is a last-resort approach to solving complex problems, and since last resorts are destinations frequented by many people when no other solutions exist, Monte Carlo is the *go-to* method.

By exploring multiple possible outcomes, wayfinding—like simulation—transforms the future from a guess to an "educated opinion." This is also why casinos frown on card counters. Counters' odds are better than those of the "blue hairs" pumping their Social Security checks into the one-armed bandits. Like people who use Monte Carlo simulation, leaders' minds operate in much the same way, combining reason and intuition. Based on a given set of actions, what is the most probable outcome? This is important to understand. Triumphant leaders determine probability not by awaiting divine intervention but by *basing it on their actions*. Once they've "taken an average" of these scenarios, they make a decision and move ahead. This explains why triumphant leaders are often perceived as more hopeful. The reason is simple: they are! Given all available information and, when necessary, making a few assumptions, they navigate the future more swiftly.

Hedging the Future

"What if . . . ?" is the mantra of wayfinding. It reinforces a leader's hope in the future by exhausting all possible scenarios and making judgments based on that information. It provides peace of mind. Hopeful leaders have trained their brains to think in future-focused simulations. As Mannie Jackson told me, "It's like consciousness: you think you are aware of something, and then as soon as you *are* aware of it, you see something new. What happens with me is that each time I reach a plateau of success, only then do I really see what is possible. Before that, it is more speculation. However, once you are there, you can actually see it. Therefore, I have two or three success scenarios running at all times. And as long as I've thought through two or three, I have hope that we can get it done." Like Jackson, one of the greatest leaders to put hope to work through wayfinding changed not only the game of baseball but the game of life. Meet Branch Rickey.

Breakmaking

When a person becomes the first at anything, look closely. Behind every triumphant leader can be found a foot jammed squarely in a door to that person's future. This spur is typically a person who believed in his or her raw and undiscovered talent long before the rest of the world agreed. People get breaks, but breaks are also given. And while we always remember who got the break, seldom do we recall who gave it. Such is the case with Branch Rickey, an unexceptional catcher for the Saint Louis Browns (later to become the Saint Louis Cardinals).

As is commonplace in our world, once Rickey failed as a player—no pennant for Saint Louis—he was promoted to management. In hindsight, getting Rickey off the field and moving him to the front office was not only the best thing for the man but perhaps also the best thing ever to happen to baseball. In the 1920s, Rickey invented baseball's minor league farm system to cultivate young players. Like many of the leaders I've interviewed for this book, Rickey was creative, but he was also thoughtful, deriving his hope and inspiration from another person, Ty Cobb.

In Lend Me Your Ears, William Safire recounts a speech given by Rickey on November 12, 1926. Addressing the Executives Club of Chicago, Rickey paid homage to his mentor in a speech titled "The Greatest Single Thing a Man Can Have." In his tribute, Rickey spoke of Ty Cobb's take-no-prisoners base-running skills, recalling a vivid game where Rickey's Saint Louis Cardinals played Cobb's Detroit Tigers. In his career, Cobb reached first base and subsequently proceeded to steal second, third, and home on six separate occasions. Not unlike Forrest Gump, he just kept running and running and running. In twenty-four seasons, a majority with the Tigers, Cobb knocked up a .366 batting average, the highest in the history of the game. For more than sixty years, he was the leader in hits. And for more than seventy years, he was the leader in runs scored. In 1936, Cobb became the first man inducted into the Baseball Hall of Fame, earning 222 out of a possible 226 votes—that's more than Babe Ruth—and retired with more records than any other player. Rickey began his speech by describing a memorable game in which, after drawing a walk in the eleventh inning, Cobb was on his way to steal second base. To quote Rickey:

> When the ball was finally thrown to second base, it hit in front of the bag and bounced over [the second baseman's] head. Cobb came down, touched second base, and angularly went on toward third without a ghost of a chance to make it. The third baseman, knowing the abandonment of that fellow Cobb—when he set out voluntarily to get an objective, he was willing to pay the price to get it—had one eye on Cobb's shiny spikes and the other eye on the ball. I then saw the quickest reflex action I ever saw in my life. That boy Cobb had reflex centers in his heels; he did not have time to telegraph his brain. He slid twelve feet in front of third base; and when the dust had cleared away, the ball had fallen out of the hands of the third baseman and was going over toward the concrete in front of the grandstand—and before we could get that ball, he scored. I saw the crowd tumbling out from every place. I said to the umpire, "Interference, interference, Tom, at third base. He did not make a slide for the base; he made a play for the ball." He paid no attention to me. They have a habit of doing that. I followed him and said, "Tom, listen to me!" "Mr. Rickey," he said. "Listen to me. Give the boy credit. He made his own breaks."

Cobb was a master wayfinder—able to reach the vicinity of his destination through observation and creativity. Cobb, like Rickey, was also a breakmaker—creating opportunities rather than waiting for them to come to him. However, what was unique about Cobb was that he created his *own* breaks. In one long and dusty twelve-foot slide between second and third base, and throughout the entirety of his career, Cobb taught his industry how to create a desired future. And it didn't involve luck.

That Thing

Rickey continued:

> As I passed the Detroit players, I did not hear a man saying, "See what luck did for us today. Old Billiken was on our side." I heard everybody saying, "He is a great player. He won the game by himself." I commenced to ask myself what it was that made a man a distinguished ballplayer. Take two men with equal ability; one of them will always stay in mediocrity and another will distinguish himself in the game. What is the difference? The more that a man asserts his own influence over his work, the less the part that luck plays. It is true in baseball that the greatest single menace that a man has is a willingness to alibi his own failures; the greatest menace to a man's success in business, I think, sometimes is a perfect willingness to excuse himself for his own mistakes. What is the greatest single thing in the character of a great baseball player? I think it is the desire to be a great baseball player, a desire that dominates him, a desire so strong that it does not admit of anything that runs counter to it, a desire to excel that so confines him to a single purpose that nothing else matters. *That thing* makes men come in at night, *that* makes men have good health, *that* makes men change their bad technique to good technique, *that* makes capacity and ability in men. *That* makes a team with 80 percent possibility come from 60 to 70 percent, *that* makes them approach their possibility; and with a dominant desire to excel, *that* simply transcends *them* into a great spiritual force. The greatest single thing in the qualification of a great player, a great team, or a great man is a desire to reach the objective that admits of no interference anywhere. *That* is the greatest thing I know about baseball or anything else.

Notwithstanding his social intolerance, Ty Cobb had *that thing*. Even in pain, Cobb was notoriously creative. He always found a way to get it done. As Grantland Rice wrote, "I recall when Cobb played a series with each leg a mass of raw flesh. He had a temperature of 103 and the doctors ordered him to bed for several days, but he got three hits, stole three bases, and won the game. Afterward he collapsed on the bench." Cobb made his own breaks, and by virtue of his actions, he showed others how to make their own as well—including Rickey.

What did Rickey learn from Cobb's wayfinding and breakmaking skills? Considered the greatest front-office strategist in baseball history, believing that "luck is a residue of design," Rickey led the Saint Louis Cardinals to nine pennants and six World Series in the 1940s. And in 1947, as general manager of the Brooklyn Dodgers, in what Rickey referred to as his "noble experiment," he broke the major league color barrier by signing Jackie Robinson—for a salary of $600 per month and a $3,500 signing bonus—and subsequently building the power-house that was the Dodger organization of the 1940s and 1950s. Branch Rickey was to Robinson what Berry Gordy was to Motown. For his work, Rickey joined Cobb in Cooperstown, home of baseball's Hall of Fame, not for his catching but rather for his breaking.

Triumphant leaders, like Rickey and Cobb, create the future. They make it happen. However, in leadership, kicking up dust is only half the battle. The other half involves showing others how to find paths of their own and mustering the courage to walk forward.

Union in the Same High Effort

Although Cobb may have won that infamous game against the Cardinals by himself, sustainable success comes only at the hands of the team. Consider: even with Cobb's drive, passion, and hard-as-nails playing style, his teams never won a World Series. Individuals can win games, but teams win championships. As Antoine de Saint-Exupéry reminds us in his book *Wind, Sand, and Stars*, "Life has taught us that love does not consist in gazing at each other but in looking outward together in the same direction. There is no comradeship except through union in the same high effort." Through wayfinding, leaders use hope, as Geoff Canada put it, "to create a plan to look people in the eye."

A Plan to Look People in the Eye

"What I always stay focused on," Canada told me, "is having a really solid plan, one that you've looked at from every angle to prepare for whatever happens. Then, after that, you can go in and look people in the eye and say, with all honesty, I believe we can do this. The 'I believe' is not just because I think we are terrific. I believe we can do it because here is a plan in place and we are going to do everything it takes to get this done. I think people recognize that I am serious about that."

Like Geoff Canada, Branch Rickey, and Ty Cobb, Napa Valley's Renaissance man used wayfinding to build one of the most successful wine brands in the world. Grab your goblet. As promised, we're going back to visit Jack.

Napa Valley's Renaissance Man

"I never graduated from college. I started at UC Berkeley. I had a football scholarship. I was in my third year. I had one more semester to go, but then this police action in Korea came about. And so I enlisted in the Air Force in the Strategic Air Command, thinking, 'When I get back, it'll be a cake walk. I can just get my degree and leave.' Well, when I got back—six years later—I had a wife and two kids. There was no way I could go back to school. I am an automobile mechanic by trade—Cakebread's Garage." Jack Cakebread, like most hopeful leaders—in his case, the entrepreneurial variety—introduced himself to the Napa Valley with grease under his fingers and from behind the lens of a camera. Cakebread is Napa's modern-day Renaissance man—one-third photographer, one-third auto mechanic, and one-third farmer.

"My dad started the garage in 1925," Cakebread told me proudly. "And so when I came back from Korea, I started working at the shop. But I got interested in photography when I was in the service. I'd take pictures to send home to show where Daddy'd been. I really enjoyed it, and so I jerry-rigged a darkroom under the stairs at the house. After the kids would go to bed, I could go in there; otherwise they'd open the door and, well, you know. After working for years without a single day off, finally, my wife, Dolores, said to me, 'You've got to have a vacation.' And so she sent some of my photographic work off to Ansel Adams. But she didn't tell me this. Ansel was holding a class. And after reviewing your work, if he thought it was worthy, you could join his class. He didn't want a bunch of point-and-shoot folks. Well, he accepted my work. I was one of seven students that he had. I worked with him for years. That got me going in photography.

"I had one-man shows at the Museum of Modern Art in Los Angeles and other places all over the country. As it turns out, a wine writer for the *Los Angeles Times* was doing a book called *The Treasury of American Wines*. The publisher saw my work hanging in a museum down there, and so they called me up and asked me if I would be interested in shooting the book. I thought, 'Well, sure.' But they didn't realize I had Cakebread's Garage to run—and I never thought to tell them anything else! And so we started.

"Nathan—the writer—would send me a list of the wineries and the winemakers and generally the kinds of shots they wanted—a vineyard shot, a cave shot, and so forth. But it was February. It was miserable weather, nothing green, just a bunch of stumps out there. And so I stopped in here because my mother knew the folks that lived here. And to be honest, I had come in to bum a bowl of soup. At the time, this was a cow pasture. There was no winery, no vineyard, no *nothin'* here. This was just open pasture. And so I said to my mother's friends, 'If you ever want to sell this place, just let me know.' Driving back to Oakland, I thought, 'Hell, they're never going to sell that place. They've lived there for fifty years! That's crazy.' Then the phone rang.

"It was a Saturday. My wife was out with her mother. They said, 'Well, we've thought it over.' And so I drove back up here again. Mind you, Andrew, I had eleven guys at the shop. It was full-service. When you take your car in, you want somebody who's going to take care of it, not just give it a sunshine job and park it out in the parking lot." He laughed as he discovered humor in his own metaphorical sketch, and with a hint of nostalgia in his voice, he repeated in a reflective and muted tone, "A sunshine job. So there I was. I had two kids in college, one in high school. I was forty-three years old, and every dime I had was invested in that shop. In fact, some of them, I didn't even have! And so I drove back up here again thinking, 'OK, I'd love to get this, but this is my top price per acre.'" Jack held out his right hand to illustrate his maximum price point. "And then," now holding out his left hand, next to but much lower than his right, he continued while looking at his left hand, "I'm gonna start here and I'll negotiate and when I get to here"—now looking his right hand—"I'm gonna quit. Well, on the way home," Jack said, aware that his left-hand price paid was now significantly higher than his right-hand maximum point of pain, "I thought, 'My God, what have I done?'

"Well, when I got home, I asked my wife, 'What did you do today?' She said, 'I got my hair fixed, went shopping. What did *you* do?' With his hand over his mouth intentionally muting his response and in a very soft and quick voice intended to slip past Dolores's ears, Jack replied, 'I bought a ranch.' Dolores immediately fired back, 'With *what?*' You see, Andrew, Dolores kept the books at the shop. She said, 'Well, tomorrow morning, we're going to go back up and you are going to tell them you just got carried away.' I felt so bad because the couple was so nice to me—in their seventies, just really gracious. So I drive back up here wondering what in the world I am going to say to this guy. I thought to myself, 'I've gotta renege on this.' So I got out of the car, walked in this house, and I said, 'You know, I just *flat* got carried away with this.' And then I reached into my pocket and pulled out my book advance. I looked at him and said, 'All that I've got is a $2,500·

advance on this book.'" Cakebread then continued with a sense of wonderment, "This *whole thing* started on a $2,500 book advance. The *whole thing!*" he exclaimed. And just to make sure I heard him, he repeated it once more: "The whole *thing!* But at the time, I was *kicking* myself for paying $800 an acre!

"But think about this," he said with a grin revealing his Irish ancestry. "Two and a half years ago, a vineyard by my house—just up the road here on the hill—was put on the market by one of the founders of MGM Studios. A guy just paid $360,000 an acre for that vineyard! Then he pulled out the old vines and put another $50,000 into replanting it. He's in at $410,000, and it has just come up the stake now. It is at least four years away from a money crop." Then, revealing an opinion shared by many in the valley—alluding to the dozens of instant-millionaire-dot-commers and other Johnny-come-latelies for whom it seems money is no object—Cakebread continued, "And this guy is no newcomer! He has been here twenty-five years. He's my neighbor—Francis Ford Coppola. I stopped kickin' myself."

Think about this: Jack's original plot of twenty-two acres cost him $17,600. Based on Coppola's price per acre, that would make Cakebread's "1973 stop for a bowl of soup" worth nearly $8 million today. Not a bad investment for a $2,500 down payment thirty-three years later. To say nothing of the additional acreage he has since purchased and the cash flow generated from operating one of the most successful, most desirable, and most beloved wineries in the Napa Valley.

"Things have changed," Cakebread continued. "We started out at 157 cases. We are up to about 95,000 now. My first sale was to Groezinger's there in Yountville, three miles down the road. Now we are in twenty-three different countries including Poland and Russia. We are now on our way into China. We're in India and Hong Kong." Jack Cakebread is an outrageously successful businessman with a heart of gold. His success is due not only to his hard work but also to his faith in himself—his hope. This guy loves life—personal and professional. To him, there is no such thing as work-life balance. It is simply life.

Cakebread then turned to hope, saying, "Hope, to me, is something that is *going* to happen. I don't hope it will happen. I *know* it will happen. I'm just hoping I can get it done before too much time goes by." For Jack Cakebread, success goes well beyond confidence and well beyond hard work. It goes to a much more profound place in the depths of a person's soul. In the spirit of Geoff Canada's philosophy—"Life is not a straight line"—Jack Cakebread found a way—and continues to find ways—to create the future even when circumstances would suggest otherwise. Cakebread is not just successful; he is triumphant. However, life has not been easy for him. In fact, life has dealt the man a heaping helping of harm, served hot in the most inopportune moments. Then again, if challenges were of our choosing—offered à la carte at the table of life—they'd eventually be removed from the menu. No takers.

Batter Up! Strike One?

"It happened right in the middle of harvest. I had about thirty tons of chardonnay sitting out there—about ten tons of it was in the press, and the darn press broke down." While overlooking his vines at the winery that bears his name, Cakebread continued, "It was a rebuilt unit. It was all that I could afford. And so I called the manufacturer for parts and he said, 'We'll have it for you in December.' And I said, well, thanks for nothing. So I looked around and finally found one up at Krug Winery. Mark Mondavi said, 'Hey, I think we have one out in the barn. Go ahead and help yourself.' And so I drove my El Camino up there and sure as heck, it was the exact model! It weighed four or five hundred pounds. I couldn't move it, of course, so I just backed the truck up and let it drop. I brought it back here, but I didn't know anything about electricity other than how to turn a light on. The unit was 440 and so I called the electrician. He said his son was up at Beaulieu Vineyard and he'd be here within twenty minutes. When he arrived, he hooked it up and—*brmmmm*—away it went!

"After harvest was over, I called Mark Mondavi and said, 'I'd like to buy it.' He said, 'Oh, just keep it. It's a piece of junk to us.' That just didn't sound right to me. And so a few days later, I called Mark again and said, 'Come on, Mark.' He wanted none of it. And so I took him a couple of cases of Reserve wine. He gave me one back, looked directly at me, and said, 'You're new in the valley, aren't ya? I'll keep this one just so I don't hurt your feelings.'

"And then there was the time I needed some half-bottles for a December harvest riesling I made in 1975. I couldn't get them, but I heard that Louis Martini might have some. And so I went up and asked him. He said, 'Sure, let's go over to the barn.' And so he started throwing them out of the hay patch to me—twenty-four cases! I said, 'What do I owe ya?' He looked at me and said, 'You're kinda new in the valley, aren't ya, kid?' My face turned red. This is the way they treat you here.

"Another time, I cut my leg when I dropped a five-gallon water bottle. I didn't know anybody up here, and so I drove back to Oakland—122 stitches. I didn't have time for 122 stitches. I needed to rack some wines. Before I knew it, here come a bunch of guys up the road from all over the valley. They had an overstuffed chair in the back of the pickup, a footstool, and two bottles of champagne. They said, 'You just point to what you want us to do today.' That's what makes this valley work." And that is what makes Jack Cakebread work—wayfinding. Strike one—getting started—averted.

Strike Two! Or Maybe Not?

When I met with Jack Cakebread at Cakebread Cellars, I had only *one* real agenda item: to get his thoughts on phylloxera, a root louse that threatened to bring the Napa Valley to its knees in the late 1980s. As Cakebread recalled, "In the middle 1980s, [the Farm Credit Bank] knew it was coming. I sat on the board for eighteen years. Our fear at that time was, What is going to happen to the growers who need to replant? They are in their late sixties and early seventies—because it is a six- or seven-year process and very expensive. We knew they were going to come to Farm Credit for a loan to fund this thing." The projected cost of replanting was $25,000 to $75,000 an acre—to say nothing of the opportunity cost of a five-year wait for new vines to bear fruit.

"Well," Jack recalled, "I told the board, 'My position is that the loan is on the land, not on the guy's life. We ain't sellin' life insurance here.' And so we went ahead and funded a lot of the applications." More than 50 percent of all the vineyards in Napa and Sonoma were replanted. To some observers, it looked like open-heart surgery. Like a scene out of a 1960s sci-fi thriller, milk cartons and grow tubes sprouted in lieu of the typical lush green vines—a scary sight to many in the know, but uneventful for most tourists. However, what they were unable to see was what hopeful leaders see with enthusiasm: possibility. To others, the tiny cartons looked like newborn children—a promising future and a clean driving record. Among the hopeful, of course, was Jack Cakebread.

"Phylloxera," Cakebread said. "It was the *greatest* opportunity that the valley has ever had and that the bank has ever had. It was an *unbelievable* opportunity!" What did Jack Cakebread see? He saw the very same thing that Thomas Edison saw when his laboratory burned to the ground in 1914—a chance to start anew. Cakebread noted, "How often in your life do you get a chance to go back and say, 'Hey, if I had this do to over again, I'd do it this way'? We had all the new technology." Cakebread Cellars spent $7,000 on multispectral imaging—the same technology NASA uses to study the surface of Mars. Not only did it take photos of its own vineyards but also of other vineyards from which Cakebread buys grapes. Talk about getting to know your vendors! The winery spent an additional $50,000 on moisture-reading-neutron-radiating probes to analyze soil thousands of feet thick from two to five million years of volcanic tuffs, cinders, and ash. (If no energy is lost when the neutrons hit, it's time to water!)

Cakebread continued with the same enthusiasm that I would have imagined Edison to have had as he walked through the ashes. "We had root stocks. We had clones of varieties you are looking at now. We had spacing. We had soil analysis that we never had before. It was just a dream!" Before phylloxera, there was only one fork in the road—only one decision vintners had to make: graft clone number three to either AxR1 or Saint George rootstock. In the period of time since most vintners had planted and the outbreak of phylloxera—in many cases, decades—twenty-five merlot clones and several new root-stock options had been introduced. For example, growers are now able to experiment with sauvignon musque, which was not previously available. In Jack Cakebread's eyes, so much more was now possible. If ordering at Starbuck's makes your head spin, just think of all the possible combinations now available to wine growers. (Yes, this is a perfect opportunity for Monte Carlo simulation.)

Better site selection techniques had been introduced, allowing for the appropriate match between a variety and the land. As Cakebread explained, "You would normally go down the road and see that the rows are all perpendicular to the highway, because that's the easiest way to turn tractors. But actually, if you take and look at this new software program, it will tell you which way to turn those rows to get the best photosynthesis to get the fruit right. So, you turn *just a little bit*, and the quality is so much better. That little stuff matters. You can also go in on the computer and you can take a look at all of your vineyards off the satellite. You can zoom right in to a couple of vines if you want. And say, 'Hey, go out and take a look at row 17—about seven vines—it looks like your emitter is plugged up.' But of course, the best thing you can do when you are farming is to leave footprints in the vineyard. Not tire tracks. Footprints."

Norm Roby, a writer for *Wine Spectator, Decanter,* and the *Wine News,* wrote of Cakebread's triumph over phylloxera, "Cakebread Cellars, one of the first hit, responded fast. By now all of its 75 acres have been replanted and it crushed its first PP [postphylloxera] Sauvignon Blanc in 1995. . . . Cakebread seized the opportunity to switch to the cooler Carneros for Chardonnay. Recent bottlings consist of 75–80% Carneros-grown Chardonnay. The bulk of the Napa plantings have been to Cabernet Sauvignon. . . . The 1995 Sauvignon Blanc, made mostly from PP grapes, was impressive." Oh, the joys of wine-speak!

The benefits, from Jack Cakebread's perspective, were endless. Whereas historically, Cakebread relied on one small area for a specific varietal, it was now able to work with vineyards to diversify—not unlike a good retirement portfolio. Bruce Cakebread, Jack's youngest son, now forty-eight, commented, "Before phylloxera, you more or less had to take what growers offered. Now, our growers who replanted according to our needs work to give us what we want in terms of quality."

For Jack, strike two was not only averted but rather involved a swing and a hit . . . a long ball . . . way, way back! Jack Cakebread, like Ty Cobb's dust-kickin', base-slidin', find-a-way-home-or-don't-come-at-all ball playin', makes his own breaks. He is a master way-finder. Where others see despair, he sees hope. And where others sit in wonder, he acts on his hope with every ounce of his heart and soul. He finds a way. Not bad for a two-time-cancer-survivin' auto-mechanic Ansel Adams protégé photo-takin' winegrower.

Miracle on Thirty-Second Street

Imagine that on your way home, you discover that your neighbors have moved in—not into the house next door but into *your* house. Although they are generally well liked among other neighbors, if for no other reason than because of their sheer size and strength, you decide never to return home. Rather, you move into the hotel down the street. In that hotel, you meet your future spouse and get married. In that hotel, you have kids—educate and raise them. In that hotel, you live out your life for the next forty-seven years. Imagine what life would be like living in this neighborhood. If nothing else, if you knew that neighbors could do this, you would arguably become adept at choosing the right neighborhood in which to live.

The "tell" in most neighborhoods is its retail stores. On Thirty-Second Street between Second and Third avenues in Manhattan, you'll find a Starbuck's, a Dean and Deluca, and a Border's bookstore. At first blush, young, urban, trendy, and sophisticated palates come to mind. Although the neighborhood at Thirty-Second Street and Second Avenue conjures up pure yuppie, on closer examination, things get a bit more intriguing. Nestled among the tree-lined streets of lower Manhattan, at 241 Thirty-Second Street, sits a nondescript brick building. If you weren't looking for it, odds are you wouldn't notice it.

It looks like every other three-flat walk-up apartment building on the island. As I climb the requisite stairs to the second-floor entry, a small brass plaque appears. It reads THE OFFICE OF TIBET AND TIBET FUND. In 1959, Tibet's neighbors, the Chinese, moved in. And so the Tibetans moved out. Among the places they landed is this small walk-up building on Manhattan's Lower East Side.

Upon entering the small foyer, many memories came rushing back to me. Not the least of which were my own experiences living in similar buildings in Chicago—one in particular in which our toaster and microwave performed only a cappella, never in harmony. The fuses would blow. At the Office of Tibet in New York, the hardwood floors are worn by at least ten generations of tenants. Creaking sounds accompany every step. The paint on the walls is eight layers thick. The lights are dim. The doors are heavy. Once inside, I was immediately met by yet another flight of stairs. As I climbed, a familiar odor grew progressively stronger. Incense. At the top of the stairs, a small room came into view. It was filled with computers, printers, and other assorted technology. Stacks of paper and books filled every open space. Five staffers worked diligently at their desks, their heads down, their eyes attending to computer screens like anthropologists viewing a newly harvested discovery.

As I passed the staff workroom, the smell of incense grew stronger. At the end of the hall, in a modestly furnished office, stood Dr. Nawang Rabgyal, representative of the Dalai Lama to the Americas and director of the Office of Tibet in Exile in New York. Rabgyal greeted me with a smile and said with a self-effacing laugh, "I don't think you will get much from me. I am only a civil servant—a bureaucrat. I am not a leader." He then proceeded to tell me that he had no other option than to take my request for a meeting. It is Tibetan tradition to be open to all who want to learn. Talk about an open-door policy.

On the wall behind his desk hung a photo of the Dalai Lama. Beneath it, in a spread organized in shrinelike fashion, are various snacks and food items from tea to assorted treats, and small plumes of scented smoke emanated from the center of the table as if my eyes were saying, 'I told you so' to my nose. It is Losar—the Tibetan New Year. It is tradition to keep food out for two weeks. Rabgyal's hospitality preceded his formality. He immediately offered me tea and biscuits. Thankfully, the food was nonperishable. Rabgyal exudes kindness, compassion, and sincerity. Then again, his behavior was precisely what I had expected from a Tibetan Buddhist. Humility.

Rabgyal's career spans the globe. He has served the Tibetan government in exile in various capacities in three different countries since 1979, including his position as director of United Nations and Political Affairs and deputy secretary and international affairs assistant in New Delhi, India. He has a master's degree in political science from the University of Delhi and a Ph.D. in history of international relations from the Kiev State University. Born in Shingri, a small village in Tibet, Rabgyal and his family escaped into exile in Nepal during 1959 when the Chinese forces occupied Tibet. India became his second home after migrating there in 1964. He's now married, lives in New York, and has a daughter.

The Most Efficient Virtual Workforce on the Planet

Since the Tibetan government in exile is perhaps the most organized group of actively hopeful followers on the planet, I had come to New York to talk with Rabgyal about hope, leadership, and the Dalai Lama. Although much has been written by and about the Dalai Lama, I had a greater interest in the nature of his followership. After all, it is insufficient to study leadership independent of followership. (And the Dalai Lama had a cold.)

What drew me to the Office of Tibet in Exile was a simple question that I hadn't the answer to: how has a nation of people, living outside its own borders, managed to survive for over four decades? Given that 70 percent of most modern organizations' value is derived from intangible assets spread across a virtual workforce, I assumed that there must be something more than compassion that the Tibetans have to teach us. After all, they have been managing virtually for the past forty-seven years.

A Sudden Act of Leadership

The Tibetan government in exile is outrageously organized. As a democracy, it has all three branches of government—executive, legislative, and judicial—fully operational. Moreover, it has a parliament, a prime minister, and voting and tax systems. Since one cannot have a democracy without a constitution, it has one of those as well. As Rabgyal explained, "We are unlike any other democracy. There was no fight. No blood was shed. The Dalai Lama gave it to us so that we could learn slowly."

Realizing that his people were going to be in a long, arduous battle for "cultural recognition," the Dalai Lama, as soon as he went into exile on September 1, 1960, introduced the current infrastructure known as the Tibetan government in exile. If you were merely to study its infrastructure, you'd be hard-pressed to know that the Tibetans are virtually homeless. In addition to all three branches of government, they have a department of education, a department of religion and culture, a department of homeland affairs, a department of security, and a department of information and international relations. Moreover, it has a strategic planning and budgeting process. The ideas come from the field. The funding comes from Dharamsala, India—the headquarters of the government in exile and home to the Dalai Lama. Sound familiar? Grants from various organizations help fund health and education, including the operation of over one hundred schools. But for administration, the Tibetans go to three sources from within their community.

In North America, every working Tibetan over six years old contributes $36 per year. In India, all who have employment give 2 percent of their salary. Both are taxes that fund the administration of programs. The second source of funding comes from the Dalai Lama's various publications and gifts given directly to him by celebrities and other organizations that support the Tibetan cause. And the third source of funding comes from businesses owned by the Tibetans. (They own and manage real assets, including restaurants and hotels.)

The Tibetans may be displaced, but they are far from disorganized and far from hopeless.

The Nature of the Struggle

Established in 1964, the Office of Tibet in New York is registered under the U.S. Department of Justice as a foreign office of the Dalai Lama. Moreover, it maintains thirteen offices of Tibet in exile, much like de facto embassies, from Kathmandu to New York, Geneva, London, Tokyo, Paris, Moscow, and South Africa. Which offices did the Dalai Lama open first? Kathmandu and New York. Why? The refugees come through Kathmandu, and the United Nations is headquartered in New York. "Save and lobby" was the Dalai Lama's strategy from the beginning.

Rabgyal told me, "I'm supposed to be the head of this office. They call me 'boss,' but I never feel like the boss. We are one family." Rabgyal explained their objectives in the following manner: "The nature of our struggle, under the leadership of His Holiness the Dalai Lama, is that we are not demanding independence; we are demanding genuine autonomy for the Tibetan culture. We are not anti-China, nor are we anti-Chinese. We are struggling for our basic fundamental right to live in peace and dignity and to preserve our culture. The essence of our culture is to be a good human being, to have a sense of caring for others. We tell our younger generations that we are a unique *culture*. We want to preserve that and contribute it within China and the world." In this regard, the Tibetans have practiced the art of wayfinding since the day the Dalai Lama went into exile. They maintain hope by planning alternative options for the future. Although some Tibetans hold complete independence as the desired goal, cultural preservation within China is an acceptable alternative. Knowing that there are multiple paths to a desired future, hope remains.

"According to Buddhist philosophy," Rabgyal explained to me, "the nature of all things is impermanent. If all things are impermanent, then all things can be changed. Imagine. In the nineteenth century, the sun never set on the British Empire, stretching from Africa to Asia. Now where is that empire? From 1917 to 1991, the Soviet Union was such a superpower." Rabgyal paused before continuing, "I studied in the Soviet Union from 1982 to 1987. After completing my studies and returning to India to work for the government in exile, I never thought such a superpower would collapse." Laughing at his self-proclaimed ignorance of how frail the situation was in the Soviet Union, Rabgyal then said, "It collapsed within two years. When everything is changeable, there is hope for the change. We need to put effort forth and to continue with good motivation. Forward. Forward. Forward. This is my belief. This is my approach. And this is my job." Forward. Forward. Forward. This mantra is shared by the Dalai Lama, who has said, "What is past is passed. The future is more important."

Rabgyal then turned to hope, saying, "Hope sustains life. Without hope, it is difficult to get on in life. It is very important, but that hope should be realistic, reasonable, rationale, and meaningful hope." And then, with a laugh that only experience could muster up, he said, "Otherwise we get stressed! As a Buddhist, we always believe that whatever we hope, one of the most important factors is to have sincere motivation. Once you have a good motivation, it gives you inner strength to pursue your dreams, no matter how hard it is." Albeit in exile, the Tibetans are actively hopeful. Recall, it took the nations of Eastern Europe nearly five decades to secure their freedom. Nonetheless, it happened.

Hedging the Future

Like the fourteenth Dalai Lama, Jack Cakebread, Geoff Canada, Charles Schwab, Branch Rickey, and Ty Cobb, triumphant leaders apply hope through wayfinding. Try this: Define a current problem or objective. Then write down the most obvious way to solve the problem or accomplish the objective. Ask yourself, if this solution were not an option, how else could you solve it, create it, fix it, or make it happen? Write down whatever comes to mind. For example, when working with clients to launch new ventures, I often ask, "Imagine that you have no budget for traditional marketing. What would you do to make this venture a success?" At first, I get the inevitable blank stare, although I have yet to be disappointed. The ideas come. Under the appropriate leadership, all humans are naturally creative. However, if you discover that your team is at a standstill, try flatlining (the topic of Chapter Eleven) and then revisit this one. It will change everyone's perspective, including yours.

11

FLATLINING

Remembering you are going to die is the best way
I know to avoid the trap of thinking you have
something to lose.

—*Steve Jobs*

This is a short chapter for good reason. The clock is ticking. What follows is not written in any leadership textbook, nor is it discussed openly in corner offices. However, the focal point of this chapter is one of the most personal, most sobering, and most privately motivating forces behind the leaders I have met. This is not an easy topic, but then again, neither is hope. This chapter is about life. Well, actually, the end of it.

To most people, nothing is as morbid as death. However, to hopeful leaders, "the inevitable" is simply another reason for their proactive behavior. It is also why, to some observers, hopeful leaders live with what appears at times to be reckless abandon. The irony is that their lives are anything but reckless. Most of their adventures are planned. As Tully Mars reflects on his dilettante lifestyle in the novel *A Salty Piece of Land*, "I believe in the aboriginal line of thinking that life's adventures are the verses and choruses of your unique song, and when it's over, you are dead. So far, I am still singing." And incidentally, so too is Tully Mars's creator, the multiplatinum-selling singersongwriter and best-selling author Jimmy Buffett.

What surprised me during the course of my research is that I never broached this topic. They did. My focus was on the life of leadership. The last thing I had expected to discuss was death. Such as Paul Orfalea's blunt reflection: "My uncle died of a heart attack when his business went under. If I weren't doing this, like him, I'd probably be dead." Or Tom McCoy's: "You know what bothers me is that I'm fifty-four. And I've had so many epiphanies in the last ten years. I'm worried I'm running out of time to communicate them all before people say, 'Why am I listening to you? You're sixty.' When I was in my thirties and forties, the last thing I would do is listen to someone in their sixties." Or Jack Cakebread's: "When my father passed away, he had no succession plan for the family business. His death was very difficult on us, both personally and professionally. I'll never forget that. I swore I would never put my kids in that situation. And so as a result, we've planned better. My greatest fear now is time." Or astronaut Jerry Linenger's: "I just hope we can get to Mars before I die. If things continue as expected, I will be in my seventies by then. I would be the right guy. Given the intensity of the radiation, they wouldn't send up a guy in his forties."

Steve Jobs, Paul Orfalea, Tom McCoy, Jack Cakebread, and Jerry Linenger have no competitor other than time. This is yet another indicator of their hopeful outlook. According to neurologist Richard Restak, "Depressed people greatly overestimate time intervals—a concrete demonstration of their frequent complaint that 'time hangs heavy on my hands.'" The opposite is true among manic patients. Time flies when you're having fun. Therefore, it should come as no surprise that hopeful leaders, while not necessarily manic, view time as their greatest threat. Death is a sober reminder of life. As Socrates is said to have observed, "Death may be the greatest of all human blessings." And then there is Geoffrey Canada.

Paul Tough, writing in the *New York Times Magazine*, calls the Harlem Children's Zone "one of the most ambitious social experiments of our time." And as David Saltzman, executive director of the Robin Hood Foundation, observed, "If this works, it'll be the best thing that's happened in a long time." HCZ's mission is to give Harlem's poorest kids a shot at the American dream. And Geoff Canada's leadership is as good as it gets. Although Geoff earned his master's degree from the Harvard Graduate School of Education, what he learned about leadership he didn't learn in school. You could say that Geoff Canada has been converted to a hopeful brand of leadership. At a very early age, Canada stood witness to an experience that would change his life. To this day, it fuels the mission of the organization he leads.

Canada speaks in a tone that reflects his mission. His voice is one of impatient will. You can feel his fight against time as he speaks. "For me, hope is a state of mind," he told me. "I am always amazed that people can be hopeful when others just give up. To me, there is no *reality* around hope, meaning that there is no time when you just sort of say this is *hopeless*, we should just give up because there is nothing we can do. I *honestly* believe in miracles."

Don't take Canada's comment about miracles the wrong way. Geoff Canada is not *waiting* for a miracle to happen. He is making it happen. This guy is one of the hardest-working souls in the city of New York. He is driven. He is passionate. He is impatient. After all, his is an important business. He is saving kids. Canada continued, "It's a funny thing: if you believe in miracles, one is always around the corner. What makes it a miracle is that by all rights and logic, it should never occur, but things like that do occur from time to time. This is why hope is important—and not just any kind of hope, but hope in really difficult, nearly impossible things. Sure, you can have lots of hope as long as it's a minor thing. 'Oh, yeah, I'm hopeful,' you say. And then something major happens. And if you haven't exercised your hope muscles, you don't know how to become hopeful again. If you are continuously hopeful in the most difficult things in life, then when something worse comes along, you say to yourself, 'Man, and I thought that last thing was bad!' When you've done this a few times, you begin to really believe that you are going to make it." And then, in an appeal—a challenge to all those who look to him for leadership—Canada continued, "So I believe that most of life is a test to exercise your hope muscles."

Then, like many others before him, Canada turned his attention to the reason for his outlook. "A lot of this I got from my grandmother. She was deeply, deeply religious. And I was deeply, deeply skeptical. She felt that part of her job was to save my soul. We used to have these very adult conversations even when I was a very young person. I kept trying to get her to define the undefinable. 'How can you have hope? How can you believe?' I would ask. We were poorer than most of the kids I work with today. Poverty is relative. I would continue to ask her, 'How can you *believe* that things are going to turn out good when there is so much bad—the little baby died and it was nobody's fault; the universe has no order; why should I believe anything good is going to happen?' Yet I could not shake her belief. And then she got sick from cancer—very painful stomach cancer. She was eventually sent home to die. I just could *not* resist going in and asking her, on her deathbed, if she still believed. And she said something to me that has stayed with me *forever*. She said, 'More than ever.' I thought, at that moment, that if you looked up *angel* in a dictionary, her picture would show up. Her words let me know the level we humans can go to and still be hopeful. I've always felt a little silly feeling hopeless when something doesn't go my way—five or six things go wrong in a given day. I just think about my grandmother, knowing she was dying, in pain, and not *at all* prepared to give up. It let me know of the relative nature of hope." And then he continued, as our conversation turned to patience, "I am very patient with young people and trying to get across points and issues, but I am very impatient with how quickly I feel we have to accomplish what we've set out to do. I feel a clock ticking."

Geoff Canada, like the many leaders I've studied, uses the word *feel* and other nonvisual and nonauditory senses to describe how he relates to the world around him. In addition to "feeling clocks ticking," I've heard things such as "tasting the future" and "smelling the fear." It's as if hopeful leaders find seeing and hearing too passive. Like most triumphant leaders, Canada opts for more active descriptions of his mission, reflecting his desire to deal the cards he plays. I can only imagine that Martin Luther King Jr. is looking on Geoff Canada with pride knowing that a contemporary soldier of King's "fierce urgency of now" shares his impatience with "the tranquilizing drug of gradualism." Canada then continued in regard to his impatience, "I find that I am much less willing to give adults time to 'get it together' because I think it ends up hurting kids. I was more patient ten years ago than I am right now. My only issue now is how long I can stay on the front lines."

The Worlds' Best Mission Statement

Geoff Canada has translated his hope into words. His mission statement is the best I have seen—ever. You know the usual catchphrases: *value-added, customer-centric, strategic partner to our clients.* Canada's contains nothing like that. His is a sober reminder of his cause and that of the organization he leads. His is not so much a mission statement as a statement of mission:

Take a Stand

Maybe before we didn't know,
That Corey is afraid to go
To school, the store, to roller skate
He cries a lot for a boy of eight.
But now we know each day is true
That other girls and boys cry too.
They cry for us to lend a hand.
Time for us to take a stand.

And little Maria's window screens
Keeps out flies and other things.
But she knows to duck her head,
When she prays each night 'fore bed.
Because in the window comes some things
That shatter little children's dreams.
For some, the hour glass is out of sand.
Time for us to take a stand.

And Charlie's deepest, secret wishes
Is someone to smother him with kisses
And squeeze and hug him tight, so tight,
While he pretends to put up a fight.
Or at least someone to be at home

Who misses him, he's so alone.
Who allowed this child-forsaken land?
Look in the mirror and take a stand.

And on the Sabbath, when we pray
To our God, we often say,
"Oh Jesus, Mohammed, Abraham,
I come to better understand,
How to learn to love and give,
And live the life you taught to live,"
In faith we must join hand in hand.
Suffer the children? Take a stand!

And tonight, some child will go to bed,
No food, no place to lay their head.
No hand to hold, no lap to sit,
To give slobbery kisses, from slobbery lips.
So you and I we must succeed
In this crusade, this holy deed,
To say to the children in this land:
Have hope. We're here. We take a stand!

When was the last time you read a mission statement like this—one that appeals not only to your intellect but to your emotions as well? Isn't this what mission statements are supposed to do—command us, not demand us—move us into action? Of course, behind Canada's statement of mission also stands a very conventional strategic plan.

"Leadership is a funny thing," he observed. "You have to know how to run a business; you have to know how to motivate others; you have to have this sense of hope about this work; and you have to have people who bring hope to the job. People keep coming up to me and saying, 'My goodness, it's been fifty years! You still have the same excitement!' But for me, this is a matter of 'Are you prepared to work—night and day, weekends if necessary, as many hours as you need, for ten or twelve years—to accomplish a goal?' If the answer is no, you are probably not the right leader for this field. You might be the right leader for some other type of work, but not this. The truth is that I'm more excited now than ever because I'm closer to the answer."

Despite the saying that it's lonely at the top, leaders actually do not sit on the top of anything. Like Geoff Canada, they sit between things. Somewhere between customers, employees, boards of directors, stockholders, players, owners, fans, students, alumni, citizens, and congregations sit leaders. Leaders are like what gerontologist Nancy Wexler calls the "sandwich generation": "Being a member of the sandwich generation is like being a slice of bologna, expected to give taste and meaning to two pieces of bread . . . your children on one side and your parents on the other." Under the mantra of "do it all," in place of a sense of accomplishment, sandwiched caregivers, like most leaders, express a feeling of guilt when they can't deliver. Gerontologists call it caregiver burnout. In leadership-speak, it's called turnover.

Getting Guilt off the Guest List

At its core, flatlining is intended to abolish every leader's unspoken *bête noire*—guilt. Time, or the lack thereof, is a sober reminder of purpose. Like caregivers, leaders risk losing hope when their expectations about the outcome of leadership are too far off, requiring the patience of a Buddhist monk to maintain. Therefore, surround yourself with other leaders. This is the fundamental reason why organizations like the Young Presidents Organization exist. YPO is the world's biggest bear hug for leadership. Join!

Finally, even though as a leader you may fly business class, you will forever remain "in the middle seat," forced to manage the expectations and divergent demands of all who look to you for leadership. Unfortunately, guilt is invited to too many funerals. Do not invite it to yours. I therefore want you to do something that may at first be difficult, but try it. I call it *flatlining*. Here goes. Think about death each day, just for a nanosecond (OK, that's long enough). Flatlining is the fastest way to remind yourself of the relative nature of your obligation, of your purpose, and of the gift of leadership that you have earned and that has been entrusted to you. Everything is relative to time. Everything. As Steve Jobs suggests, "Your time is limited, so don't let it be wasted living someone else's life. Have the courage to follow your heart and intuition. You've got to find what you love. Do what you believe is great work. If you haven't found it, keep looking. Don't settle."

Time is one thing that no one has figured out how to stop—not even Albert Einstein. When describing his theory of relativity, Einstein quipped, "When a man sits with a pretty girl for an hour, it seems like a minute. But let him sit on a hot stove for a minute, and it's longer than any hour. That's relativity." Nothing is a more effective mental diuretic than the thought of one's own death. Think about it. Now move on. Put hope to work.

Part Three

PUTTING HOPE TO WORK

Do more than belong: participate.
Do more than care: help.
Do more than believe: practice.
Do more than be fair: be kind.
Do more than forgive: forget.
Do more than dream: work.

*–Attributed to American college
administrator William Arthur Ward*

12

CURB STEPPING

What I essentially did was to put one foot in front
of the other, shut my eyes, and step off the ledge.
The surprise was that I landed on my feet.

—*Katharine Graham, on becoming*
president of the Washington Post

Imagine yourself on a walk. It's a beautiful summer day. You're on
your way to a tall vanilla latte. You arrive at a crosswalk. The signal
is red, so you wait and exchange pleasantries with a man who is waiting to cross as well. You then look up, and as expected, the walk signal turns green. You proceed. However, halfway across the street, you
look back and see that the man is still standing on the curb, looking
down at his feet. You wonder to yourself, "Does he realize that the
walk signal has turned green? Maybe he's sight-impaired? Perhaps
he's just daydreaming?" Satisfied with your own reasoning, you continue on your way. Ten minutes later, on your way home, you return
to the same crosswalk. You stop, look across the street, and see the
same man standing there. He is still staring at the curb. Nor does it
look like he's ever looked up. He's neither daydreaming nor sight-
impaired; he's phobic.

The man suffers from two paralyzing fears: anablephobia, the fear
of looking up, and agyrophobia, the fear of crossing the street. Imagine suffering from the inability to see what is in front of you coupled
with the inability to step off the curb. While the man at the crosswalk
may seem strange, ask yourself, "How often do you find those around
you looking down—caught in the moment—versus looking up—

focused on the future? And how often do those around you, even though fully aware of an opportunity, stand still in the face of it? All teams, organizations, and, at times, humans suffer from the fear of looking up and the fear of taking action. To make matters even more challenging, when we do act, it is not uncommon to feel repulsed by the very thing that attracts us. It's called approach-avoidance conflict. It is a very human phenomenon. In fact, you may have some experience with it.

"I Love You, You're Perfect, Now Change"

Have you ever been attracted to someone and then discovered that you can't stand the person once you are in his or her company? Or perhaps you know someone who has married, divorced, remarried the ex, and divorced the ex a second time, only to marry someone just like the previous spouse. Why do we do this?

Psychologist Kurt Lewin was the first to experimentally investigate approach-avoidance conflict. His research has shown that as we approach an object of desire—a person, for example—feeling repelled has a greater effect on our emotions than the feeling of attraction. Simply, the closer we get, the less desirable the person becomes. The title of the long-running off-Broadway musical describes approach-avoidance conflict the best: *I Love You, You're Perfect, Now Change*. The reverse is also true. The farther away we get from the person, the more attracted we are: absence does indeed make the heart grow fonder. And in similar manner, we often react the same way to objectives. You really want to win that new account, get that promotion, and retire early. However, you also know that each of these objectives requires more work, less sleep, and a smaller mortgage (and hence a smaller house). Although we are attracted to the future, we are also repelled by it. At times, it's just too overwhelming, and as we approach it, we have a tendency to focus on what is wrong versus what is right. Hopeful leaders manage this phenomenon by breaking down apparently impossible tasks into bite-sized actions. They miniaturize the future. It's easier to digest that way. I call it *curb stepping*. Recall the

Polynesian wayfinders. They referred to this phenomenon of future miniaturization as "getting inside the box"—breaking down a lofty goal into bite-sized pieces and then vociferously chewing it! It should come as no surprise that the greatest wayfinders are often the best curb steppers. Among them is Jack Cakebread.

Dining Alone

"When I got into the wine business," Cakebread recounted, "I would come home, go down to the library, and look in the newspaper morgue. I'd look up the restaurant reviews—usually Wednesdays or Thursdays—in, say, Cleveland. I'd go down the list, and I'd see the same restaurants being mentioned, four or five of them. So I'd call them. I'd say, 'My name is Jack Cakebread, and I'd like to make a reservation.' At one I'd do an early lunch. At the others, a late lunch, early dinner, late dinner, and so on. 'And by the way,' I would say, 'I'm bringing my own wine,' so I'd ask, 'What's the corkage?' They'd say, 'Fifty cents.' (Try that now!) I'd then get the 'red eye' out of Oakland to Cleveland. I'd get in there early—6:00 A.M. I'd go to a hotel—they'd rent you a room for a morning. I'd get a shower, a shave, put the suit and tie on. And then I'd go call on these guys. I'd look at their menu. I'd look at my wine. I'd look at the menu prices, because you don't want to have a $12 entrée with a $30 bottle of wine. Then I'd see if there was a fit on their wine list. Now mind you, I was sitting there with three bottles of wine in front of me. It doesn't take very long—a single with three bottles of wine—before somebody is going to come out and say, 'What the hell is going on here?' Sure enough, the chef or owner or wine buyer would come out. I'd introduce myself. They'd taste the wine. And I'd say, 'Would you put this on your menu?' They'd say, 'These are really nice.' My response was, 'Well, who's the distributor in town?' They'd tell me. Once I got a consensus on a name, I'd go home. I would take the red eye on Sunday in order to get back down to the garage. I'd get out of my suit and tie and get things going down there—order parts, everything. About 10:00 A.M. on Monday morning, I'd call up Cleveland, George Hammer &

Sons. And after spelling my name for them fourteen times and explaining who I was and what I was doing, I'd say, 'I have orders for thirty-four cases of wine. Would you be interested in handling it?' They'd say, a bit surprised, 'Well, uh, yeah.' George Hammer & Sons is still my distributor, thirty-three years later. That's how you build it—one at a time—in person."

Looking out into the future, Jack Cakebread stepped off the curb. Triumphant leaders put hope to work by breaking the future down into small, manageable steps rather than daunting leaps of faith. One city and thirty-four cases of fine wine kept the dream alive. Of course, those small steps must also be the *right* steps. Nothing gets distributors to believe in your cause more than throwing them business that they didn't have to get on their own!

As Cakebread reflects, "People look at my vineyards, my brand, and my success today and say, 'I could never do that.' However, what they have not seen are the nineteen years my wife and I worked three jobs—I on my tractor tilling the fields and taking photos and she back at the garage. The garage, my photography, and Dolores's support are responsible for this place."

Cakebread Crumbs: Three Irons in the Fire

"Why are you here?" I asked. Cakebread's response: "My only other option is—I retire. When you retire, that's doing what you want to do when you want to do it. And I've been doing that for thirty-three years." He laughed. "We ran the shop and the winery and the photography business and the vineyard management business for nineteen years. We went back and forth every day. Dolores used to say, 'You live in Napa Valley. You just sleep in Oakland.'"

"So," I asked, "what was your original vision?"

"Well, it's embarrassing to talk to B-school people," Cakebread responded, "because when I got into this business, I went to UC Davis and took extension classes on viticulture. I knew trees or, as my wife used to say about our vines, 'Look at all those short trees out there.' That was in 1974. Then, in 1983, I was accepted to the Graduate School of Business at Stanford. I thought, 'This is getting pretty complicated.' I picked up some business sense. I went down and really learned from those guys. I really did." However, Cakebread's will to lead emanates from generations of what seems to be a hopefully genetic predisposition.

"My great-grandfather came around the Horn on a sailing ship from England," Cakebread noted. "He was illiterate. He wasn't stupid; he just wasn't educated. He signed his name with an X. He came over here with his new bride. She was fourteen; he was fifteen. They worked their way over and walked up from San Francisco to the gold fields to make his fortune in gold. Well, he never did. He ended up as a hard-rock coal miner right outside of Pittsburg, California. He had thirteen children, four of whom died. Five boys and four girls survived. He gave each child a quarter section, one of which went to my grandfather. That's 160 acres! Do you know how much mining that is? However, during the Depression, they lost it all. My grandfather was down to his last twenty acres and Bank of America was going to repossess. And so my dad stepped up and signed the note—$6,000, more money than I could ever imagine. I couldn't believe it. And so my dad put me on the tractor up there where we planted almond trees. I was nine years old, and so they put big extensions on the controls. And that is how I got into agriculture. When the Korean War thing came around and I had to leave, my father leased it out to a guy. When I got back, the guy hadn't even pruned it. That's like never cutting your lawn! It took me about three years to get it back looking good, and then my dad sold it. I was thirty-seven years old. It broke my heart. But then this photo shoot came up, my father had since passed away, and so I had my hands full at that shop. I was the line mechanic. I was the body and fender guy. I was the painter. But my father never really sat me down and said, 'Jack, this is how you really run a business.' Having worked with my father for a long time and now that I am working with my sons, I have been on that side of the desk and now I am on this side of the desk. I say to my sons, 'I know exactly what you are thinking.' The philosophy I have, Andrew, is that when you start up a business as an entrepreneur, there are some things that you have to know are going to happen to you. One is that the company is going to grow and you have been doing everything—cleaning the latrine, turning out the lights, doing the production, doing sales, traveling, doing all this stuff. But as your company grows, you need to know that you have to have somebody come in and answer the phone. You can't just let it ring. And in those days, we didn't have voice-mail. They finally came out with a recording machine, which was a pain in the neck. I was in the office, in the shop, in the vineyard. I was all over the place. My original phone sat in the back of my 1967 El Camino. It sat behind the seat and weighed two hundred pounds. You pushed a button to talk and released it to listen. It was hooked up to the horn in the vineyard. I'd jump off the tractor, and it would be Dolores, calling me from the shop, saying, 'Now, what do I do next?' And that is how we did it.

"I've always been in business for myself. I've always signed the front of a paycheck, always—except one time. They told me, 'Under no circumstances, Jack, because the secretary of the treasury had to sign it.' That's when I was in the Air Force. I have always been my own person. The only partner I got is my wife. Nothing would ever happen around here without her. But if you're in something that you wake up in the morning and you can't wait to get to work, you've got a winner! If you enjoy what you're doing, you'll never work another day in your life. Ever."

The Two-Minute Rule

Think like Jack Cakebread. Miniaturize the future. Practice curb stepping. Try this. Write down a desired objective. Then ask yourself, "What *one thing* can I do in the next two minutes to work toward this goal?" That's right, two minutes. Think no further. This may involve calling someone who can help or pulling together a team to discuss the burning question you need answered. Step off the curb. Do something—anything. Get it started.

Selling Hope

Of course, getting started is only half the battle. To make hope happen, you need to get the word out. Since triumphant leaders think about hope differently, it should come as no surprise that they also communicate differently. They use the voice of hope.

13

THE VOICE OF HOPE

The hero is really a puppet. The *storyteller* is the
one who inspires us.

—*Robert Schmidt*

Keep information simple, and people will remember it. This sounds
good, but it doesn't work. Consider the following deceptively simple
sentence. "George Washington was a Revolutionary general who led
the Continental Army to victory." This is likely how you were taught
social studies in high school—a series of allegedly easy-to-remember
single sentences. However, consider the evidence. According to a
study conducted by Washington College, "Only 46 percent of the
800 adult Americans surveyed could identify George Washington as
the Revolutionary general who led the Continental Army to victory.
And when asked who they thought was America's greatest president,
only six percent named Washington, ranking him seventh among all
U.S. presidents." However, over 91 percent of adult respondents were
familiar with the story of Washington and the cherry tree. Stories are
memorable. Facts aren't. Use stories.

Is it any wonder that Jimmy Buffett's lyrics are so memorable:
"He went to Paris lookin' for answers to questions that bothered
him so." Buffett is a storyteller. It should therefore come as no surprise that in addition to his enormous success as a singer-songwriter,
he is one of only six authors in the history of the *New York Times's*
Best-Seller Lists to reach number one in both fiction and nonfic-
tion. The others were John Steinbeck, Ernest Hemingway, William
Styron, Irving Wallace, and Dr. Seuss. So much for "wasting away

in Margaritaville." Storytelling works. For example, consider the purest form of storytelling: gossip.

People are endlessly fascinated with people—their dreams and their dirty laundry. In fact, the magazine with one of the largest circulations in the world is aptly titled *People*. *People's* combined sales—nearly $500 million a year—are second only to *TV Guide* (yet another indicator of the spirit of our age). Moreover, according to Magazine Publishers of America, the five top-grossing magazines in single-copy sales are all about us, quite literally: *Us Weekly*, *National Enquirer*, *Woman's World*, *Star Magazine*, and *People*. (Incidentally, the *Harvard Business Review* ranks number eighty-six.) We like to learn, but *man*, do we *love* to gossip.

Gossip is extremely well organized and fundamentally decentralized. It is managed by the most creative department in most organizations—the rumor mill. When leaders fail to communicate their beliefs and expectations—their hope—the rumor mill does it for them. So how then can you communicate hope? You have three options.

Communicating Hope

Hope involves expectations. And expectations make the world go around. In fact, Wall Street has its very own word for expectations management. It's called *guidance*. However, in addition to guidance—a form of financial storytelling—leaders have three means by which to communicate hope.

The first involves conventional communication: internal memos and meetings. While these may be appropriate methods by which to manage day-to-day operations, they are insufficient means by which to inspire the future. Communicating a reason to believe with a flip-chart is like drinking Latour from a plastic cup. You know the content is there, but you can't get past the packaging. Therefore, leaders have a second and much more dramatic opportunity to communicate hope: martyrdom.

Recall from the Burson-Marstellar study of CEO turnover mentioned in Chapter Three that "investors view a new CEO as a sign of hope." CEOs are not alone in this regard. We welcome new coaches, generals, and politicians, who, for no other reason than their novelty, send a message of hope in the future. But why wait until your departure to communicate hope? You do have another option. It is the voice of hope: storytelling, the most effective form of human communication.

All Kinds of Minds

I once pitched Charles Schwab on the idea of a Schwab Leadership School. His response: "I had a conversation with the dean of a local business school. He was talking about what he wanted to do, and I gave him some ideas on what I thought he should do. I told the dean that if you want leaders, enroll students who have shown leadership in different ways in earlier aspects of their lives. Enroll students who are great communicators. It's all about SAT scores and boxes with you guys. Scores and boxes don't make for great leaders. All my experiences with great leaders are about passion, belief, hard work, and communication. Whether you are a religious leader, a business leader, or a government leader, you must understand all that you can about the subject matter, but you have to couple that with *unbelievable* communication skill. I would seek to get students who have both the passion and the skill to develop into great communicators. Because *that* is the leadership that everyone looks for. It doesn't mean they have to be the smartest guys in the room. Sustained leadership comes only from people who live out their values and their beliefs and are able to communicate them extremely well."

Schwab's wisdom is the result of his involvement as cochair of an institute called All Kinds of Minds. "The institute," he explained, "devotes its energies to helping teachers in the high school and lower schools to understand that kids don't all learn the same way. My involvement with All Kinds of Minds has helped me learn about people. This understanding has led me to understand the power of diversity—diversity in how people process information. If you cannot communicate your beliefs to a diverse set of people, with different backgrounds and perspective, you are never going to make it as a leader. You've got to be deeply empathetic and deeply understand-ing to the world of differences." Storytelling provides the means by which to appeal to the world of differences. Stories are the best form of time travel.

As Geoff Canada, CEO of the Harlem Children's Zone, told me, "I find that stories help people begin to bridge connections—between today and the future, and between my role and theirs. When our kids say, 'You know, I feel the same way,' that is the beginning of a con-nection. And that is what you need to lead. You need to connect with people in a way that they *believe you* when you tell them some-thing. I have found that it is harder to *tell* kids something and have them believe you than to *share* something with them and have them believe that. Basically, as a leader, when you tell people things, they say to themselves, 'Well, you don't know how I was thinking' or 'You don't know what I went through.' Stories fill in the blank. Stories an-swer a question that all people have: 'What does this have to do with me?'" Geoff Canada shares stories of experience. The following is one such story he shared with me.

"I was in my office, talking with a security person who was having a tough time as a young African American man. I was trying to tell him that he needed to be more serious about his job and how serious we are here." At this point in the story, as if to underscore Canada's mission, the sound of police cars and screaming ambulance sirens arose in the background. Canada proceeded to talk through the noise as if it weren't there—as if he had grown accustomed to it. He continued, "As I was talking to the security guard, one of the kids from the sixth grade came in and said how much he admired me and that he hoped one day he could come work for me. He was so serious!" Canada invited the child over to a wall in his office where pictures of Harlem Children's Zone kids from the past several years were displayed. Canada pointed to one of the photos and asked the child, "Do you know who this per-son is?" The boy said that he did not. Canada asked him to think a bit harder: "Think of security," he hinted. Canada's voice became infused with infectious enthusiasm: "The boy's eyes opened wide, like turning on a light!" It was a photo of the security guard when he was about twelve years old. Canada continued his conversation with the boy, saying, "You know, he now has his college degree, and he's a good guy. We are always hoping our kids will come back and help."

Canada, in that moment, employed a story that immediately connected that child's dreams with reality. In that moment, he created the future for that child. In the child's mind, no longer was the future as ambiguous, uncertain, and unattainable as it may have seemed before. He could see the future standing squarely in front of him in the form of someone else who had followed a similar path. And in the security guard's mind, his job had instant meaning. Narrative storytelling, especially from personal experience, makes hope tangible.

If your charge is to get others aligned with and working toward a shared but ambiguous future, storytelling is a powerful tool. Stories help people conceptualize the future. They are the voice of hope. Consider the anatomy of the following stories—as told by John Steinbeck, David Ogilvy, and Elbert Hubbard.

The Weight of Leaders' Words

George Milton and Lennie Small were roving ranch hands with a shared dream—to someday own a farm. In John Steinbeck's novella *Of Mice and Men*, Lennie makes a frequent request of his leader: "Tell me about the rabbits, George!" It's not as if Lennie couldn't remember the story. In fact, he knew it well. However, for Lennie, hearing the story from his leader, George, gave him hope in the future. Although Steinbeck's tale is tragic, the rabbit story makes a seemingly impossible future somehow more attainable. However, it's not the story alone that matters. *Who* tells the story is as important. When told by leaders, stories hold more meaning. Lennie needed to hear the story from not just anyone. He needed to hear it from his leader, George. Leaders' words weigh more.

Ego-Speak

According to adman David Ogilvy, "If you always hire people who are smaller than you are, we shall become a company of dwarfs. If, on the other hand, you always hire people who are bigger than you are, we shall become a company of giants." This is a great story. However, consider how Ogilvy could have communicated his opinion about hiring practices in his firm. In a nonstorytelling format, it might have sounded something like this: "Hire good people. In fact, hire people smarter than you. Don't let your ego get in the way. It will be good for us all." When told in a nonstory format, you can imagine his advice causing more harm than good.

Ogilvy, like most triumphant leaders, spoke to the inner voice of his audience—"What will happen if my boss discovers that my employees are 'better than I am?'" Although most people capable of building great teams eventually become the best leaders, Ogilvy realized that not everyone thinks this way. Therefore, he told a story.

The Greatest Leadership Story Ever Told

The greatest leadership story ever told in print may well be Elbert Hubbard's story "A Message to Garcia." This leader's lament is thought to have achieved a larger circulation than any other literary work attained during the lifetime of the author. Great stories like Hubbard's are the wrapper in which triumphant leaders share the gift of hope.

In Hubbard's "Message," Cuba was a hostile region in the years leading up to the Spanish-American War, and President McKinley needed to get a message to an insurgent leader in the territory. His name was Garcia. Rowan was the man who would carry this message from McKinley to Garcia. If captured, Rowan would face certain death at the hands of the Spanish. However, knowing the risks of the situation and the objective of his leader, Rowan accepted the challenge, carried the message, found Garcia, returned alive, and confirmed delivery of the message. He succeeded. Hubbard's message is simple:

"The hero is the man who does his work—who carries the message to Garcia." What Hubbard also communicated through Rowan is a leader's desire for creativity and resourcefulness among his followers. Although McKinley gave Rowan the objective, he did not tell him how to get the job done—namely, how to find Garcia. Hubbard's appeal is for his employees to be more like Rowan, to find a way to get the job done using their own ingenuity. What is most remarkable about the story of "A Message to Garcia" is what happened after Hubbard published it in the March 1899 issue of *Philistine* magazine.

When he wrote it, Hubbard gave so little thought to the piece—despite the investment of a whole lot of emotion—that he published it without a title. After it ran, however, orders came in for back copies of the March issue of *Philistine*. Hubbard had no idea why people were calling. However, the phone kept ringing. First, a request came in for fifty copies and then a hundred, two hundred, a thousand, ten thousand. By now more than forty-five million copies of Hubbard's "Message" have been sold. Why is it so popular? Hubbard wrote a prescription for every leader's lament in the form of an eight-page story.

How to Tell a Great Story

First, throw away your visual aids. You don't need them. Did Abraham Lincoln use a flipchart at Gettysburg? Did Martin Luther King Jr. use a dry-erase board on the steps of the Lincoln Memorial? Did Mother Teresa require an LCD projector in the slums of Calcutta? However, who will ever forget "Four score and seven years ago . . . ," "I have a dream . . . ," or Mother Teresa, who wrote, "We ourselves feel that what we are doing is just a drop in the ocean. But if that drop was not in the ocean, I think the ocean would be less because of that missing drop." In place of slides, use metaphors to help people visualize your points. In lieu of flipcharts, use personal experiences to frame your vision. And in spite of a room full of gadgetry, turn off the LCD projector, turn on the lights, look into your audience's eyes, and have a conversation.

Consider the Context

Environment matters. Seek the appropriate venue to tell your stories. Whether you choose to tell it at a speech you are giving at an annual conference, face-to-face with a colleague, or in an informal setting, avoid distractions. Why does this matter? It goes back to expectations. People are not always expecting to learn or to be inspired. The environment will determine their level of interest, engagement, and participation. Like celebrating a special occasion at a fine restaurant, the table you choose matters. Much like customizing a marketing message based on the media in which it will be distributed, you must tailor your story to the environment in which it will be shared. Never forget that expectations management is hope management.

Take a Look Around

Tom Henry is the benevolent pastor of Saint Pauls United Church of Christ in Chicago. In response to my curiosity about where he gets material for his sermons, he responded, "I am an observer. If you just pay attention, there are great stories all around. When I see something happen, I make a quick note. I write it down. Then, later, I use that story to create my sermons. You never know when a sermon will fall into your lap." Tom Henry is not alone. Consider many of the funniest comedians. They are actually not joke tellers. They are observant storytellers who simply hold a mirror up to the comedy that is life on earth. Consider Bill Cosby's dentist visit, Eddie Murphy's ice-cream man, or Jerry Seinfeld's master of your domain. Think like Cosby, Murphy, Seinfeld, and Henry. Observe.

Create a Theme

Unlike jokes, stories typically follow a logical progression. They practically finish themselves. And they are born from a theme. Consider Winston Churchill, one of the all-time great storytellers. Churchill always spoke to a theme. For example, his "blood, sweat, and tears" phrase came from a radio talk on a singular theme—sacrifice. Why is Churchill so often quoted? He was branding while other politicians were still marketing. He understood the need for a theme. In fact, once, when served a sloppy dessert, Churchill is said to have ordered, "Take away this pudding: it has no theme." In addition to a theme, stories used to "manage uncertainty"—stories of hope—typically take on two forms that you may wish to try, namely, "slay the dragon, save the princess" and the Trojan Horse. Here is how they work.

Star Wars, Lord of the Rings, the defeat of communism, the American Revolution, and even Scooby Doo have one thing in common. On the one hand, you have the princess—possibility. On the other hand, where there is a princess, there is often a dragon lurking—the challenge. Great stories—stories of triumph, of good versus evil, of overcoming the odds—tell this simple tale. Slay the dragon. Save the princess.

Of course, princess-and-dragon stories work only when there is an obvious nemesis—a known competitor or a disruptive trend, for example. However, when no nemesis is obvious or available, you have to change the dialogue. Therefore, a second storytelling format often used by triumphant leaders to communicate hope is what I call the Trojan Horse format. This format is particularly relevant in two scenarios: (1) you want to motivate people to act on something that they have previously ignored (for example, repeal of the estate tax), or (2) you are attempting to launch a new idea (for example, construction of the Golden Gate Bridge).

Reframe the Debate

If you want to change the status quo, you must first help people understand the gravity of the current situation—why should they care? This is where stories come into play. In the early 1990s, in an attempt to influence voter sentiment, Republican pollster Frank Luntz suggested that conservative legislators begin referring to the estate tax as the "death tax." For many, the word *estate* implies wealth. There-fore, to the majority of Americans who do not consider themselves rich, the expression "estate tax" didn't mean much. Death, on the other hand, now *that's* something that gets our attention.

Through his research, Luntz discovered that the expression "death tax" rekindled voter sentiment much more than "estate tax" did. Luntz reported that "85 percent of Americans in the six states we've surveyed either want the Death Tax completely eliminated or significantly reduced." Luntz's Trojan Horse story reframed the debate. However, language alone is insufficient. Stories must be communi-cated to be effective. Therefore, to distribute their story, pro-repeal groups created the "Death Tax Pizza Fund."

Although they protested the repeal, William H. Gates Sr. and Chuck Collins recount the pizza fund phenomenon in their book *Wealth and Our Commonwealth: Why America Should Tax Accumulated Fortunes.* The pizza fund was created from the basic precept that gov-erns most high school class president campaigns. Pizza is a motivator. It is reported that death tax pizza funds began in the offices of the antitax advocacy group 60 Plus in Arlington, Virginia, and quickly spread across the Potomac, making their way into House Speaker Newt Gingrich's office. In offices across Washington, D.C., anyone who uttered the words *estate tax* was fined $1. The money collected in fines was then used to buy pizza for the office. "Woe to the innocent office intern" who uttered the forbidden phrase, Gates proclaimed. The *death tax* phrase eventually made its way out of the special-interest groups and onto talk shows, into advertising, and finally into the title of the "Death Tax Elimination Act of 2000." The Trojan Horse story pushed the repeal cause forward.

The reason Trojan Horse stories work is that they do not attempt to change *what* people believe; rather, they change how people *talk about* what they believe. In moments of uncertainty—when the future is unclear—triumphant leaders make hope more accessible by chang-ing the debate. They create Trojan Horses to carry the message. Like Luntz, Joseph Strauss was a mastermind of the Trojan Horse format.

Sell the Implications, Not the Idea

Joseph Strauss was known as the drawbridge king. With one very well-known exception, the majority of his four hundred bridges were uneventful projects. Strauss realized that the only way to get the impossible done—to build a bridge across the Golden Gate, the entrance to San Francisco Bay—was to tell a better story than one of mere transportation. So he told a story of opportunity. Driving from town to town in Marin County, California—north of San Francisco and disconnected from it by the bay—Strauss drummed up support for the bridge not by selling its travel benefits but by promising great wealth to the landowners of Marin. Strauss built a Trojan Horse because transportation was not as compelling. Why? First, many citizens of Marin were farmers. They had no need to get to the city as often as a bridge would allow. Second, when they did have a need to get to San Francisco, they already had a way—the ferry system. Therefore, Strauss had to tell a better story. He told that story. The bridge got built. Incidentally, at the time of writing this book, the small town of Tiburon, California—on the southernmost tip of Marin County—was declared one of the most expensive ZIP codes in America by *Forbes* magazine. Strauss was not only a storyteller; he was right.

Care

Pablo Casals, the world-renowned cellist and humanitarian, once suggested, "The capacity to care is the thing that gives life its deepest significance and meaning." Stories work because they are real. In this disposable world, people crave authenticity. Illustrate your empathy, but don't rely solely on an inspirational quote. Richard Nixon is said to have directed his speechwriters, "Never give me a naked quote. Put it in a little story." Or consider Martin Luther King's dream. King's most famous speech, delivered on August 28, 1963, from the steps of the Lincoln Memorial, packs a punch not for its oft-quoted line "I have a dream" but rather for what led up to and followed it. His dream had flames of withering justice, lights of hope, and mighty streams all nestled among Georgian red hills and perched high atop snow-capped mountains. King did not rely on a naked quote. He told a great story. Quotes communicate insight, but stories make the future meaningful. Speak from your heart. Share your stories.

Manage the Mill

As for the rumor mill, use it. Think like a viral marketer. For example, when the soft drink maker Red Bull first introduced its product in the United States, it sought to create buzz prior to its launch. Therefore, it resorted to a very creative marketing campaign. Among other tactics designed to get the word out, it filled trashcans outside nightclubs frequented by the brand's target customers with empty cans of their product. As clubgoers exited the clubs, they would invariably see heaping piles of Red Bull cans and subsequently think, "What's that? Red Bull? Never heard of it, but it must be good. I should try it." Mind you, the product wasn't even available in the United States at the time. Like most things in life, if you can't get it, you want it even more. That is the anatomy of buzz—creating and distributing stories that move people to act. And buzz isn't just for selling products. It's for selling hope. Create an internal buzz campaign. Manage the mill, or it will manage you. Recall the challenge of facial expressions. People know when you are angry, upset, or disappointed. How will they know of your hope? Tell stories.

14

FREAKING IN

He that lives in hope dances without music.
—*George Herbert*

My two-year-old son, Charlie, dances without music. It seems he's written his own soundtrack to accompany his very busy life. It's a soundtrack comprised of anything that has a rhythm to it. In homage to Dr. Seuss, to the chug-chug-chug of our washer he does shrug. Charlie shakes his head from side to side like a bobble-head doll. He thinks he's funny. My wife and I think he's the next Johann Sebastian Bach.

Like many young children, he also talks to himself. While countless parents and teachers mistake this jibber-jabber as inattentiveness or at times a symptom of the very voguish ADHD, it is an essential part of cognitive development. Psychologist Laura Berk has found that among children under ten years old, private speech can account for 20 to 60 percent of the remarks made on any given day. Although it may appear that the child is undisciplined, he is actually using chatter to master new skills and to learn to control his behavior.

The importance of private speech was first documented in Russia in the 1930s by a prominent psychologist named Lev Vygotsky. Due to the Cold War, educators and psychologists were kept from understanding his contributions until recently. Under Stalin's regime, anyone who thought too much about anything attracted persecution. Academics were a nuisance. The Communist party declared Vygotsky a rogue and a threat to society. Subsequently, he became not only the target of the Stalinists but also of the psychology community. Recall that fear works. Before he could distribute his findings in 1934,

Vygotsky died of tuberculosis. By 1936, the party had banned all of his published works. However, it took two men of stature to shield Vygotsky's contributions for over half a century.

In addition to Stalin, the larger-than-life reputation of Swiss theorist Jean Piaget kept the mouths of children shut. In the 1920s, Piaget claimed that private speech played no role in cognitive development. His eminence gave Vygotsky less prominence. Piaget deemed chatter egocentric and evidence of an immature mind. In other words, Piaget believed that the self-chitchat served primarily as an accompaniment to a child's day. He believed that it might also stimulate speech in another child, but neither child really cares or understands what the other is saying. There is no communication happening. Preschool teachers, although in disagreement, suffered the fate of Vygotsky. They had no voice. And then Stalin died. Enter Nikita Khrushchev. Denouncing Stalin's terror tactics, he promoted intellectual freedom. By 1953, Vygotsky's twenty-year ban had ended, and within the decade, English translations of his work appeared in the United States, soon to be supported by a team of researchers at Harvard University. By the 1980s, studies on private speech had increased 300 percent, and most of them supported Vygotsky's findings. So why is private speech so important? And what is actually happening?

Say, for example, that a child is attempting to insert a Barney DVD, or as my son calls it, *ah-ah,* into his parents' DVD player, although he doesn't quite know how. Turning to his mother for assistance, she agrees to help. As Mom puts the DVD into the player, she explains what she is doing to the child. It may go something like this: "First, we push the *open* button. Then we place the *DVD* in the tray. Next, we close the *tray*. And finally, we hit the *play* button." The child records elements of his mother's instructions into his private speech and then later uses them to guide his own efforts. "The most significant moment in the course of intellectual development," Vygotsky wrote, "occurs when speech and practical activity, two previously completely independent lines of development, converge." Unlike Piaget, who claimed that egocentric chatter diminishes as children learn to communicate, Vygotsky proposed the opposite—that communication begets private speech. Piaget had the cart before the horse. So what does all this have to do with hope, triumph, and leadership? Everything. Here is the punch line.

According to Vygotsky's findings and those of numerous independent studies, as children gain mastery over their behavior, private speech does not diminish; it merely goes inside. As children use private speech to learn how to live in the world around them, they begin to omit words and phrases. Once a child understands how to play the Barney DVD on his own, he will no longer verbalize "open, DVD, tray, play." However, he will *think* them. Only if there is something he still does not understand will he continue to verbalize that word. Say, for example, hitting the play button hasn't registered with him. He will *only* verbalize the word *play*. Just as the squeaky wheel gets the oil, the puzzling word gets spoken. Over time, as children grow older and eventually become adults, they start to *think* words rather than say them. Private speech becomes the inner voice—the same voice, incidentally, that accompanied me in London on the day that Brainball and Booth Girl taught me that nothing mattered.

The need for private speech never disappears. When we encounter difficult situations in our lives, private speech pays us a visit. It is a tool. It helps us overcome. It also helps us learn. In this regard, those who succeed against the odds, those who use hope to their advantage, think words directed at the task at hand. Like a child saying to himself, "open, DVD, tray, play," hopeful individuals use private speech often to achieve their desired objective. However, private speech, albeit private, is not isolated. In other words, private speech is an effect. Communication is the cause.

In a study of thirty-six low-income Appalachian five- to ten-year-olds, Laura Berk and one of her graduate students, Ruth Garvin, discovered that most utterances were for self-guidance. In other words, they weren't random. They were directed. By analyzing recordings of children in the classroom, on the playground, in the halls, and in the lunchroom, Berk and Garvin observed that most children talked to themselves while working alone on challenging tasks and when no one, particularly the teacher, was around to help them. The Harvard studies lent even more insight into the role of communication and self-directed speech. Whereas Berk and Garvin studied lower-income families, Harvard researchers studied middle-class families. At age ten, when more than 40 percent of the Appalachian children's private speech remained audible, less than 7 percent of the private speech of the middle-class children was out loud. Why? This led to a striking discovery by Berk and Garvin. Middle-class parents converse with their kids much more often than the Appalachian parents, suggesting the reinforcing effect of communication and learning. The middle-class kids had progressed faster than the lower-income kids and had learned to manage challenging tasks because of the preponderance of communication from their parents. In this regard, leaders, like parents, although they may feel hopeful, need to work harder to communicate hope. If not, assuming you are unable to broadcast an image of your brain to all those who look to you for leadership to show your "true feelings," your followers can only rely on inference and much more stealthy means to translate your thoughts into meaning. That is why we have nonverbal communication coaches and cosmetic surgery at our disposal. If you don't feel good, at least look your best!

In subsequent studies Berk conducted with children with ADHD and with learning disabilities, her findings were similar. Most remarkable among ADHD children was that they did not exhibit less private speech. In fact, they used more. The only difference found between the groups was that ADHD children took longer to internalize the audible speech, suggesting that they have difficulty paying attention to themselves as much as to everyone else. In other studies, muttering first graders did better at second-grade math, jibjab second graders performed better once they entered third-grade math, and so on. Overall, the children who moved most rapidly from audible sounds to inner speech were also most advanced in their ability to focus attention and control motor activity. Private speech improves performance. However, Berk's discoveries go beyond providing insights for putting hope to work in the face of a challenge by offering one additional insight for leadership.

In studies of the mother-child relationship, children with authoritative mothers—mothers who are warm and loving yet exert some control and direction to help the children—illustrated more exceptional improvements in mastering progressive tasks. Berk discovered that private speech acts as a mediator of sorts between the mother and the success of the task at hand. Yet another observation by Vygotsky confirmed some sixty years later. Private speech helps followers internalize and execute the directions of their leaders. Mantras matter.

The Art of Distributed Leadership

Whether he is aware of it or not, Hector Ruiz, CEO at Advanced Micro Devices, is a subscriber to Vygotsky's principles. Through the use of language—namely, some very simple and easy-to-understand organizational mantras—he has engaged the employees of AMD on a very basic level. He knows how to lead from within his followers. Ask anyone at AMD about "getting a ticket from Hector," and they will tell you that Ruiz gives out two types of figurative tickets: a parking ticket and a speeding ticket. Parking tickets are given to those who do nothing or sit still when opportunity knocks or challenges present themselves. Speeding tickets are given when an employee either thinks a little too far out of the box or moves faster than the company is able to go. Which is the worse kind of ticket to get from Hector Ruiz? A parking ticket. In the spirit of innovation, competition, and speed to market, Ruiz has created a culture of private speech. When confronted with a challenge, many at AMD silently think to themselves, "Will I get a parking ticket or a speeding ticket for this?" Organizational mantras, like private speech among children, help organizations direct themselves through impossible situations. It is what I call the art of "freaking in." Why hold an emergency conference call when in a challenging situation? Distribute motivation. Teach your followers to lead themselves. Let your organization babble. Teach them to freak in.

In addition to the private-speech studies of children by Vygotsky, Berk, and others, corroborating evidence also comes from the world of competitive athletics. In 1977, Michael Mahoney asked a group of gymnasts at Pennsylvania State University what they thought about and what they said to themselves during competitions. As it turned out, those most successful—those who qualified for the Olympic team—were no less plagued by doubt and anxiety than their less successful teammates. In other words, winners worried as much as losers. However, the difference between the two was the presence of private speech, audible or silent, among winners and its absence among losers. The Olympic qualifiers constantly encouraged themselves, through internal conversations, more than those who did not qualify.

Private speech carries hope. Whether leading a team against a formidable foe or attempting to sink a twelve-foot putt, private speech, when focused, deliberate, and positive, works to improve human performance. Consider its role with yips, quips, and the game of golf.

Yips, Quips, and the Game of Golf

"There is a force in the universe that makes things happen, and all you have to do is get in touch with it. Stop thinking, let things happen, and be the ball." This is the wisdom of golf pro Ty Webb, played by Chevy Chase, in Harold Ramis's cult film *Caddyshack*. In an attempt to help amateur golfer Danny Noonan, Webb suggests this Zen-like mantra as a remedy to Noonan's struggling putting game. Like "Use the force" from *Star Wars* and "I think I can" from *The Little Engine That Could*, "Be the ball" has become a part of our culture—and all but unavoidable on golf courses around the globe. Ramis isn't alone in his illustration of Vygotsky's principles in the game of golf. Through a unique combination of precision timing, humor, and bellyaching one-liners, one man—a leader on and off the stage—earned his name, Bob Hope.

According to the celebrated entertainer, he told jokes to fund a seventy-year obsession with the game of golf. "Golf is my profession," he once said. "Entertainment is just a sideline. I tell jokes to pay my greens fees." Born Leslie Townes Hope in Eltham, England, in 1903,

Bob Hope left England for America in 1907 when, according to Hope, "I found out I couldn't be king." Bob was a great promoter—not only of Hope but also of hope. In the history of show business, no individual traveled so far, so often, to entertain so many. From World War II through the 1991 Persian Gulf War, Hope traveled over two million miles to entertain over eleven million American military personnel. His omnipresent goodwill gave the phrase "There Is Always Hope" two literal meanings. Bob Hope was a natural leader. People followed him because he followed them. Film critic Vincent Canby wrote in Hope's obituary, "There was nothing Bob Hope loved more than an audience, and audiences responded in kind, particularly soldiers facing combat who desperately needed a laugh. Once, he chartered a yacht for a cruise in Canadian waters. It was one of the few formal vacations he ever took. However, he found he could not stand the serenity. He cut the cruise short and returned to Hollywood with the comment, 'Fish don't applaud.'" No wonder the world's most hopeful entertainer lived to be one hundred.

Ironically, the two things Bob Hope enjoyed most—joke telling and golf—are central to hope, the virtue. Humor gives hope. Golf takes it. Golf requires extreme mental acuity and endless acts of courage simply to survive eighteen holes with one's ego intact. It also involves private speech. Enter the yips (aka choking).

The Yips

They affect one-fourth to one-half of all mature golfers, including professionals such as Harry Vardon, Bobby Jones, Ben Hogan, Sam Snead, Bernhard Langer, and Sam Torrance. Perhaps you've experienced them. Here's a test. Have you ever missed a crucial putt under pressure or been in an endless putting slump? If so, you might be suffering from a case of the yips.

Since the early 1900s, the yips have cost professionals golfers millions of dollars in prize money and the average hack an afternoon's worth of a damaged ego. Once known as "the jumps" and "whisky fingers," the yips is a movement disorder. In the 1920s, the word *yips* was confined to an obscure people dwelling in L. Frank Baum's fictional Land of Oz. In the 1940s, the yips in golf became known as "the jitters," a reference to a drunk's tremors.

The science of the yips gained momentum following the 1996 Masters after Greg Norman lost a final-round six-shot lead to Nick Faldo. So awestruck by the "wheels falling off" Norman's game, the NBC television program *Dateline* subsequently bankrolled a study of choking in golf.

A team of scientists at the Mayo Clinic, led by Dr. Debbie Crews from the Department of Exercise Science at Arizona State University, departed from earlier research by suggesting a prominent role of psychological factors rather than neurological factors. Crews's research consisted of an EEG ("brain wave") study of ten amateur golfers with an average of five years' golfing experience and with handicaps ranging from 11.5 to 26. The task consisted of twenty five-foot putts to establish a baseline, followed by a second trial of twenty putts on condition that the golfers who improved won $300 while golfers who performed worse than baseline would have to pay $100.

The field split, with half doing better and half doing worse. Based on the EEG patterns, Crews and crew discovered that the pattern of brain activity of successful golfers and unsuccessful golfers differed significantly. Among successful golfers, brain activity was spread evenly across both hemispheres, while among unsuccessful golfers, brain activity was concentrated in the left hemisphere.

According to Crews, the increased left-brain activity among unsuccessful golfers was anxiety related. She attributes the successful golfers' brain pattern under pressure as a consequence of critical right-brain processing (they could "see the future" more clearly in their mind's eye). Having discovered that unsuccessful golfers are dominant in the left hemisphere, Crews encourages the use of imagery, relaxation techniques, and target focus as ways to promote right-brain activation. This, in part, is not only a contribution to the game of golf but refutes Chevy Chase's mantra "Be the ball" as a secret to success. Based on Crews's findings, you should, if anything, seek to "be the cup"—focus on the target and imagine the ball falling into it.

Although the jury is still out on the role of emotion and its link to the yips, the golf community is sold on Crews's findings. In fact, she was awarded the First Annual Golf Science Award from *Golf Magazine* and the World Scientific Congress of Golf.

In the lonely moments of critical decision making, Vygotsky, Berk, Mahoney, Crews, and Nicklaus have taught us the virtues of private speech in translating our hopes in the future into our actions in the present. They have taught us the art of freaking in. Among the superfreaks, I was most moved by the story of Jerry Linenger, the Mir cosmonaut who was stranded on the Mir space station for five months as it spiraled out of control. Private speech not only helped him succeed in his career. It saved his life.

"Gonna Put Out That Fire and Gonna See My Boy"

Jerry Linenger is as good as they come. Raised in a blue-collar family near Detroit and educated at the U.S. Naval Academy, Linenger's drive far overshadows his education, even though he holds a Ph.D. and an M.D. He's the father of four and is simply as good as the earth (although at times I wonder if the earth is as good as he is).

Linenger and I met in his hotel suite in downtown Chicago. He was in town to give a speech. When I arrived, he was clearly in the middle of something and said, "I've gotta get my work done and then we can talk." His work, I noticed, entailed finishing ironing a shirt he had begun ironing before I arrived. Finish what you start. Jerry Linenger knows commitment—no doubt one of the primary reasons for his unusual success.

Knowing his story long before I sat down with him, and he knowing mine, I opened our conversation with a single word: "Hope." Linenger was right there with me. No doubt, he had thought about this word often. Citing his mantra, which was written on a piece of paper on the table between us, he responded, "Hope is what gets you out of bed in the morning." Putting his notes aside, he then lent these words: "Hope is not 'Keep your fingers crossed.' It is 'I'm ready for this,' 'I can handle it,' 'I am prepared,' 'I've been here before,' 'I know what to do.'" No pretense. No ego. Jerry Linenger gets it done.

Astronaut Linenger came onto my radar screen due to a very specific and well-publicized situation he encountered while on the space station Mir. Fire. In fact, it was a fire so vicious that it nearly killed him and his crew of Russian cosmonauts. I wanted to know how he thought, felt, and behaved in that precise moment. Considering that 1.8 million American adults aged eighteen to fifty-four are agoraphobic, intensely fearing and avoiding any place or situation where escape might be difficult, his experience on Mir was the perfect petri dish in which to study hope. He said to me, "Oddly, I became very calm, almost too calm. My pulse actually dropped." Yes, he actually stopped and took his own pulse. I don't know about you, but I have a hard time waiting to read my pulse under even the most benign circumstances. "For me," he said, "it seemed as if time slowed down. I found myself staring at the flames shooting at me. I could feel the heat. The smoke began to fill the station. I knew to be cautious and methodical. After all, I had been trained for these types of situations." What came next in our conversation I found most compelling. "In the challenges of life," he said, "the *easiest* thing to do is to have confidence in yourself; however, knowing how your partners will react is hard. How do I communicate my hope in the future in that very moment?" Confidence is demanding. Hope is commanding. Confidence may help sell cars, but hope enrolls others to believe.

Linenger continued, "After what seemed to be an eternity, I had to shake myself up a bit, to get myself motivated and to get my pulse up. However, while trying to motivate myself, I thought, 'This is it.' I started thinking to myself. I said good-bye to my son and apologized to my wife for not being there to help raise him." At first, Linenger surrendered to fear—but not for long. As Jodi Foster's character Clarice says to Anthony Hopkins's Hannibal Lecter in *Silence of the Lambs*, when he asks her how she feels, "Scared at first. Then—exhilarated." Linenger continued in a voice as if he were back on Mir, as if the fire were right there in the room with us (in fact, I thought I could even feel the heat). "Then something came over me and I thought, 'I'm gonna put out that fire and I'm gonna see my boy again.' And then I said it again. This time out loud. 'I'm gonna put out that fire and I'm gonna see my boy!'" Linenger didn't freak out. He freaked in. He used private speech to put hope to work. And his hope, like the fire, glowed so brightly in him that his Russian comrades became hopeful as well. They derived their hope from his, and together they put out the fire. Together they survived.

Jerry Linenger now lives with his wife and family in a small town in northern Michigan. He sees his boy every day, and he still talks to himself. He told me that each and every morning, he wakes up, takes a deep breath, and counts his blessings for the air he breathes. This, of course, means a lot coming from a man who, at one point aboard Mir, due to an equipment malfunction, had to use his own urine and that of his comrades to make oxygen. As Linenger commented, "One of the best parts about earth is that you don't have to make your own air here." I ended our conversation by asking him what he will do next. "First," he said, "I want to teach my kids to have the same frame of mind that I have had since returning to earth. I want them to see the borderless world that I saw from space, but I don't know if I want them to be astronauts. Mostly, I want to give them the hope I have always had. Then," he continued with an infectious passion reflected prominently on the surface of my skin, "Mars."

Triumphant leaders provide their teams with simple, memorable, and actionable mantras—"private speech"—thereby distributing decision making throughout the organization. When creating the future, losers freak out, but the triumphant freak in. Go forth. Have no shame. Create a mantra. Talk out loud! And, as I suggested to Lee Stacey, senior vice president for the New York Jets, and other sports industry luminaries at General Sports and Entertainment's annual Sports Executive Leadership Conference, although I wouldn't recommend Gandhi's passive resistance as the mantra for the Jets, they should create one relevant to the organization and the situation at hand. Help others rise to the occasion. Teach them the art of freaking in.

15

SHINE

Come on you raver, you seer of visions, come on
you painter, you piper, you prisoner, and shine!
—*Pink Floyd*

After hours of intense study in the neuroanatomy lab at the Indianapolis School of Medicine, medical student Frank Meshberger reposed among the pages of a book on artist Michelangelo di Lodovico Buonarroti Simoni. As an aspiring obstetrician-gynecologist studying neuroanatomy, Meshberger must have found solace in Michelangelo's own paradox. While he adorned the ceiling of Saint Peter's Sistine Chapel with over 5,800 square feet of frescoes in four short years, making twenty generations of painters green with envy, Michelangelo hated to paint. In fact, his loathing of painting was further exasperated by his fervent desire to return to sculpting the tomb of Julius II. I find quiet comfort in knowing that even divine Renaissance men believed that the grass is always greener.

Back in Indianapolis, Meshberger stumbled on a three-page foldout of the *Creation of Adam*, one of Michelangelo's most recognized and most beloved works of art. Though not an art critic, Meshberger was immediately taken by the shape of the image surrounding God and the angels. Although he had never seen the painting before, Meshberger was as familiar with the *Creation of Adam* as McDonald's forty million daily visitors are with its Golden Arches. Could it be that nearly five hundred years since Michelangelo created his masterpiece on the ceiling of the Sistine Chapel, Meshberger would see what three million rubbernecking visitors per year had overlooked?

Where others saw angels in flight carrying God in a mantle with his right arm reaching toward Adam, Meshberger saw something much more controversial. He saw a secret yet arguably very deliberate message. Here among the many rooms housing the Vatican Museum's five-hundred-year-old art collection, including the Cappella Niccolina with paintings by Beato Angelico, the Appartamento Borgia decorated by Pinturicchio, and the Sistine Chapel with its frescoes created by the most notable fifteenth-century Umbrian and Tuscan masters, Michelangelo left a message that may reflect more than the artist's interpretation of God.

Where others saw angels, Meshberger saw what he had been working on all day: an anatomically, and eerily, accurate image of the human brain. After hours of staring at images of the human brain, was Meshberger's own staring back at him? Perhaps. However, Meshberger's observation was not temporary, nor was it malicious. In other words, he had no beef with the Vatican. In fact, Meshberger assumed that his epiphany was anything but novel. Certainly someone must have made a similar observation? Or so he thought.

After graduating from medical school, Meshberger occasionally shared his observation with friends and family, although he never encountered anyone who was familiar with a "brain theory." It was not until 1988, with the Sistine Chapel restoration project under way, that Meshberger decided to do further research into Michelangelo's private life. Meshberger's fixation raised a lot of questions, not the least of which was how Michelangelo would be so well versed in the complexity of human anatomy, much less neuroanatomy, to depict the brain in such detail. After all, he was a reluctant painter and an avid sculptor, not a pathologist. Or was he?

As Meshberger would soon discover for himself, the divine Michelangelo had an artistically curious appetite for dissecting cadavers. I suppose you don't get the title "Renaissance man" for nothing! Michelangelo's anatomical interest is best described in Giorgio Vasari's book *The Lives of the Artists*, where Vasari writes, "For the church of Santo Spirito in Florence, Michelangelo made a crucifix of wood which was placed above the lunette of the high altar, where it still is.

He made this to please the prior, who placed rooms at his disposal where Michelangelo very often used to flay dead bodies in order to discover the secrets of anatomy." Given his occupation of carving bodies *from* stone, I suppose a likely preoccupation would be carving cadavers *on* stone. In fact, given his anatomical interest, it would seem more shocking for images of human organs not to find their way onto one of his many canvases.

Meshberger returned to the *Creation of Adam*. This time, he overlaid an image of the human brain onto a life-sized image of the painting. Even more stunning than his original observation, Meshberger discovered that not only can you see the outline of the surface of the brain, but you can clearly see the basilar artery, the brain stem, the optic chiasm, and the pituitary gland, each accurately represented among the angels and image of God. God's arm stretches outward toward Adam in what looks to be the prefrontal cortex, considered the most creative and human area of the brain. In a lounging position, you see Adam reaching toward God with his left arm. Although their fingers appear to touch, they do not. This gap, according to Meshberger, is much like a synaptic cleft, suggesting that Adam is already alive.

An angel with a sad expression on his face sits below God's arm. This area correlates with the area of the brain that is often activated on PET scans when a person experiences a sad thought. In place of the limbic system, the emotional center of the brain—often considered the anatomical manifestation of the soul—God's image is superimposed.

Could it be possible that Michelangelo painted a human brain on the ceiling of the most powerful place on earth at the time in an act of artistic defiance, like a modern-day graffiti artist leaving midnight messages on the subways of New York? Perhaps. And if so, what does all this have to do with hope and leadership? Everything.

The original scope of work for the Sistine Chapel ceiling project called for a rendering of the Twelve Apostles. However, Michelangelo told Pope Julius II that this would be a terrible waste of space, prompting Julius to give Michelangelo the freedom to paint more or less

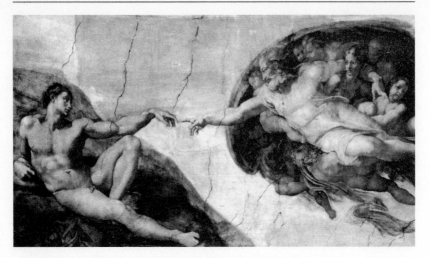

Creation of Man or *Human Brain* on the ceiling of the Sistine Chapel

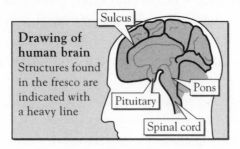

Drawing of the human brain

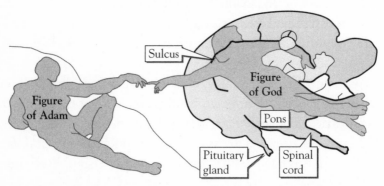

Michelangelo's fresco with overlay by Frank Meshberger

whatever he wanted. And so he did. He painted the human brain. Although there is no way to interpret Michelangelo's original intent, simply because we haven't the luxury of asking him directly, Meshberger has certainly given art critics something new to debate among the pages of the *New York Times*. Whether or not Michelangelo's intent was to draw a human brain or whether it was a sheer coincidence, like clouds forming into the profile of John Kennedy, Meshberger's discovery would not be surprising to the likes of leaders such as Nelson Mandela, Vaclav Havel, or Martin Luther King Jr., each of whom was well known for his campaign of symbols. These men used symbols to make the intangible more accessible. They used symbols to communicate hope.

The Will to Win

Like Michelangelo, triumphant leaders often look for, reflect on, and use symbols to raise the collective consciousness needed to win. Because of the intangible nature of hope, symbols provide a mechanism by which to make hope actionable. They are expressions of will. From wishing on a star to throwing coins in fountains, we have created tangible outlets for our beliefs—real-world ways to affect our fate. In fact, even simulated-life gamers have caught on to the importance of will as a basic human expression. Remember the video game Sims 2 I spoke of earlier in the book? In addition to new features allowing for the creation of goals and aspirations, its developers have also added a "free will" option. This option allows a Sim to make decisions as expressions of that person's desire. Say a Sim decides to place a dish on the floor. This may not make logical sense, but it is an expression of will, good or bad. Throughout history, triumphant leaders have employed symbols in order to make things happen to their liking. In fact, if you look closely enough, you can even find traces of hope in a sandwich.

Mandela's Sandwiches

It is home to at least 132 bird species. Because of its unique location just seven miles off the coast of Cape Town, South Africa, the environment provides an unusually safe and sheltered haven for a number of endangered species, some of which have moved here form the nearby mainland to breed. A tourist favorite, which was introduced in 1983 after it was nearly brought to extinction in the 1800s, is the African penguin, known formerly as the jackass penguin. Just off the coast, between the island and Cape Town, heaviside dolphins, Cape Fur seals, and southern right whales play. The island itself is home to more than twenty species of mammals, including ostriches, geckos, and tortoises. The climate is Mediterranean. Winds blow. In spring, flowers bloom. It's beautiful. Welcome to the hellhole of inhumanity.

For four hundred years, Robben Island was a destination favored by social outcasts and political troublemakers. Its visitors didn't come here of their own volition; rather, they were sent here against their will. Those who came to Robben Island were prisoners of their own thoughts and therefore, according to the island's operators, must be purged of their opinions.

During the apartheid era, Robben Island became known for the institutional brutality inflicted on political dissidents, social misfits, and assorted outcasts. The mission of those who ran the island was straightforward: crush morale. And so they tried and failed. What was once the nastiest, darkest, and most malignant blemish on the skin of humanity is now an international symbol of freedom, personal liberation, and the triumph of the human spirit. Instrumental in this shift of public opinion is one man, the island's most recognized former resident, Nelson Mandela. Throughout his twenty-seven-year stay on the island, Mandela was aware that he had lost his freedom but regarded it always as a temporary loss; his hope in the future remained strong. Though he had none of the luxuries afforded a free man, Mandela led. Though isolated, he communicated. Though caged, people followed him. Mandela liberated himself and his nation through applied hope, but how did he do it? Hope is all that he had. Or was it? Like Michelangelo, Mandela used symbols. They became his greatest leadership asset.

As a leader, particularly in a situation where the future is ambiguous, if not dark, everything becomes a method of communication. Why? Because hope is intangible; therefore, triumphant leaders work to make hope more accessible to those who look to them for leadership. To triumphant leaders, hope is in everything. Everything sends a message—even sandwiches. That's right, sandwiches. As Mandela wrote in *Long Walk to Freedom*, "The challenge for every prisoner, particularly every political prisoner, is how to survive prison intact, how to emerge from prison undiminished, how to conserve and even replenish one's beliefs. Our survival depended on understanding what the authorities were attempting to do to us, and sharing that understanding with each other. . . . The authorities' greatest mistake was keeping us together, for together our determination was reinforced."

As far as Mandela was concerned, as a leader, he had all that he needed at his disposal. His dignity, the company of others, and hope in the future. Although he hadn't the support of administrative staff or line managers, he chose to lead. He just had to be more creative about *how* he led. Mandela recognized the strategy of his oppressors very early—crush morale—as well as the tactics they deployed to strip prisoners of their dignity—uniforms, songs, and stale sandwiches. This is all that Mandela needed to play their game. To Mandela, if the authorities could use these symbols to their advantage, he could too. And so he did.

Mandela writes:

We were having our lunch under the shed when this warder wandered over. The warder had an extra sandwich, and he threw it on the grass near us and said, "Here." That was his way of showing friendship. On the one hand, he was treating us as animals to whom he could toss a bit of slop, and I felt it would undermine our dignity to take the sandwich. On the other hand, we were hungry, and to reject the gesture altogether would humiliate the warder we were trying to befriend. I could see that the comrade who had befriended the warder wanted the sandwich, and I nodded for him to take it. The strategy worked, for this warder became less wary around us. He even began to ask questions about the ANC [the African National Congress, Mandela's political party, outlawed at the time]. By definition, if a man worked for the prison service, he was probably brainwashed by the government's propaganda. He would have believed that we were terrorists and Communists who wanted to drive the white man into the sea. But as we quietly explained to him our non-racialism, our desire for equal rights, and our plans for the redistribution of wealth, he scratched his head and said, "It makes more bloody sense than the [Nationalists]."

Using symbols as weapons, Mandela won the war of will. In his effort to "conserve and replenish" the beliefs of his followers, in the many moments of uncertainty and on his long walk to freedom, he used everything from songs to trousers. Song lyrics became Mandela's version of "internal memos," and trousers preserved the inmates' dignity. When Mandela successfully coaxed a pair of long pants from a prison guard, to wear instead of the obligatory shorts, Mandela demanded that *all* prisoners be given trousers. Same pants, same rights. Equality in everything.

For twenty-seven years, where others saw stale fish soup, Mandela saw a chance to lead. Like Mandela, triumphant leaders use symbols to make hope more tangible. In the Silicon Valley—a land of dreams and dogfights—one such leader keeps a lighthouse at the White House. Meet Tom McCoy.

McCoy's Lighthouse at the White House

It's a modern-day David-and-Goliath tale. Some would say it's an impossible fight. Then again, that's what makes it such a great leadership story. Welcome to the fast-paced, cutthroat world of high science and advanced technology. Welcome to the world of semiconductors. It's Advanced Micro Devices versus Intel. The score: Intel, 80 percent; AMD, 15 percent—market share, that is. However, AMD, the much smaller and nimbler microprocessor manufacturer, headquartered in Sunnyvale, California, continues to nip away at the heels of Intel's core processor business. But how? What keeps these guys motivated?

Nearly every businessperson with indoor plumbing is familiar with the principles espoused by the former chairman of Intel, Andy

Grove, and his leadership mantra, "Only the paranoid survive." However, what about the underdog? What about AMD? It's one thing to lead a company with 80 percent market share but quite another to inspire the hearts and minds of the underdog. So how does AMD's leadership keep its employees on task? Hope and a whole lot of ingenuity must come into play.

To test my assumption and satiate my curiosity, I traveled to Sunnyvale to meet with AMD's chief administrative officer, Tom McCoy. According to his job description, McCoy is responsible for "leading those functions that help create, sustain, and promote the AMD culture and core values." Needless to say, McCoy's responsibility for "culture" is what drew me to him. Though he is not the formal leader of AMD—he's not the CEO—I had learned through friends working for AMD that he holds the attention of AMD's many thousands of employees. Why? Through his words and actions, Tom inspires people. He is a great communicator.

When I arrived at AMD's offices, I was immediately taken aback by the architecture of the building. My first Meshberger-like reaction was, "Haven't I seen this before?" And then it hit me: it looks like the White House in Washington, D.C. And then I thought, "It makes perfect sense. If you're going to take on Intel, why not do it from a building that resembles the home of the leader of the free world?" As I entered the lobby, the next thing that caught my attention was a photo of Lance Armstrong, heroically displayed, shrinelike, in a cabinet near the receptionist's desk. "Of course," I thought, "if you're going to take on Intel, why not have the world's greatest athlete in tow?" Although Team Armstrong and the building's architectural design are appropriate reflections of its mission, it was determination, compassion, and thoughtfulness of the leader I was soon to meet, Tom McCoy, that best explains AMD's sustained relevance in the marketplace.

When introduced to McCoy, I asked him the same question I had asked all the others (one you should know by now): "Why do you do it? Why are you here?" His response, like Charles Schwab's, reminded me why people are attracted to those who can communicate so very well. "AMD is a big manufacturing company. We have these incredible monuments to what is the current roll-up of the ingenuity of the human race in these fabs. The technology inside a leading-edge semiconductor wafer fab is the most complicated machinery man has ever devised. And the products that are made by companies like AMD and Intel, processors, are the most complicated machines on earth. When you think about the ability today to build the equipment to make these kinds of products and you imagine all the people in the history of the world who have contributed to innovation that ultimately rolls into these functioning devices, it is overwhelming. When you see these tools being installed that are half as big as boxcars and cost about $50 million a pop and you peer inside and you look at the aggregate engineering—physics, chemistry, electrical engineering, material sciences, design, paint, and all that is embodied in this thing—and then you think about all the people in the world who have touched something in their mind that is now comprehended in this tool, it is overwhelming. It's like standing in front of a big skyscraper and asking, 'How do they do this?' Well, you know what, people do this. People. Somebody has to have a vision. Why is vision important? Because vision leads the leaders. You have to imagine. You have to inspire. And every day, you must think about how to keep it going. Now that I've seen this one in my mind's eye and I can see that that's going to get done, what can I imagine now? This all rises and falls on leadership. Therefore, people crave leadership.

"So why do I do it?" McCoy paused to ask himself. "I have to confess, there are days when I mutter to myself, 'Why couldn't I have been content to be a clerk in a paint store? I'd read my magazine and every once in a while if somebody needed help picking out a color, I'd be there.'" He finally did answer the question: "Destiny. I think it's what I'm supposed to be doing."

McCoy is driven deeply by his faith in God and in man. You can feel it in his words. He understands, as a leader, that if you don't make your beliefs and your will to win visible to those who look to you for leadership, they will look for those things elsewhere. Ultimately, they will come to their own conclusions about what you believe, how you think, and how you feel. That's right. They'll just make it up. (Remember, the best-selling magazines in the world are about gossip.) All touchpoints matter.

The Attitude of Your Posture

"Leadership starts before you get in the door," McCoy observed. "I am grateful for a remark that somebody once made to me a number of years ago. She said, 'You know, Tom, when you get out of your car and you walk across the parking lot, people are looking at you. They are looking at the attitude of your posture. They are looking at the pace of your step. They are looking at the countenance on your face. And so if you're walking across this parking lot and you're stressed and you're down, a lot of people are going to know. So you ought to think about that.' It was a very mature, constructive piece of advice. We don't realize or appreciate our influence on other people. How small things can make a difference. Language, bearings, attitudes, accountability—this stuff matters." McCoy is not paranoid. Quite the contrary, he is aware of how leaders communicate, even when they do not mean to do so.

Hopeful leaders communicate not only through their words but also through their actions, even those that may seem irrelevant, personal, or private. Although the paparazzi may not chase them down freeways, leaders, like Hollywood actors, live in glass houses and therefore must be mindful to their outlook "because," as McCoy put it, "their dreams are on the line." Leadership not only involves managing objectives, time, and money but also managing the aspirations of the people who follow you. McCoy continued, "The people who work here at AMD don't just have jobs; they have dreams, they have mortgages, they have things they want to do with their lives. Your people can sense your underlying attitude no matter what you do or say. Verbalize your expectations. People need to hear that you believe in them and want them to succeed. You must be a prophet of *their* success. You must be hopeful, and you must act on that hope. And so," he continued, "you communicate a vote, even in the parking lot, to the people who are looking to you for leadership. You are communicating in everything that you do. It is not easy to keep that frame of mind. This is one of the reasons why at times leadership is a lonely exercise. Because it is rare that you can visibly show your own fears, your own stresses, and also your own dream. Even dreams sometimes, if they are really ambitious, are hard to communicate because you have to find the opportunity for credibility. That all sums up for me, because like you, I am in the business of teaching and preaching about leadership. The greatest leaders understand their capability to change the environment and literally by force of will enable things to happen."

Return of the Jedi

At the end of our first meeting, as I was packing up my things and we began walking out of the boardroom, Tom looked at me and said, "Hey, I want to show you something." We walked to his office. Once inside, it became suddenly clear to me why he was so interested in this book and so passionate in our conversations. In McCoy's office hang two paintings. One is by the "artist of light," Thomas Kinkade. The other is a Kandinsky. The Kandinsky is colorful and abstract. In it, the artist portrays a brave warrior slaying a dragon. This needs no explanation. As I turned to look at the second painting, I experienced a *Brady Bunch*–like flashback transporting me to an earlier conversation we had had. In it, Tom observed, "Life is a storm. For most people in the world, there are more stormy days than there are days of clear sky. That is an easy thing to forget when you are enjoying the good life here in the good old USA. For many people, life is a sea of uncertainty, a constancy of fear—fear being the most powerful negative influence in the universe—and that is why people crave leadership. And that is why leaders really need to think about who they are and where they stand. Because people want to know who you are— who you are and where you are. Because you, as the leader, are the beacon of hope. You are the place where the harbor is. People want to steer in your direction but will do so only when they believe in you. They want to know that if they follow you, they are going to be OK.

You have to give them a way of thinking that enables them to make decisions when they don't know what to do. Your hope in the future breeds confidence among those who look to you for leadership."

The soundtrack in my mind then faded out as the paintings came back into focus. Kinkade's depicts a lighthouse in a foggy harbor, showing the way for distant ships. McCoy's wife gave it to him (behind every great man . . .). In fact, the painting inspired a pivotal speech that McCoy delivered at an AMD conference shortly after the terror attacks of September 11, 2001. He called the speech "Lighthouses of Leadership." At the time, AMD's stock price was sitting at $5 a share and morale was low. In the speech, McCoy spoke of values, of responsibility, and of hope. People continue to talk about McCoy's speech. It worked. As McCoy put it, referencing yet another David-and-Goliath tale, "We had a *Return of the Jedi* year. Needless to say, now the empire is striking back!" He laughs. There is no question that McCoy loves the competition. Before I left his office and while reflecting on the uncertainty of foggy harbors and distant ships, I asked, "What is the name of the Kinkade painting?" "Beacon of Hope," he replied. So why does AMD remain relevant in such a highly competitive industry? Leadership. There is a lighthouse at the White House. As a measure of McCoy's words, it is worthy of note that nearly a year passed between my first meeting with Tom McCoy and the publication of this book. In that time, AMD made a significant market share grab against its formidable foe (Intel) while simultaneously launching an ambitious initiative in cooperation with the United Nations and MIT to introduce a $100 laptop to help deliver on its mission to "make technology affordable to the world" and was recognized by the Environmental Protection Agency as one of the EPA's "green power partners." Hope works when you work in the pursuit of it.

One Heartbeat

Twenty minutes. That is all that separated Jack Cakebread from financial ruin. As Jack recalled, "I've come close to bankruptcy. I had my heart in my throat in 1978. This one guy said, 'I'll pay you for the wine in thirty days—$32,000.' It was every dime I had. Three years. He never paid me. At the time, I was also shooting photographs at pro football games—the NFL. I remember shooting the game, but I don't remember a thing about the game, nothing. I was so worried because I was going to have to come up here to the bank and tell them, 'I've lost my home, my business, I've lost everything because of this $32,000.' And so I'm driving up and thinking, 'It's all over. It's through. I'm forty-eight years old and I'm done.' And so I thought, 'I'd better stop by the post office and just check.' And so I did. As I was looking through the bills, there it was—$32,000. I was within twenty minutes of going out of business. My stomach churned for months after that. I thought to myself, 'Why did you ever let yourself get there?' I had faith in myself, but I was doing it all—too much. My philosophy now—and one that I share with everyone—is that this place has one heartbeat. Whether you are working in the vineyards or in the office, we are all in this together. That's how you grow a business and keep it going."

A firm believer in formal education, yet equally proud of his bootstrap success, Cakebread shared a story with me about his one heartbeat in action. As he recalled, "One of the students from Stanford who participated in Cakebread U. asked me once, 'In 1997, you had a big year—not only quality but quantity. It was a great year. But in 1999, you had a real short crop. What do you do then?' In fact, we were off 27 percent in 1999. I said to him, 'In '97 we had a good year. So you take that money, you put it in a coffee can, and you put it under your bed. And then in '98 and '99 when you need it, you take it out and you pay the bills with it.' The professor rolled his eyes and said, 'Geez, Jack!' He didn't like my response. But here I am." One heartbeat.

Shackleton's Games

Emotions are the key to survival, not just for humans but also for dogs. Professor Marc Bekoff at the University of Colorado studies dogs, specifically their smiles. According to Bekoff, dogs do in fact smile. They smile through play. And play is more than just fun. Play is joy and pleasure. Forms of play depend on how the species lives. Among carnivores, predatory play is aggressive. Dogs that live alone play with things. And if the dog has no one or nothing to play with, it will chase its tail. Just as we, when bored, scribble on paper and twiddle our thumbs, dogs find ways to play. Play is important. It makes dogs, and us, feel good. However, while play is fun, it is also a way in which animals learn to take on life's challenges. Play is an exercise in will-building. Although we'd like to think we are a more advanced species than dogs, if there is one thing we share in common it is play.

Games are will-builders. They exercise the mind and the spirit. They are why we are so drawn to competitive sport. It thrills us. Triumphant leaders, throughout history, have known this and therefore have used games to focus their teams, their organizations, and in some cases their crews. Among the most hopeful is explorer Sir Ernest Shackleton.

During his early twentieth-century expedition to Antarctica, games not only helped Shackleton focus the efforts of his crew and sustain their capacity to work but also ultimately helped him and his crew maintain the will to survive. Unfortunately, however, the dogs didn't make it. Shackleton and his crew ate them. The crew had no other choice. And the dogs had no other option.

Imagine for a moment that the year is 1914. The place is London, England. It is an unusually sunny Saturday afternoon. With your tea in hand and biscuits by your side, you open a local newspaper and find the following ad: "Men wanted for hazardous journey. Small wages. Bitter cold. Long months of complete darkness. Constant danger. Safe return doubtful. Honour and recognition in case of success. Signed: Ernest Shackleton." Shackleton allegedly placed this newspaper ad to solicit crew members for his 1914 Imperial Trans-Antarctic Expedition. Would you have responded, or would you like some more tea? I for one could use a spot of Earl Grey when you get a moment. Twenty-seven men signed on. The Trans-Antarctic Expedition is one of the greatest survival epics in the history of man. For Shackleton, the journey began long before he placed his brutally honest recruiting ad.

In 1901, Shackleton joined Robert F. Scott's Discovery expedition and six years later would return on his own. Within one hundred miles of the South Pole, skin-splitting frostbite and near starvation forced Shackleton to turn back. Norwegian Roald Amundsen conquered the South Pole in 1911, much to Shackleton's dismay. Shackleton's response was to raise the bar. Due to Shackleton's well-executed skill at marrying well—his wife, Emily, was loaded—he had the time and the money to plot another expedition. This one involved another unrealized goal: to be the first to cross the frozen continent on foot. Extreme sports are nothing new.

His ship set sail in August 1914 with Shackleton at the helm. While the world was focused on war, a three-hundred-ton Norwegian-built schooner named after Shackleton's family motto *Fortitudine vincimus*, "By endurance we conquer," headed down the River Thames. Four months and twelve thousand miles later, ice appeared. The *Endurance* spent the next six weeks smashing through a thousand miles of the frozen sea. By January 29, 1915, the ice had conquered the *Endurance*. However, it hadn't conquered Shackleton. Stuck in the ice yet still intact, Shackleton and his crew sat aboard their crippled ship a relatively short hundred miles from their destination. Imagine: stuck in and on the ice (sure to melt within months) thirteen thousand miles from home. As Alexander H. Macklin, one of the surgeons aboard the *Endurance*, wrote, "It was more than tantalizing, it was maddening."

In this moment, one of the greatest leadership stories of all time was about to be written. Realizing that his dream was no longer viable, Shackleton gathered his men together and announced a new plan: wintering. Mind you, spring was as long as nine months away. How would he maintain the will of his crew? How would he keep their faith in him and in each other? Simply, how would they survive? Among other things, Shackleton used games. Not just any games, but games designed to promote camaraderie, hope, and fortitude. From racing sled dogs to wagering cigarettes and chocolate on various challenges, including who could do the best impersonations, Shackleton continued to exercise the mind, body, and spirit of his crew. As Macklin wrote, "Shackleton displayed real greatness. He did not rage at all, or show outwardly the slightest sign of disappointment." And then, cracking sounds began.

The ship was giving way to the pressure of the frozen sea. Macklin's diary entry reads, "I do not think I have ever had such a horrible sickening sensation as I had whilst in the hold of that breaking ship." Shackleton's secondary strategy, wintering, had run its course. Therefore, like most triumphant leaders, Shackleton announced yet another new plan: ocean camp.

Using timbers from the splintering ship, the crew built a makeshift galley on the ice and filled it with food. As the men watched from their linen tents, nine months from the day the ice brought their journey to a standstill, on October 27, 1915, the *Endurance* sank. Insomnia visited Shackleton that evening. All night, he thought. And then morning came. As their leader, Shackleton knew that his men would be looking to him for yet another plan. The question on each of their minds at this point certainly must have been "Now what?"

The morning after three hundred tons of the finest Norwegian design fell into the sea, Shackleton approached his men and launched his fourth directive with the assurance, poise, and assumptive coolness of David Mamet's star salesman, Ricky Roma, saying, "Ship and stores have gone—so now we'll go home." Imagine. You are thirteen thousand miles from home. You've waited nine months for a spring thaw. Your ship has sunk. At this point, your boss looks at you and says, 'Let's go home.' Say nothing of walking! What would you do? If you were among Shackleton's crew, six months from this announcement, you would walk. And so they did.

On April 9, 1916, having fashioned lifeboats from the wreckage of the formerly magnificent *Endurance*, Shackleton and his crew began their pursuit of Elephant Island—the nearest landmass. After seven days, intense rainstorms, and one hundred miles, the men arrived, some barely alive. It is here that Shackleton and five volunteers took to the sea again, this time in the largest lifeboat, *James Caird*. On April 24, 1916, the smaller crew sailed in pursuit of South Georgia Island, 650 nautical miles to the north, while the other men remained on Elephant Island. Hurricane-force winds and twenty-foot waves accompanied their journey. Roland Huntford, Shackleton's biographer, described the *James Caird* as "a cockleshell that was like an insect swimming in a tidal wave."

Among the volunteers was navigator Frank Worsley. Had his sextant readings been wrong by a mere one degree, the *James Caird* would sail off course and be lost to the sea. With screws wedged in their boots for traction, the men reached South Georgia Island only to meet their next challenge. They were on the wrong side of the island. The whaling port was a twenty-two-mile glacial mountain hike away. So they walked. And walked. And walked. Thirty-six hours later, they arrived. For the time being, they were safe. Now, however, they must return to save the remaining crew still stranded on Elephant Island. Of this experience, Shackleton wrote, "If anything happens to me while those fellows are waiting for me, I shall feel like a murderer."

After three unsuccessful attempts, Shackleton reached Elephant Island on August 30, 1916, four months and six days after the *Caird* had left. With lifeboats as shelter, the twenty-two castaways on the island were singing songs to hold on to the last threads of hope and sanity. (Perhaps Mandela was familiar with Shackleton's journey.) After retrieving his remaining crew, among them the surgeon, Macklin wrote, "I stayed on deck to watch Elephant Island recede in the distance. . . . I would still see my Burberry [jacket] flapping in the breeze on the hillside—no doubt will flap there to the wonderment of gulls and penguins till one of our familiar [gales] blows it all to ribbons." No one died. Shackleton, through his intellect, emotion, and the use of games to exercise the will of his men, may not have attained his original objective, but, as *Time* put it, he "defined heroism."

Years later, the geologist on Shackleton's 1907 expedition, Raymond Priestley, reflected, "For swift and efficient travel, give me Amundsen; for scientific investigation, give me Scott; but when you are at your wits' end and all else fails, go down on your knees and pray for Shackleton."

Nirenberg's Stars of Discovery

As a kid, he loved to play in the Florida swamps. He was, and continues to be, endlessly curious. He is an intellectual journeyman finding glory in the journey of discovery as much as in the destination of
answers. Marshall Nirenberg shared this story with me about his fascination with tinkering and learning. "I remember, as a very young
child, sitting on the rug in the living room at my mother's feet. She
was reading. I was putting together an erector set. When I finished
building, I said with a great deal of excitement, 'Mom. Look what I've
made!' She responded, 'What is it, Marshall?' At which point I said,
'I don't know. What does it look like?' She looked at it and then at
me and said, 'Marshall, you have to begin with an idea of what you
are going to create and then build it—not the other way around.'"
However, what she didn't realize is that Marshall's mind works differently from most. Sure, answers matter, but it's the process of discovery and the search for insight that thrills him most.

Since the 1940s, Marshall Nirenberg has been an adept observer
of the environment. Like Charles Darwin on the HMS *Beagle* generations before him, while playing in the swamps as a kid, Nirenberg
meticulously tracked and documented his observations of insects,
birds, and plant life. He would continue this process of discovery for
the next sixty years (including his current fascination with fruit flies).
And then, in the spring of 1961, from his laboratory at the National
Institutes of Health in bustling Bethesda, Maryland, Nirenberg embarked on a process of discovery that would lead to one of the greatest achievements in modern science. And for it, in 1968, he would
win the Nobel Prize. A long way from his mother's rug and Florida's
swamps, Marshall cracked the genetic code.

Born April 10, 1927, in New York City, Marshall Nirenberg
spent his formative teenage years in Orlando, Florida, and then studied zoology and chemistry at the University of Florida in Gainesville.
He went on to earn a Ph.D. in biological chemistry from the University of Michigan in Ann Arbor in 1957. A fellowship with the

American Cancer Society drew him to the National Institutes of Health, where he joined the staff in 1960. At age seventy-nine, he still maintains a laboratory in the National Heart, Lung and Blood Institute. At present, Nirenberg is using advanced digital scanning technology to study the genetic development of neural networks in the brains of fruit fly embryos. As he said to me, "Although I had earned my Ph.D. working on carbohydrate transport through cell membranes, I switched into nucleic acids because that is where the action was." Imagine, working years to earn a degree in one field, only to switch to an entirely different field in which nearly all of your preparation and training is irrelevant. Nirenberg explained, "I wanted to work in a field that was really important and exciting. I wanted to play with the big boys—the best biochemists in the world. It was the hottest field in the world with really experienced biochemists with big labs and lots of people. I was working alone, all by myself—that's dangerous—but there I was, thinking, 'I don't know a thing about this. What chance do I have of being successful?' But I didn't think that for long. I thought if I didn't do it then, when would I do it? I went into science to have fun, to discover, to explore. I wanted to discover something new, something important."

It would take Nirenberg two years of training—on his own—to get up to speed. Imagine, as a newly minted Ph.D., making your life's discovery—not to mention one of the greatest contributions to modern science—within your first seven years in the profession. So much for experts! Moreover, once he had cracked the code, he looked for another swamp to explore. "Once we had deciphered the code, at that point, I felt a need to switch fields. It became too easy for me. Now I am in a field that is a morass, where there are few answers and a lot of questions—neurobiology. I love it." You can take a kid out of the swamps, but you can't take the swamps out of the kid.

Like all great discoveries before his, Nirenberg's cracking of the genetic code was met with mixed reviews. In December 1961, the *New York Times* wrote that "the science of biology has reached a new frontier leading to a revolution far greater in its potential significance than the atomic or hydrogen bomb." Other observers were not as enthusiastic. Arne Wilhelm Kaurin Tiselius, himself a Nobel laureate, had a different opinion: this knowledge, he proclaimed, could "lead to methods of tampering with life, of creating new diseases, of controlling minds, of influencing heredity, even perhaps in certain desired directions." However, knowing this to be the case, Nirenberg maintained his will. I also asked Nirenberg, as I asked Charles Schwab, why he still does what he does. He responded simply, "The thing I enjoy most is thinking." Thank God.

In the science of discovery, where failure is far more common than success, hope is required. As Nirenberg remarked, "Most experiments don't work. So as a scientist, you are always failing. However, when we discovered that messenger RNA is required for protein synthesis, it was like walking into a toy store." "However," I asked him, "before things started working, how did you maintain the will to continue?" Nirenberg responded, "I had a habit. I would come home each night, and after supper, I would read journals, open a notebook, and start thinking about problems at hand and possible experiments in the lab, and one thing would lead to another. As ideas came to me, I would [assign] stars, in a sort of self-evaluation of my own ideas. From my training and experience, I would give some ideas more stars than others. Some were terrible and some were mediocre, but some were so thrilling; I would get excited about them. When you think of something new and then think of the ramifications, it's incredible. I would jump up and run to my wife and share them. I wrote the ideas, in this field and in others, just as fast as they came to me, one after another. Before I knew it, I would have twenty pages of ideas. Ideas are cheap, you know. However, I would experiment with only a few. I continued to work through two technicians. I would write an experiment each night, and the next day we did it. What I regret, however, in retrospect, is that I stopped working with my own hands. That's not a good thing. You need to stay in touch." Like Schwab's American dream and Mother Teresa's drop in the ocean, Nirenberg's stars of discovery fueled his hope in the future and in himself. Triumph is rarely awarded on the first attempt. *Einmal ist keinmal,* the Germans say: once is never.

Deciphering Leadership

Nirenberg and I then turned to leadership. No longer is he alone in the lab. Nirenberg observed, "I look for three things in postdoctoral fellows—high energy, intelligence, and a positive outlook. I learned very early in my career that you can't be too critical of those who work for you—at least not consistently critical. I remember when I was a graduate student attending a University of Michigan biochemistry seminar. We would take turns reading selected papers. At the first seminar I had to give, I got very interested in it, and at the end of my presentation, I suggested what the next step should be to the work presented in the paper. Apparently, this was not such a good idea. Later, one of the professors told me that I shouldn't offer what to do next and that I should simply present the paper. I couldn't help it. After reading every paper, I always thought, 'What would the next step be?' Therefore, I am not too critical of my postdoctoral fellows." This is a man who is not only brilliant but also knows a thing or two about leadership. What he failed to mention during our conversation is that after working under his leadership, not one but two of his postdoctoral fellows have won the Nobel Prize. In addition to managing the omnipresent fear of failure that lives below the surface of most scientists' egos, Nirenberg welcomes competition. He claims it made him more diligent in his greatest discovery. Nirenberg's anecdotal account of competition is also supported scientifically.

Remember Brainball and the day that nothing mattered? In addition to having players compete, researchers also had them cooperate in order to examine which state of play—competition or cooperation—would create greater levels of stress. In a cooperative state, watching Brainball played cooperatively is like watching a tennis match where players never score a point. No one wins and no one loses. In Brainball, which scenario, competition or cooperation, do you think decreased players' stress levels? In a surprising discovery, using galvanic skin response (GSR) sensors, the researchers found that while playing the game actually reduced overall stress levels, it was competition, not cooperation, that lowered stress levels the most. In fact, not only did competition reduce stress for all players, but women actually found competition to be more fun! And so too did Nirenberg.

Conversations with God

At the end of our conversation, Nirenberg turned to a topic that I would have never expected. It seemed out of place—particularly coming from a man of science, a man who had spent the past seventy-nine years of his life trying to prove things, a man who, one would think, requires scientific evidence in order to believe *anything*. From the heart, mind, and soul of one of the world's living treasures came these words: "While I was working on deciphering the code and as I ran the experiments, it was like asking God, 'Is this what you meant? How about this?' And God would respond. If the experiment failed, it was as if he was saying, 'Not quite, Marshall.' So I would keep on. I realized, then, that not everyone has the opportunity to have conversations with God. I did." Stars, hearts, and lighthouses—look for symbols to develop, express, and communicate will. Like God, they are in everything. And then, as Wisdom advised Khalil Gibran in "The Visit of Wisdom": "Advance and never halt, for advancing is perfection. Advance and do not fear the thorns in the path, for they draw only corrupt blood."

No Damn Miracle

In closing, since I teach at Northwestern University, I would be remiss not to mention our year of hope—the year our Wildcats made the trip to the big house of college football, the Rose Bowl. Although many people thought it was a miracle, Northwestern credits applied hope. In fact, just as the 2005 White Sox adopted Journey's *Don't Stop Believin'*, the 1995 Wildcats adopted Frank Sinatra's *High Hopes* and sang it from camp to California.

In the first game of the season, the Wildcats played what was thought to be a warm-up game for Notre Dame's Fighting Irish—one of college football's most legendary winning schools versus one of its most famous losers. This is the stuff of legend, a Cinderella story. Before the game, Northwestern's coach, Gary Barnett, told his team, "When we win, don't carry me off the field. Act like you've been there before." He thus planted the seed that they could win, he believed in them, he believed in them so much that he had already began planning the victory celebration, and winning is nothing more than meeting expectations. In what is recognized as one of the biggest wins in Northwestern's history, the Cats beat the Irish, 17–15. In a storied season, the Wildcats continued upset after upset all the way to New Year's Day.

On January 1, 1996, fifty thousand fans poured into the Rose Bowl, including members of the Wildcats' 1949 Rose Bowl team. Southern Cal took an early lead and by halftime led 24–10. In the third quarter, the Wildcats scored the first four times they had the ball, and by the fourth quarter, the Wildcats led, 32–31. Although the Wildcats won the Big Ten that year, on this day and in this game, Southern Cal prevailed, 41–32. Considering that Northwestern hadn't posted a winning season in over two decades, this was a very triumphant year for the team, the school, and generations of Northwestern alumni. To underscore the point—that hope is not solely the domain of the miraculous—the Wildcats players, in the postseason, wore T-shirts that read THIS WAS NO DAMN MIRACLE! Applied hope was responsible for their success. Needless to say, when invited by Jay Leno to appear on *The Tonight Show*, what song do you suppose they sang?

That Constant Burr of Agitation

Remember that hope, as defined and used by the leaders you've met in this book, is as far from wishful thinking as you can get. Their hope involves believing deeply, seeing further, thinking conditionally, and acting willfully to make things happen. And as a leader, you cannot let hope reside with you alone. As Tom McCoy explained, "A leader's number one day-to-day responsibility is to communicate hope. If, as a leader, you do not feel hopeful, you are not cut out for the job of leadership. As a leader, you need to be looking for reasons to be hopeful even when circumstances would suggest otherwise. If you do not have that constant burr of agitation under your saddle encouraging you to search for a way out, a way around, and a way to succeed, those who look to you for leadership will know it immediately. And," Tom continued, "it is insufficient for you alone, as a leader, to be hopeful. Hope must manifest itself among the team in order to be effective. The team holds the dream."

The Courage to Believe

Choose hope. But also know that by opting to use the most sustainable form of human motivation, it is also the most challenging. Odd as it may seem, it takes courage to be hopeful. As Simon Peter advised, "Always be ready to give an explanation to anyone who asks you for a reason for your hope" (1 Peter 3:15). As Peter suggests, it is best to assume that as a hopeful person, you will forever be an oddity to others. Since they cannot see your hope, people need a reason to believe it. However, heed the words of William Blake: "When I tell the truth it is not for the sake of convincing those who do not know it, but for the sake of defending those who do." Don't waste your time on converting the fatalists. Seek out the hopeful, the willful, and the courageous. They already know the truth, but they need your leadership in order to win.

Moreover, while we recognize that there is always hope, we often forget about hope once we have accomplished what we had hoped to achieve. Like a professional football player's silent shout of "Hi, Mom" into the television cameras following a touchdown, hope, like Dad, is often forgotten in the trappings of success. In hope's place, we opt to credit hard work, intelligence, and often luck rather than the power of belief, imagination, and will. It's as if we are reluctant to give ourselves credit for the dream that gave rise to our will to work in pursuit of that dream. The irony of hope is that everyone loves a dreamer, but no one wants to be called one.

However, all outrageously successful people, at some point in their journey, were dismissed by doers as dreamers. However, the joke is on the doers. Because what the doers often overlook is that they are employed by a dreamer who found a way. Truth be told, in moments of uncertainty, we look to the *hopeful doer*—the problem solver, the creative one, the person who can find a way out. When it *really* matters, we turn to hopeful leaders like flowers reaching for the sun.

Hopeful leaders turn the unbelievable into the expected. As the late movie critic Gene Siskel, a die-hard Chicago Bulls fan, once said of Michael Jordan's supreme talent (or words to this effect), "People keep saying how *unbelievable* he is. You'd think after they have seen him do so many unbelievable things season after season, game after game, and shot after shot, they'd begin to believe." When the ball was in Jordan's hands, saving the game at the buzzer was not only believable but expected.

Becoming More Human

I have learned a great deal during the two years of writing this book—not the least of which is humility. I am deeply indebted to the leaders who have inspired the pages of this book—mostly for their generosity, but selfishly for their hope not only in themselves and in those around them but also in this project and in me. If you take nothing else away from this book, be vulnerable to possibility—let down your guard—and have the courage to believe in the power of hope. As a fellow Chicagoan commented while reflecting on the age in which we live today, Studs Terkel observed, "Now we're vulnerable. But now maybe we're more human."

Learning to See with Your Heart

To be human is to hope. To hope is to see with your heart. And to lead in the face of uncertainty is to have the courage to act on your seeing heart—to create the future rather than waiting for it to come to you. In these definitive moments of leadership, be awake to possibility; when in doubt, go inside for guidance and leave the screen door open for sustenance; when it is said by those who have tried and failed that it can't be done and by those who have feared to listen that it will never work, learn to believe; and when you ultimately, finally, and with every ounce of your being make your decision and place your bet on a future so abundant in promise that you can taste it, choose hope, rise, stand up tall on the shoulders of the giants who have come before you; throw off the bowlines; unleash the hounds; step off the curb; and shine.

Epilogue

I have a confession to make. When I first contemplated the idea of a leader's hope as a competitive advantage and voiced the concept to others, I was met with a few quizzical looks. This didn't really surprise me; I wasn't entirely sure of the thing myself. After all, I had painstakingly convinced myself that my success was exclusively the result of hard work and lucky breaks. Finding room for hope would require a little psychological redecorating. However, soon after I realized that taking on hope was a nearly impossible task, I moved forward. After all, isn't that the purpose of hope—to help us walk in the direction of the future even though it may be uncomfortable? Albert Einstein may have said it best, "If at first the idea is not absurd, then there is no hope for it." Who can argue with Albert? Therefore, I bridled my skepticism by funding my optimism.

Adding to my intrigue was a sense of professional responsibility. If I were to claim expertise in anything—which I aspire never to do—it is *newness*: new products, new services, and new ways of doing business. Since it is my responsibility to help organizations create things that do not exist, hope has always lingered in my thoughts, for at its core, strategic innovation is the business of the impossible—what is impossible to believe, to create, to save, to fix, to solve, to achieve. And since the impossibility business contains supersized portions of ambiguity, creativity, measured risk taking, and an omnipresent fear of failure, over time I have developed a keen interest in the facility of the human mind and the capacity of the human spirit to achieve the impossible. As I've learned, "impossible" is a highly subjective concept. To some people, it represents the absolutely unattainable; to less pessimistic others, it means probabilistically unachievable; yet to a few triumphant souls, as Art Berg noted, "The impossible just takes a little longer."

Therefore, I suppose you could say that I was destined to write about hope. Without hope, we never move beyond the past and into the future and ideas never move beyond the silly and into the realm of the sensible. As Herman Melville suggested, "It is not down on any map; true places never are." I decided to give hope a chance. I had hope for hope and therefore wrote this book. And am I glad I did. Like Geoffrey Canada's grandmother, I believe now "more than ever." And I trust that you do too. However, this book leaves a question unanswered, a question as mysterious, as unexplored, and as relevant to leadership as hope. It is a question that I am currently seeking to answer. Stay tuned.

Notes

Chapter One

Aristotle is quoted in James Golden, Goodwin Berquist, William Coleman, and J. Michael Sproule (eds.), *A Rhetoric of Western Thought*, 8th ed. (Dubuque, Iowa: Kendall/Hunt, 2003), p. 74.

Henry Gannett's words are from David Zaslowsky and T. H. Waktins, *These American Lands* (Washington, D.C.: Island Press, 1994), p. 287. Gannett was a surveyor of the Wyoming Territory in the 1870s and director of the U.S. Geological Survey. He is also noted for his expeditionary travels with John Muir. "The Alaska coast is to become the showplace of the earth," he predicted in an essay in a 1901 issue of *National Geographic*. He concluded his essay with the quote about waiting until you are old to visit Alaska.

Bertrand Russell wrote *New Hopes for a Changing World* (New York: Simon & Schuster) in 1951; the quote is from pp. 10–11.

Details regarding the 7-Tesla MRI are from Pamela McDonnell, "NYU School of Medicine Attracts a Powerful MRI Machine," New York University Medical Center and School of Medicine, Oct. 7, 2003 [http://www.eurekalert.org/pub_releases/2003-10/nyum-nyu100703.php].

Chapter Two

Charlie Chaplin's line is from the movie *The Great Dictator* (1940), in which he portrayed Adenoid Hynkel, dictator of Tomania.

Robert van Weperen is quoted on page 2 of the article "Artefacts as Research," by Sarah Ilstedt Hjelm, of the Interactive Institute, the makers of Brainball [http://smart.tii.se/smart/publications/pubs/ArtefactsAsResearch.pdf].

For information on the Snowdon, Danner, and Friesen study, see Deborah Snowdon, *Aging with Grace: What the Nun Study Teaches Us About Leading Longer, Healthier, and More Meaningful Lives* (New York: Bantam, 2002).

William Buchholz's observation is from "The Medical Uses of Hope," *Western Journal of Medicine*, 1988, *148*, 69.

Details of Dr. Maruta's study can be found in Toshihiko Maruta, R. C. Colligan, M. Malinchoc, and Kenneth P. Offord, "Optimists vs. Pessimists: Survival Rates Among Medical Patients over a 30-Year Period," *Mayo Clinic Proceedings*, 2000, *75*, 140–143.

Information on C. Richard Snyder's study is derived from "Hope Is an Important Key to Student Success," a University of Kansas Office of University Relations press release in connection with publication of Snyder's book, *The Psychology of Hope*, Mar. 16, 1999 [http://www.ur.ku.edu/News/99N/MarNews/Mar16/hope.html].

The effect of hopeful managers on subordinates is explored in Suzanne J. Peterson and Fred Luthans, "Does the Manager's Level of Hope Matter? Preliminary Research Evidence of a Positive Impact," [http://64.233.187.104/search?q=cache:eaIbqSDFmEAJ:cobacourses.creighton.edu/MAM/2002/papers/Peterson.doc+%22Manager%27s+Level+of+Hope%22&hl=en].

Thomas Edison is quoted in Charles R. Swindoll, *Hand Me Another Brick* (Chicago: Nelson, 1978), p. 83.

Harry Emerson Fosdick, of the Union Theological Seminary, preached the sermon "Procrastination" at the First Presbyterian Church in New York City around the year 1925.

The history of Outward Bound is recounted at the organization's Web site [http://www.outwardbound.org].

The story of Walt Disney and the creation of Mickey Mouse is from "Mickey Mouse Hits a Milestone: Disney Symbol Turns 75," CNN.com, Nov. 18, 2003 [http://www.cnn.com/2003/SHOWBIZ/Movies/11/18/mickeyat75.ap].

Adolph Ochs's management during the Great Depression is recounted in Susan E. Tifft and Alex S. Jones, *The Trust: The Private and Powerful Family Behind the* New York Times (New York: Back Bay Books, 2000).

Details regarding Muhammad Yunus and the Grameen Bank are from the bank's Web site [http://www.grameen-info.org].

Chapter Three

Barack Obama's words are from his keynote speech, "The Audacity of Hope," delivered at the 2004 Democratic National Convention in Boston on July 27, 2004.

The information on job loyalty is based on Bureau of Labor Statistics, "Employee Tenure in 2004," Sept. 21, 2004 [http://www.bls.gov/news.release/tenure.nr0.html]. On why people leave their jobs, see Leigh Branham, *The 7 Hidden Reasons Employees Leave: How to Read the Subtle Signs and Act Before It's Too Late* (AMACOM, 2005), and Keeping the People, "Q&A with the Author, *The 7 Hidden Reasons Employees Leave*," *Keeping the People Report*, Mar. 2005 [http://www.keepingthepeople.com/newsletter/vol-03-winter-2005.html].

The statistics on workplace fatalities can be found in Bureau of Labor Statistics, "Census of Fatal Occupational Injuries, 2004" [http://www.bls.gov/iif/oshwc/

cfoi/cfch0003.pdf]; those on the Walker Information National Employee Bench-marking Study were reported by Fisher Vista, "Statistics" [http://www.fishervista.com/statistics.htm]. The rise in the risk of heart attack on Mondays was documented in a *British Medical Journal* study cited in Cable News Network, "Monday Morning Bad for Your Health," Feb. 3, 2005 [http://edition.cnn.com/2005/BUSINESS/02/03/monday.pressure].

The details on average CEO tenure and on market reaction to new corporate leadership are from Matt Krantz, "Ousting CEOs Often Boosts Stock Price," *USA Today Online*, Feb. 10, 2005 [http://www.usatoday.com/money/companies/management/2005-02-10-departing-ceos-usat_x.html], which is also the source of the quote by Leslie Gaines-Ross.

Steve Zika was kind enough to share Advanced Micro Devices' "in-house mantra" with me.

Ulrich Kraft told the story of Jancy Chang in "Unleashing Creativity," *Scientific American Mind*, Apr. 2005, pp. 16–24. Steven Smith is quoted on page 18 of that article. The Air Force fighter pilot study and the Guilford study on thinking are discussed on pages 19–20.

Chapter Four

Vaclav Havel's words are from Vaclav Havel and Karel Hvizdala, *Disturbing the Peace*, trans. Paul Wilson (New York: Knopf, 1990), pp. 181–182.

The study "Self-Fulfilling Prophecies: The Synergistic Accumulative Effect of Parents' Beliefs on Children's Drinking Behavior," by Stephanie Madon, Max Guyll, Richard Spoth, and Jennifer Willard, appeared in the Dec. 2004 issue of *Psychological Science* and is discussed in the article "Two Self-Fulfilling Prophecies Are Stronger, and More Harmful, Than One." Medical News Today, Jan. 4, 2005 [http://www.medicalnewstoday.com/medicalnews.php?newsid=18577].

Dr. Nawang Rabgyal has recently been transferred from his position as the director of the Office of Tibet in Exile in New York to a new role as "additional secretary" in the Department of Information and International Relations at the Central Tibetan Administration in Dharamsala, India.

Information on the White Sox and Ozzie Guillen is from John Shea, "Managing Spotlight: Chicago's Guillen Keeping Things Loose and Fun," *San Francisco Chronicle*, Oct. 25, 2005, p. C1 [http://sfgate.com/cgi-bin/article.cgi?f=/c/a/2005/10/25/SPGL2FDK0O1.DTL].

Regarding the popularity of Dante's books, at the time of this writing, his *Inferno* ranked number 19,841 in sales on Amazon.com, *Purgatory* ranked number 165,917, and *Paradiso* ranked number 235,442.

Chapter Five

Thomas Patterson's observations are from "Why Is News So Negative These Days?" History News Network, Dec. 2, 2002 [http://hnn.us/articles/1134.html], one of a series of articles based on his book *The Vanishing Voter* (New York: Knopf, 2002).

Peter Jennings's quote is from "The Bad News Campaign," *Media Monitor*, Mar.-Apr. 1996, pp. 3–6.

Amos Tversky and Daniel Kahneman published their research results in "Judgment Under Uncertainty: Heuristics and Biases," *Science*, 1974, *185*, 1124–1131.

Anthony Reading's observations are from *Hope and Despair: How Perceptions of the Future Shape Human Behavior* (Baltimore: Johns Hopkins University Press, 2004), p. xii.

Barbara L. Fredrickson sets forth the reasons why negativity trumps positivity in "The Value of Positive Emotions," *American Scientist*, 2003, *91*, 330–335.

Robert Schrauf is quoted in an article by Lee Dye, "Why Do Humans Have More Words to Describe the Negative?" Feb. 2, 2005 [http://abcnews.go.com/Technology/DyeHard/story?id=460987&page=1].

Robert B. Zajonc published his research findings in "Attitudinal Effects of Mere Exposure," *Journal of Personality and Social Psychology Monograph*, 1968, *9*, 1–27. The quotation is from page 2.

Pablo Picasso purportedly made his remarks in a conversation with his artist-lover Françoise Gilot in 1946.

The photographs of Duchenne de Boulogne's experiment are from *The Mechanism of Human Facial Expression* (Paris: Renard, 1862).

Steven Johnson's book *Mind Wide Open: Your Brain and the Neuroscience of Everyday Life* (New York: Scribner) was published in 2004.

The excerpt about Lewis and Clark is from Randy J. Larsen, "Emotion and Cognition: The Case of Automatic Vigilance," *American Psychological Association Online*, Nov. 2004 [http://www.apa.org/science/psa/sb-larsen.html].

The report by the neuroscientists invited to Dharamsala by the Dalai Lama was published by Antoine Lutz, Lawrence L. Greischar, Nancy B. Rawlings, Matthieu Ricard, and Richard J. Davidson under the title "Long-Term Meditators Self-Induce High-Amplitude Gamma Synchrony During Mental Practice," *Proceedings of the National Academy of Sciences*, 2004, *101*, 16369–16373 [http://www.pnas.org/cgi/content/full/101/46/16369].

Sharon Begley's comment is from "Scans of Monks' Brains Show Meditation Alters Structure, Functioning," *Wall Street Journal*, Nov. 5, 2004, p. B1.

Chapter Six

Milan Kundera's words are from *Ignorance: A Novel*, trans. Linda Asher (New York: HarperCollins, 2002); the epigraph is from page 12, the later quote from page 13.

Elizabeth Barrett Browning's famous lines are from *Sonnets from the Portuguese*, published in 1850.

Peter Schweizer's comments are from "Ronald Reagan's One Big Thing," *Hoover Digest*, Fall 2002 [http://www.hooverdigest.org/024/schweizer.html].

Vaclav Havel made his "calm as a morgue" comment in a letter to Dr. Gustáv Husák dated Apr. 8, 1975.

The mandate against jazz is reprinted from Josef Skvorecky, *Talkin' Moscow Blues*, ed. Sam Solecki Lester and Orpen Dennys (Hopewell, N.J.: Ecco Press, 1990), pp. 86–97. Skvorecky explains, "I read them, gnashing my teeth, in Czech translation in the film weekly *Filmovy Kuryr*, and fifteen years later I paraphrased them—faithfully, I am sure, since they had engraved themselves deeply on my mind—in a short essay titled 'I Won't Take Back One Word.'"

Chapter Seven

Charles Lutwidge Dodgson, using the pen name Lewis Carroll, wrote *Through the Looking Glass* in 1872.

Christopher Columbus's character spoke these words in the film *1492: Conquest of Paradise*, written by Roselyne Bosch, directed by Ridley Scott, and released by Touchstone Pictures in 1992.

The Aristotle quotes are from "Aristotle's Golden Mean of Midlife," a column by Mike Bellah posted on his Best Years Web site [http://www.bestyears.com/aristotlemean.html].

Karel Hvizdala published *Disturbing the Peace* as a book-length interview with Vaclav Havel. The quotation is from the English edition, translated by Paul Wilson (New York: Knopf, 1990). As described in the preface of the book, when Karel Hvizdala first proposed the idea of a book-length interview to Vaclav Havel in 1985, Hvizdala was living in West Germany, Havel in Prague, and neither of them could visit the other. Havel liked the idea because it would give him a chance to reflect on his life as he approached fifty; he accepted. They worked on the book over the next year, communicating by underground mail. According to Hvizdala, the first approach, in which Havel sent written responses to the questions, did not satisfy either of them: the answers were too much like essays. So Hvizdala sent Havel a batch of about fifty questions, and between Christmas and the New Year, Havel shut himself in a borrowed flat and came out with eleven hours of recorded answers. Hvizdala transcribed and edited them and then sent the manuscript back to Havel with some supplementary questions ("for drama," Hvizdala says). Havel prepared a final version with some new material in it, completing it in early June 1986.

Jim Stockdale's observations are from a conversation with Jim Collins, recounted in Collins's book *Good to Great* (New York: HarperBusiness, 2001), pp. 83–86.

The *Princeton Review* named DePaul University students the happiest in the nation in 2003. The statistics on smiling and laughter are from "As I See It: Keep Laughing," by Victor Rozek, citing work reported by Bill Strubbe writing in *Body Sense* [http://www.itjungle.com/tfh/tfh110804-story04.html].

The work of social scientists David G. Myers and Robert E. Lane was reported by Barry Schwartz in "The Tyranny of Choice," *Scientific American*, Apr. 2004, pp. 70–75.

Bobby McFerrin wrote the maddeningly catchy "Don't Worry, Be Happy," one of the big hits of 1989.

In the World Health Organization's 2001 World Health Report, *Mental Health: New Understanding, New Hope*, the WHO found that unipolor depressive disorders are the single largest cause of disability in the world (11.9 percent), followed by adult-onset hearing loss (4.6 percent) and iron-deficiency anemia (4.5 percent) [http://www.nimh.nih.gov/outreach/Roundtable2003message.pdf].

Winston Churchill made his remark about buildings in a speech to the House of Commons (meeting in the House of Lords) on Oct. 28, 1943. He was speaking in favor of reconstruction of the House of Commons, which had been destroyed by wartime bombing in 1941.

Information about brainwashing is based on Jeff Stryker, "How Brainwashing Came to Life and Thrived," *San Francisco Chronicle*, Aug. 1, 2004, p. E1 [http://www.sfgate.com/cgi-bin/article.cgi?f=/c/a/2004/08/01/INGRR7UIJ31.DTL&hw=How+Brainwashing+Came&sn=001&sc=1000].

The quotation from William J. Byron's *Answers from Within: Spiritual Guidelines for Managing Setbacks in Work and Life* (New York: Macmillan Spectrum, 1998) is from page 261.

Part Two

Geoffrey Canada's remarks are from a personal conversation on May 9, 2005.

Chapter Eight

John Perry Barlow's words are from his eulogy for Cynthia Horner, delivered at the Brechin Church, Nanaimo, British Columbia, Apr. 22, 1994.

Phil Mickelson's story is from his personal Web site [http://www.philmickelson.com/facts/bio.php]. The Peter Kessler anecdote and the extract following it are from Chris Lewis's article "How Mickelson Rescued a Sport: An Omnipotent Woods Would've Drained Golf of Drama," which appeared in the online issue of

Sports Illustrated dated Aug. 17, 2005 [http://sportsillustrated.cnn.com/2005/writers/chris_lewis/08/17/inside.golf/index.html].

The statements about Thomas Paine are based on John A. Schutz, "Common Sense," The American Revolution Home Page, n.d. [http://www.americanrevwar.homestead.com/files/OTHER.HTM].

Chapter Nine

Carl Sagan is quoted in Judson Polling, *Do Science and the Bible Conflict?* (Grand Rapids, Mich.: Zondervan, 2003), p. 21.

The Illinois lotto advertising campaign, including the slogan "Somebody's gonna lotto; it might as well be you!" was created by the Bayer Bess Vanderwarker advertising agency.

Information on the experiments conducted by Solomon Asch and by Gregory Berns is based on Sandra Blakeslee, "What Other People Say May Change What You See," *New York Times,* June 25, 2005, p. F3.

The list of people with dyslexia is from Davis Dyslexia Association International, "Famous People with the Gift of Dyslexia," Oct. 11, 2005 [http://www.dyslexia.com/qafame.htm].

The discussion of W. Edwards Deming's theory is based on information gleaned from the W. Edwards Deming Institute Web site [http://www.deming.org] and from Mary Walton's book *The Deming Management Method* (New York: Perigee, 1986).

The *Wine and Spirits* 2005 poll results can be consulted online at the Cakebread Web site [http://www.cakebread.com/articles/Wine&Spirits_05.pdf].

Chapter Ten

Branch Rickey's speech to the Executives Club of Chicago is reprinted in William Safire, *Lend Me Your Ears: Great Speeches in History* (New York: Norton, 2004). The epigraph at the start of the chapter is from that speech.

Information on Ty Cobb and the quote by Grantland Rice are from The Baseball Page.com, "Ty Cobb," Oct. 26, 2005 [http://www.thebaseballpage.com/past/pp/cobbty]. Details on the career of Jackie Robinson are from Jean West, "Branch Rickey and Jackie Robinson: Interview Essay," The History of Jim Crow [http://www.jimcrowhistory.org/resources/lessonplans/hs_in_robinson_rickey.html].

Antoine de Saint-Exupéry's words are from *Wind, Sand, and Stars* (Orlando, Fla.: Harcourt, 1992), p. 215. The book was originally published in 1939.

Chapter Eleven

Steve Jobs's observations cited throughout this chapter are from the commencement speech he gave at Stanford University on June 12, 2005. The full text can be read at http://news-service.stanford.edu/news/2005/june15/jobs-061505.html.

The words of Tully Mars are from Jimmy Buffett's novel *A Salty Piece of Land* (New York: Little, Brown, 2004), p. 3.

Paul Tough's comment is from page 3 of his article "The Harlem Project," which appeared in the *New York Times Magazine* on June 20, 2004. The David Saltzman quote is from page 4.

Martin Luther King Jr.'s words are from his famous "I Have a Dream" speech, delivered on the steps of the Lincoln Memorial in Washington, D.C., during the March on Washington, Aug. 28, 1963.

Geoff Canada's poem "Take a Stand," reprinted here in its entirety with the kind permission of its author, was written Feb. 14, 1996.

Nancy Wexler's observations on the "sandwich generation" are examined in Terri M. Tallman and Patricia H. Holmes, "Caregiver Burnout," Senior Series, Ohio State University Extension, Apr. 1998 [http://ohioline.osu.edu/ss-fact/0145 .html].

Albert Einstein's quip explaining relativity is from *And I Quote: The Definitive Collection of Quotes, Sayings, and Jokes for the Contemporary Speechmaker,* by Ashton Applewhite, William Evans, and Andrew Frothingham (New York: St. Martin's Press, 2003), p. 40.

Chapter Twelve

Katharine Graham's quote is from her autobiography, *Personal History* (New York: Knopf, 1997), p. 341.

Kurt Lewin introduced his ideas about conflict in *A Dynamic Theory of Personality* (New York: McGraw-Hill, 1935).

Chapter Thirteen

Robert Schmidt's observation is from "Why Write About Superheroes?" posted at the Web site of *Blue Corn Comics* on Aug. 23, 2001 [http://www.blue corncomics.com/whyhero.htm].

The Washington College Prize and poll was conducted Feb. 7–10, 2005, by Washington College's C. V. Starr Center for the Study of the American Experience; the results are posted at http://starrcenter.washcoll.edu/poll.

Jimmy Buffett's lyrics are from "He Went to Paris," from the album *A White Sport Coat and a Pink Crustacean,* copyright © 1973 by Jimmy Buffett, and "Margaritaville," from the album *Changes in Latitudes, Changes in Attitudes,* copyright © 1977 by Jimmy Buffett. Reprinted with permission.

John Steinbeck's short novel *Of Mice and Men*, originally published in 1937, was reissued by Penguin Books in 1993.

The source of David Ogilvy's quote is an interesting story in itself. Each new office manager hired by his advertising agency, Ogilvy & Mather, was given a set of Russian nesting dolls; inside the smallest of the dolls was a slip of paper with the famous quote on it. Ogilvy himself tells the story in *Ogilvy on Advertising* (New York: Crown Books, 1983), p. 41.

Mother Teresa's widely quoted comment is from "Carriers of Christ's Love," in *A Gift for God: Prayers and Meditations* (New York: HarperCollins, 1996), p. 40. The essay was originally published in 1975.

Frank Luntz's work on the "death tax" was reported by the Public Broadcasting System in a *Frontline* special titled "The Persuaders." A transcript of the interview with Luntz, conducted Dec. 15, 2003, was posted at the PBS Web site on Nov. 9, 2004 [http://www.pbs.org/wgbh/pages/frontline/shows/persuaders/interviews/luntz.html].

In *Wealth and Our Commonwealth: Why America Should Tax Accumulated Fortunes* (Boston: Beacon Press, 2004), William H. Gates and Chuck Collins credit Jim Martin, president of the 60 Plus Association, with renaming the estate tax the "death tax."

Forbes' study of the most expensive ZIP codes was conducted by DataQuick Information Systems of La Jolla, Calif. The average home price in Tiburon was $1.01 million as of Sept. 6, 2003 [http://moneycentral.msn.com/content/invest/forbes/P62020.asp].

Pablo Casals's comment on life's meaning is from Sir John Templeton's *Wisdom from World Religions* (West Conshohocken, Pa.: Templeton Foundation Press, 2002), p. 164. Nixon's instruction to his speechwriters is from William Saffire, *Lend Me Your Ears: Great Speeches in History* (New York: Norton, 1997), p. 23. Martin Luther King Jr.'s "I Have a Dream" speech was delivered on the steps of the Lincoln Memorial in Washington, D.C., during the march on Washington, Aug. 28, 1963.

Chapter Fourteen

George Herbert's words are attributed to him by Beverly Elaine Eanes in *Joy: The Dancing Spirit of Love Surrounding You* (Mahwah, N.J.: Paulist Press, 1995), p. 20.

Laura E. Berk published "Why Children Talk to Themselves" in the Nov. 1994 issue of *Scientific American*, pp. 77–83. Her work with low-income children was reported in Laura E. Berk and Ruth A. Garvin, "Development of Private Speech Among Low-Income Appalachian Children," *Developmental Psychology*, 1984, *20*, 271–286. Her studies with ADHD and learning-disabled children were published as Laura E. Berk and M. K. Potts, "Development and Functional Significance of Private Speech Among Attention-Deficit Hyperactivity Disordered and Normal Boys," *Journal of Abnormal Child Psychology*, 1991, *19*, 357–377, and Laura E. Berk and S. Landau, "Private Speech of Learning Disabled and Normally Achieving Children in Classroom Academic and Laboratory Contexts," *Child Development*, 1993, *64*, 556–571.

Lev S. Vygotsky's statement is from *Mind in Society: The Development of Higher Psychological Processes* (Cambridge, Mass.: Harvard University Press, 1978), p. 24.

Michael Mahoney's gymnasts study is documented in Michael J. Mahoney and Marshall Avener, "Psychology of the Elite Athlete: An Exploratory Study," *Cognitive Therapy and Research*, 1977, *1*, 135–141.

Caddyshack was released by Warner Bros. in 1980.

Vincent Canby's obituary ran under the heading "Bob Hope, Comedic Master and Entertainer of Troops, Dies at 100" in the *New York Times*, July 29, 2003. Curiously, Canby himself had died in 2000 but had already prepared his obituary for Hope.

Discussion of the yips and the Mayo Clinic study of the phenomenon is based on Geoff Magnum, "The Neuropsychology of Golf Putting," Putting Zone, Nov. 2002 [http://www.puttingzone.com/Dystonia/yipsstudy.html].

The statistic on agoraphobia in the U.S. population is from National Institute of Mental Health, "The Numbers Count," NIH Publication 06-4584, Feb. 3, 2006 [http://www.nimh.nih.gov/publicat/numbers.cfm].

Chapter Fifteen

Pink Floyd's lyrics are from "Shine On You Crazy Diamond (Part I–V)," copyright © 1977 by Pink Floyd. Reprinted with permission.

The story of Frank Meshberger and Michelangelo's *Creation of Adam* is based on Frank Lynn Meshberger, "The Interpretation of Michelangelo's *Creation of Adam* Basilar Neuroanatomy," *Journal of the American Medical Association*, 1990, *264*, 1837–1841, and on British Broadcasting Corporation, "The Mystery of Michelangelo's *Creation of Adam*," Feb. 14, 2002 [http://www.bbc.co.uk/dna/h2g2/A681680].

The quote from Giorgio Vasari's *Lives of the Artists* (New York: Penguin, 1991), translated by George Bull, is from pages 332–333 of volume 1.

Nelson Mandela's words are from his autobiography, *Long Walk to Freedom* (Boston: Back Bay Books, 1995), pp. 390 and 419.

The story of the *Endurance* and of British polar explorer Sir Ernest Shackleton is based on Second Story, "The *Endurance*" [http://www.kodak.com/US/en/corp/features/endurance/home/index.shtml] and on Alfred Lansing, *Endurance: Shackleton's Incredible Voyage* (New York: Carroll & Graff, 1959).

The *New York Times*' comment on Nirenberg's work was reported in National Institutes of Health, "Papers of Nobel Scientist Marshall Nirenberg Added to 'Profiles in Science,'" May 2001 [http://www.nih.gov/news/pr/may2001/nlm15

.html]. Arne Tiselius's take is from "The Marshall W. Nirenberg Papers: Public Reactions to the Genetic Code, 1961–1968," at the U.S. National Library of Medicine at the National Institutes of Health [http://profiles.nlm.nih.gov/JJ/Views/Exhibit/narrative/publicreaction.html].

Kahlil Gibran's words are from *The Vision: Reflections on the Way of the Soul*, trans. Juan R. I. Cole (New York: Penguin, 1998), p. 41.

Details of the Northwestern Wildcats' 1995 football season are from the article "On This Day in 1995 . . . ," written by Louie Vaccher for *WildcatReport*, Sept. 2, 2005 [http://northwestern.rivals.com/content.asp?CID=450038].

William Blake's quote on the purpose of truth is from a footnote in his book *Milton, a Poem: The Illuminated Books of William Blake* (Princeton, N.J.: Princeton University Press, 1993), p. 224.

Studs Terkel made his comments at his ninetieth birthday celebration on May 16, 2002; see Chicago Historical Society, "Studs Terkel's 90th Birthday," 2002 [http://www.studsterkel.org/bday.php].

Epilogue

Art Berg titled his award-winning final book *The Impossible Just Takes a Little Longer: Living with Purpose and Passion* (New York: Morrow, 2002).

The Melville quote is from *Moby Dick* (New York: Oxford University Press, 1988), p. 49. The novel was first published in 1851.

Further Reading

The works listed here inspired my thinking for this book. You may find them of interest as well.

A&E Television Networks. *Ellis Island*. Produced by Greystone Communications, Inc., for the History Channel, 1997.

Baylis, Trevor. *Clock This: My Life as an Inventor*. London: Headline, 1999.

Cawthon, David. *Philosophical Foundations of Leadership*. New Brunswick, N.J.: Transaction, 2002.

Cousins, Norman. *Head First: The Biology of Hope and the Healing Power of the Human Spirit*. New York: Penguin, 1989.

Cox, Richard. *Sport Psychology: Concepts and Applications*, 5th ed. New York: McGraw-Hill, 2002.

Curry, Lewis, C. R. Snyder, David Cook, Brent Ruby, and Michael Rehm. "Role of Hope in Academic and Sport Achievement." *Journal of Personality and Social Psychology*, 1997, 73, 1257–1267.

Dingfelder, Sadie. "Creativity on the Clock" *Monitor on Psychology*, 2003, 34(10), 56.

Follett, Ken. *On Wings of Eagles*. New York: Signet, 1983.

Fredrickson, Barbara. "The Value of Positive Emotions." *American Scientist*, 2003, 91, 330–335.

George, Jennifer, and Jing Zhou. "Understanding When Bad Moods Foster Creativity and Good Ones Don't: The Role of Context and Clarity of Feelings." *Journal of Applied Psychology*, 2002, 87, 687–697.

Goleman, Daniel, Richard Boyatzis, and Annie McKee. "Primal Leadership: The Hidden Driver of Great Performance." *Harvard Business Review*, Dec. 2001, pp. 42–51.

Groopman, Jerome. *The Anatomy of Hope: How People Prevail in the Face of Illness*. New York: Random House, 2004.

Gross, Daniel. *Forbes' Greatest Business Stories of All Time*. Hoboken, N.J.: Wiley, 1996.

Havel, Vaclav, and Karel Hvizdala. *Disturbing the Peace*, trans. Paul Wilson. New York: Knopf, 1990.

Hellman, Hal. *Great Feuds in Medicine: Ten of the Liveliest Disputes Ever.* Hoboken, N.J.: Wiley, 2001.

Hitt, William. *Thoughts on Leadership.* Columbus, Ohio: Battelle Press, 1992.

Hubbard, Elbert. *A Message to Garcia.* South Melbourne, Australia: Lothian Books, 1997. Originally published 1899.

Kanter, Rosabeth Moss. *Confidence: How Winning and Losing Streaks Begin and End.* New York: Crown Business, 2004.

Klein, Amy. "Hope, If Not Optimism." *Reconstruction Today,* Autumn 2004.

Koestenbaum, Peter. *Leadership: The Inner Side of Greatness.* San Francisco: Jossey-Bass, 1991.

Linenger, Jerry. *Off the Planet: Surviving Five Perilous Months Aboard the Space Station Mir.* New York: McGraw-Hill, 2000.

Loeb, Paul Rogat. *The Impossible Will Take a Little While: A Citizen's Guide to Hope in a Time of Fear.* New York: Basic Books, 2004.

Luthans, Fred, and Susan M. Jensen. "Hope: A New Positive Strength for Human Resource Development." *Human Resource Development Review,* 2002, *1,* 304–322.

Mipham, Sakyong. *Turning the Mind into an Ally.* New York: Riverhead, 2003.

Morgan, David. *Essentials of Learning and Cognition.* New York: McGraw-Hill, 2002.

National Geographic. "What's in Your Mind?" Mar. 2005, pp. 2–31.

Neese, Randolph. "The Evolution of Hope and Despair." *Social Research,* 1999, 66, 429–469.

Peterson, Suzanne, and Fred Luthans. "Does the Manager's Level of Hope Matter? Preliminary Research Evidence of a Positive Impact." *Organizational Behavioral and Theory Track,* forthcoming.

Phillips, Donald. *The Founding Fathers on Leadership: Classic Teamwork in Changing Times.* New York: Warner Books, 1997.

Pinsky, Robert. *The Life of David.* New York: Nextbook, 2005.

Porter, Lyman, Gregory Bigley, and Richard Steers. *Motivation and Work Behavior,* 7th ed. New York: McGraw-Hill, 2003.

Raines, Dennis. *Principles of Human Neuropsychology.* New York: McGraw-Hill, 2002.

Reading, Anthony. *Hope and Despair: How Perceptions of the Future Shape Human Behavior.* Baltimore: Johns Hopkins University Press, 2004.

Restak, Richard. *Mozart's Brain and the Fighter Pilot.* New York: Three Rivers Press, 2001.

Schneider, Benjamin, Paul Hanges, Brent Smith, and Amy Salvaggio. "Which Comes First: Employee Attitudes or Organizational Financial and Market Performance?" *Journal of Applied Psychology,* 2003, 88, 836–851.

Schweizer, Peter. "Ronald Reagan's One Big Thing." *Hoover Digest,* Fall 2002 [http://www.hooverdigest.org/024/schweizer.html].

Seligman, Martin E. P., and Mihaly Csikszentmihalyi. "Positive Psychology." *American Psychologist*, 2000, 55, 5–14.

Snyder, C. R. *The Psychology of Hope: You Can Get There from Here*. New York: Free Press, 1994.

Snyder, C. R. *Handbook of Hope*. San Diego, Calif.: Academic Press, 2000.

Snyder, C. R., and others. "The Will and the Ways: Development and Validation of an Individual-Differences Measure of Hope." *Journal of Personality and Social Psychology*, 1991, 60, 570–585.

Snyder, C. R., and others. "Development and Validation of the State Hope Scale." *Journal of Personality and Social Psychology*, 1996, 65, 321–335.

Spiro, Howard. *The Power of Hope*. New Haven, Conn.: Yale University Press, 1998.

Taper, Bernard. *Cellist in Exile: A Portrait of Pablo Casals*. New York: McGraw-Hill, 1962.

Tifft, Susan E., and Alex S. Jones. *The Trust: The Private and Powerful Family Behind the* New York Times. New York: Back Bay Books, 1999.

Van Dulken, Stephan. *Inventing the Twentieth Century: One Hundred Inventions That Shaped the World*. London: British Library Board, 2002.

Walton, Mary. *The Deming Management Method*. New York: Putnam, 1986.

Watson, Peter. *The Modern Mind: An Intellectual History of the Twentieth Century*. New York: HarperCollins, 2001.

Wiley & Putnam's Emigrant's Guide: Comprising Advice and Instruction in Every Stage of the Voyage to America. Fort Washington, Pa.: Eastern National, 2001. Originally published 1845.

Yukl, Gary. *Leadership in Organizations*, 5th ed. Upper Saddle River, N.J.: Prentice Hall, 2001.

Acknowledgments

I first of all thank all who gave so generously of their time in helping me write this book: entrepreneur Charles Schwab; physician and author Deepak Chopra; Mir astronaut-cosmonaut Jerry Linenger; Harlem Children's Zone founder and CEO Geoffrey Canada; Advanced Micro Devices' chief administrative officer Tom McCoy; entrepreneur Paul Doyle; Vosges Haut-Chocolat founder Katrina Markoff; Jose Kuri; vintner Jack Cakebread; Kinko's founder Paul Orfalea; Nobel laureate Marshall Nirenberg; Saint Pauls Church pastor Tom Henry; representative to His Holiness the Dalai Lama and former director of the Office of Tibet in Exile in New York Nawang Rabgyal; past international chairman of the Turnaround Management Association, partner with the law firm of Cairncross & Hemplemann, P.S., John Rizzardi; former senior vice president of Honeywell and owner of the Harlem Globetrotters Mannie Jackson; Association Forum of Chicagoland president Gary LaBranche; and Wally Scott. These individuals were chosen as much for their differences as for their similarities. I have always found contrast, if not more insightful, certainly more interesting. I also thank my clients whose unique leadership has indirectly influenced this book. Special thanks also go to Bob Calder, Tim Calkins, Jack Domet, Rick Kolsky, Drew Mendoza, Marilyn Jacobson, and John Ward for your friendship and your contagious belief in others. To my "brain trust" of neuroscientists and behavioral, organizational, and social psychologists, thanks for your gentle nudges: Jim Belasco, Edward Bowden, Mark Jung-Beeman, Fred Luthans, Hal S. Shorey, Rick Stalling, Paul M. Hirsch, and Catherine M. Ruvolo. I thank the most influential doctor in my life, this one is a physician—a courageous immigrant who fled persecution in exchange for the American dream—and to the most influential nurse in my life—a midwestern farm girl with a zeal for learning, pride in the U.S. Air Force, and an insatiable love of big-city life: my folks, M. T. and Rosemary Razeghi. Their work, actions, and beliefs have contributed significantly to this collection of thoughts on hope, leadership, and success. Thanks go too to my reviewers and mentors, many of whom interrupted their busy lives to wade through the chaos of earlier versions of my ideas and ultimately this book: Cindy Razeghi, Sara Bailey, JoAnne Doering, Christopher Eastwood, Christian Foy, Bethany Frick, Bill Frick, Erik Gilbert, Michael Hogg, Judd Hoekstra, Andrew Keyt, Debbie Krupa, Santiago Kuribrena, Alan Razeghi, Amy Razeghi, Emily Razeghi, Cheryl Read, Arlyn Rubash, Kathleen Rubash, Kevin Rubash, Marge Rubash, Dean Savoca, David Schmahl, Matthew Schwingel, Kevin Stapleton, Tom Stat, Mike Varon, and Steve Zika. Also, special thanks go to Andy Appleby, Ken Blanchard, Lance Armstrong, James Rootes, Lee Stacey, and Bill Stapleton. To my literary agent, David Hale Smith, thank you for your tenacity. To my manager, Bobi Seredich, thank you for your life-balancing acts of creativity. And to my editor, Susan Williams, and her team at Jossey-Bass, who from the very beginning of this project have anticipated my many questions before they even occurred to me—thank you. Furthermore, I would be remiss not to thank the always and actively hopeful crew at Starbuck's on the corner of Clark and Deming who kept me caffeinated for days on end as I wrote this book. Also thank you Sean Tehrani of Sage Restaurant and my friends at Kabuki for your hospitality. And finally, I'd like to thank an organization that has been an eternal source of inspiration for me during this project—the doctors, nurses, and staff of Children's Memorial Hospital. I wrote a majority of this book with you outside my window—quite literally—and inside my heart. For your work, thank you.

A.J.R.

The Author

ANDREW J. RAZEGHI is a writer, educator, and adviser to organizations on growth strategy and innovation. As founder of the Andrew Razeghi Companies, LLC, he works with organizations seeking growth through the creation and introduction of new ideas. His work spans industries, from consumer packaged goods to health care, tourism to media, and nonprofit organizations to professional sports teams. He also speaks to thousands of people each year at trade association and organization events on topics related to leadership and innovation.

Razeghi is also an adjunct associate professor at the Kellogg School of Management at Northwestern University and has taught the capstone M.B.A. course on strategy and organization at the Graduate School of Business at Loyola University, Chicago. Shortly after the fall of communism in Central Europe, he was invited to be among the first American professors to teach free-market economics at the University of Economics, Prague, Czech Republic.

In addition to his work as an educator and adviser, Razeghi is a review panelist for the Wright Centers of Innovation at the National Academies of Science in Washington, D.C.; a thought leader with the Knowledge Dialogue; and an advisory board member of Americans for Informed Democracy (AID), a nonpartisan 501(c)(3) organization working to raise global awareness on more than five hundred university campuses and in nearly a dozen countries. AID seeks to build a new generation of globally conscious leaders who can shape an American foreign policy appropriate for our increasingly interdependent world.

Razeghi earned his master's degree in financial derivatives from Loyola University, Chicago, where he graduated Beta Gamma Sigma. He earned his undergraduate degree in international business at Bradley University in Peoria, Illinois, and studied modern popular culture at Richmond University, London. He lives in Chicago with his wife, Cindy, and son, Charlie.

For more information, visit http://www.andrewrazeghi.com.

Index

Ward, W. A., 173
Washington, G., 183
Wayfinders: Dalai Lama as, 161–162; as
    having a plan, 149; Jack Cakebread as,
    149–157; Ty Cobb as, 129d, 145–149.
    See also Triumphant leaders
Wayfinding: breakmaking through, 141,
    145–147; described, 141–142; hedging
    for the future approach of, 162–163;
    on Thirty-Second Street, 157–159;
    triumphant leaders' use of, 142–143;
    "what if. . .?" mantra of, 144–145
Wealth and Our Commonwealth: (Gates
    and Collins), 192
Webb, Ty (fictional character), 200
Weperen, R. van, 21
Western ideology, 79
Western Journal of Medicine, 17
"What Other People Say May Change
    What You See" (*New York Times*),
    115
WHO's *Mental Health: New Understanding,
    New Hope* report, 92, 242
Will to win, 211
Wind, Sand, and Stars (de Saint-Exupéry),
    148–149

Wine and Spirits (magazine), 130
Wine News (magazine), 156
Wine Spectator (magazine), 156
Wishful thinking, 86–88
Woods, T., 104
Workplace fatalities, 238–239
World Health Organization (WHO),
    91–92
World War II torpedoed ships, 20–22
Worsley, F., 224
Wright, W., 27

Y

The yips, 201–203
Young Presidents Organization (YPO),
    171
Yunus, M., 23

Z

Zajonc, R., 49–50
Zappa, F., 69
Zeitgeist: disposability of modern, 28–29;
    meaning of, 25–26; of our age, 26–27;
    porteur de sens (bearer of meaning)
    response to, 30–31